IMPACT

CFDA

ABRAMS,
NEW YORK

IMPACT

50 YEARS *of* THE COUNCIL OF FASHION DESIGNERS OF AMERICA

CONTENTS

PREFACE
DIANE VON FURSTENBERG

IMPACT is what American fashion is about.

To make an impact is to have a direct effect. As the president of the Council of Fashion Designers of America, I can happily confirm that we have had a direct effect on the business of American fashion for the past fifty years.

There is something magical about the way this group was founded back in 1962, in a small room off of Seventh Avenue. It was the brain trust of twenty passionate designers who were motivated to create a safe haven for the members of their community. They sought to protect and promote their own.

Nearly half a century later, through triumphs and failures, with businesses made and broken, that small assemblage has evolved into a modern family of over four hundred members. Along with fashion, accessory, and jewelry designers, it includes creative directors and industry provocateurs.

While growing, the CFDA has also galvanized. We mentor and nurture new talent in many ways, we work with business in the industry, and we publish books about the culture of fashion. We take to Washington to make sure that artistic integrity is kept intact by establishing anti-piracy laws. We do it. A collective as one.

True to the original missive of this organization, we continue to celebrate and support each other through scholarships, awards, and grants. Philanthropic initiatives have been equally as important. During our tenure we have raised nearly $100 million in the fight against AIDS and breast cancer. When natural disasters strike in neighboring or distant countries, the CFDA is always there with a plan to lend a helping hand.

We are a family—a design family, an industry family, a supportive family.

I can't wait to see the amazing things that this creative, inspiring, determined group will achieve in the next fifty years.

FOREWORD

CATHY HORYN

The first designer I ever knew was Bill Blass. We met on the opening night of the Detroit Auto Show in 1987. He had come to town, with his tux, to promote the latest Bill Blass edition for Lincoln-Mercury, and because I was the fashion writer for *The Detroit News*—and relatively new on the beat—I went to Cobo Hall to meet him. Seeing this handsome son of a gun, who walked and talked like Gable if Gable had gone to Eton, you would have no trouble believing that he loved nothing better than a long drive, a cigarette on his lips. But Bill had absolutely no aptitude for driving, and nothing—not the flats of his native Indiana, not four years in the army in World War II—had made a difference. The guys at Lincoln obviously knew that Bill's charisma—and, of course, his name—could sell cars. That night, as he wheeled me around the convention center, grunting in mock surprise at one god-awful outfit after another, I really wasn't thinking about any of that. I just hoped that other designers were going to be like him.

Later, whenever I went to New York for the shows, I would drop by his office at 550 Seventh Avenue. Bill was always kind to the out-of-town press, which had done so much to help his career in the sixties and seventies, when he traveled the country widely doing trunk shows. I cherish my friendship with him for many reasons, but the most meaningful to me as a writer is that he turned me on to a period in American fashion when everything seemed to intersect.

As Patricia Mears states in her essay accompanying this invaluable history of the Council of Fashion Designers of America, the years 1940 to 1945 were a bonanza to American fashion. With Paris houses virtually shut down by the war, new American talent emerged and thrived, while established stars like Clare Potter and Claire McCardell continued to make simple and innovative clothes. Yet by 1962, the year that Eleanor Lambert founded the CFDA, the story had opened up considerably. Now you had a historical moment being shaped by a dashing group of designers, a few influential editors who were by no means lap dogs, some astute money men, and this swinging bunch of socialites who didn't have the slightest hang-ups about seeing their names in print. Yes, the clothes were great and, yes, designers were becoming household names (blah blah), but more to the point, you had this incredibly vital story, set around the personalities and ambitions of a handful of key figures, at the very moment when fashion was beginning to acquire status and cultural importance in New York. It had the dimensions of a novel. Anyway, that's how I saw things when Bill would talk of his friendships with John Weitz and the sexy, and ultimately self-destructive, Jacques Tiffeau, or the arrival of

Oscar de la Renta on the scene and his subsequent marriage to the worldly Francoise de Langlade; there were the gossipy lunches with Donald Brooks and John Fairchild of *Women's Wear Daily*, the rise of Diana Vreeland at *Vogue*, the striking presence of society women like Chessy Raynor, Nan Kempner, Louise Grunwald, and D.D. Ryan, and the still relatively modest lifestyles with time for pleasure. By the end of the sixties, you had the emergence of Halston as a dress designer, complete with his European-styled entourage.

It was an era when everything was personal—the feuds as well the dreams—and it set the stage for the big businesses and vast fortunes that would follow in the late seventies and eighties, changing forever the dynamics of our industry. Indeed, if there is a natural bookend to this special era in American fashion, it would be the Versailles showdown in 1973—again the brainchild of the dauntless Ms. Lambert.

When I first began covering the collections in New York, in 1986, I was dimly aware of the CFDA. Actually, what most of us writers knew were the Big Five—Bill, Oscar, Calvin Klein, Ralph Lauren, and Donna Karan. We gamely schlepped around the Garment District, wedging ourselves into showrooms, climbing filthy stairs to see new designers we had heard about by word-of-mouth (I still recall visiting a young Ricky Vider in a shoebox space), running over to the Plaza or the Pierre to catch Bob Mackie or Carolyne Roehm and clothes blazing with Lesage beadwork, and trooping down to SoHo to see Marc Jacobs or Stephen Sprouse, or a new guy named Isaac Mizrahi doing these amazing colors. If it occurred to some of us to complain about this inconvenient setup, I don't remember. We were having too much fun.

Like many writers, I grumbled a little when the CFDA created the centralized tents in Bryant Park, sure that some creative, grime-coated spirit would be sacrificed to convenience. I was wrong. A trace of Garment District grit remained. And I think the modest, realistic, endlessly cheerful Stan Herman was a kind of miracle to the organization and the industry in general. Or perhaps, as we say, timing is everything. Under the energetic leadership of current president Diane von Furstenberg, and thanks to groundbreaking ideas like the CFDA/Vogue Fashion Fund for young talent and substantial scholarships awarded on behalf of Geoffrey Beene and Liz Claiborne, the CFDA has set a standard for the global fashion community. The new home at Lincoln Center reflects that. Each of us has a separate relationship to fashion; each of us dreams and thinks about it differently, and each remembers why we joined the party in the first place. I hope you will enjoy this journey of fifty years as much as I have.

THE COUNCIL *of* FASHION DESIGNERS *of* AMERICA: A HISTORY

PATRICIA MEARS

INTRODUCTION

For the first time in the history of American fashion, leaders in all branches of creative design both East and West Coast, representing clothing, textiles, millinery, footwear and jewelry, have banded together and formed a national honorary and ethical society. Its purpose is to gain recognition for fashion design as an important expression of American art and a representative aspect of American culture, and to project the fashion arts as a means of gaining world appreciation for America's contribution to world civilization. The organization is called the Council of Fashion Designers of America (CFDA). [1]

The statement above, issued in a press release by the legendary fashion publicist Eleanor Lambert, dates to early 1963, just a few months after the CFDA was formed and its charter filed with the Secretary of the State of New York. With a membership of just over fifty of America's leading fashion design talents, its goals were lofty from the outset, and its primary mandate was the recognition and promotion of fashion design talent based in the United States.

Over the next five decades, the CFDA membership rolls swelled into the high hundreds, and its activities, outreach, and influence expanded exponentially. Celebrating its fiftieth anniversary in 2012, the Council of Fashion Designers of America, Incorporated, officially describes itself as:

A not-for-profit trade association that leads industry-wide initiatives and whose membership consists of more than 400 of America's foremost womenswear, menswear, jewelry, and accessory designers. In addition to hosting the annual CFDA Fashion Awards, which recognize the top creative talent in the industry, the organization offers programs which support professional development and scholarships, including the CFDA/Vogue Fashion Fund, the Geoffrey Beene Design Scholar Award, the Liz Claiborne Design Scholarship Award, and the CFDA/Teen Vogue Scholarship. Member support is provided through the Business Services Network, a group of companies offering designers strategic opportunities.

The CFDA's high-profile membership and its newsworthy activities have mirrored not only the ascendancy of American fashion's global influence, but also the increasing interconnectedness of leading fashion capitals, manufacturing centers, and consumers in every corner of the world. It has thus moved away from the purely design-oriented, art-immersed objectives of its first charter, based on that of the American Institute of Architects, and a grant-based structure, its initial funding having come from the federal government—specifically, a grant from the National Council on the Arts. Today, its activities are more business-focused and philanthropic, its membership larger and more egalitarian, and it is professionally run. Even though it was built upon the foundation of older organizations, the CFDA's core mandate was to reject the mind-set of those organizations that sought to hinder individual talent. The CFDA has never strayed from its primary mission: to encourage and advance creativity in fashion in America.

The short history presented here documents the evolution of the CFDA from its inception in 1962, its early promotional efforts, and its strong ties to the arts to the growth of its educational programs, its support of worthy causes, its own awards ceremony, its stewardship of fashion week, and its support of designers. It is a chronicle of the individual and collective efforts of the founders, select presidents, and executive directors, who have so diligently worked to shape the CFDA.

We have a wealth of primary sources on the creation and the early years of the CFDA due to the fact that Eleanor Lambert, the CFDA's early champion and chief architect, kept an extensive archive of letters, telegrams, working notes, and newspaper clippings. Now part of the Special Collections in the Library at the Fashion Institute of Technology, this mostly unpublished material is a rich and invaluable resource that provides a clear idea of how the CFDA was created and grew. Information in the archives also demonstrates how closely Lambert aligned the early programming of the CFDA with the performing and fine arts; she clearly believed that fashion was a worthy creative entity on par with other artistic disciplines. It should be noted that Lambert was also the publicist for many of the designers both before and during their CFDA memberships, a fact that seems not to have hampered her activities.

This is, of course, far from an all-encompassing history of the CFDA. The intent is to communicate the general development of the organization's growth and to highlight its more colorful programming as a small part of a visually rich publication that is companion to the *Impact* exhibition organized by the Museum at FIT. The brainchild of the current president, Diane von Furstenberg, *Impact* is an ode to the most illustrious efforts of CFDA's many members as they celebrate its fiftieth anniversary.

AMERICAN FASHION: A BRIEF HISTORY

Before launching into the history of the Council of Fashion Designers of America, it is important to understand the climate in which it emerged. Its primary goal, as noted, was to advance the notion of American designers. Today, in an era dominated by the designer label, it is perhaps difficult to comprehend how seminal the CFDA was in creating the platform for such recognition. The CFDA arose during one of the culturally richest periods in the history of the United States. It was in this environment of bourgeoning creativity that America became a nexus of global fashion—with New York City at its epicenter.

From the mid-nineteenth to the mid-twentieth century, the American fashion machine was enormous and possessed the largest and most advanced manufacturing system in the world. Clothing manufacturers had a strong grip on the American fashion industry and few, if any, had interest in promoting domestic design talent. These manufacturers, as well as the leading fashion editors of the day, strongly supported the notion of French-designed apparel. Ironically, American-made clothing was readily purchased by consumers in the United States, and it was often more compelling than French haute couture. Unlike "artistic" high styles from Paris, American fashion encompassed clothing types positioned along a wide spectrum that represents nearly every type of

sophisticated design made throughout the twentieth century, from inexpensive sportswear and separates to blue jeans and uniforms, luxurious ready-to-wear, and costly, custom-made gowns.

For the individual designers of these clothes, the road to recognition was a long one. Prior to the onset of World War II, there was an incipient movement in the United States to dispel the notion that American fashion was little more than a copier of Parisian haute couture or a manufacturing megalith that produced only casual and functional clothing. Independent designers, such as Jessie Franklin Turner (1910s to the 1930s) or Elizabeth Hawes and Valentina (beginning in the 1920s), were couturieres who designed mostly custom-made clothing. But they were very few in number.

The idea to promote American talent on a larger scale and beyond the production of exclusive, made-to-order fashion began to gather momentum during the interwar years. As early as 1932, for example, innovative retailer Dorothy Shaver of Lord & Taylor featured American designers in the store's advertising as part of her promotion of young talent. Hawes, Clare Potter, and Claire McCardell were a few of the names Shaver advanced. There were also many associations that promoted American fashion in the 1930s: Custom Tailors' Club, Garment Retailers of America, New York Modern Designers' Club, Retail Millinery Association, the Fashion Group, and the Fashion Guild. American design was featured in two World's Fairs: in 1933 in Chicago and 1939 in New York. Yet even with these efforts, the influence of the Parisian couture was profound.

When the outbreak of World War II cut off access to Parisian haute couture, American manufacturers and magazine editors had no choice but to focus on domestic design. While a comprehensive history of American fashion would be too complex to detail here, most accounts view the period from 1940 to 1945 as a golden age in which many of the best and most important designers this country has ever produced emerged from anonymity. They would become the first members of the CFDA, and they included Norman Norell, Pauline Trigère, Ceil Chapman, and Jo Copeland.

However, after the war ended, French fashion regained much of the ground it had lost in the 1940s, and because of the Parisian resurgence, the rise of American designers, especially those who did not own their own companies, began to fade. According to designers who witnessed the inception of the CFDA, such as Bill Blass,[2] it was in the early 1960s that the beginnings of a change could be felt on Seventh Avenue, the heart of New York fashion. Blass echoed the sentiments of Eleanor Lambert,

the woman who had made it her life's mission to change the American fashion status quo. Lambert stated that a designer "must above all have encouragement to pursue fashion as an artistic as well as commercial endeavor, to be lifted above 'hack work' when his talents warrant."[3]

Few Americans were interested in or even aware of the plight of fashion designers at the time. Lambert, understanding their malaise, enlivened the story of American fashion in an effort to change the collective mind-set. In testimony before Congress on Thursday, October 31, 1963, she elucidated what can almost be described as the Hollywood version of fashion design history: "We think of creative American fashion as a recent development. Some people date it after the last war," she said. "It has actually been more like the 100 Years War. Probably the first gun in the war of fashion independence was fired by the celebrated anti-slavery crusader, Harriet Beecher Stowe." Lambert quoted an 1848 essay by Mrs. Stowe, who wrote "'. . . the genius of American life is for simplicity, and absence of ostentation. . . . It requires an army of girls to emancipate us from the decrees and tyrannies of alien fashion. . . . Forward, girls! You can, if you will, yet save the republic!'"[4]

The remainder of her speech was more temperate, but she continued to stress the need for both an independent American voice in fashion as well as an environment in which to cultivate high-end talent and to promote individual designers by name. Those designers who had emerged from the manufacturers' backrooms to make names for themselves in America—first Norell and Trigère, and later, Blass and Geoffrey Beene—were part of

a wave that followed the template set by McCardell in the late 1930s. With Lambert, they were casting American designers as "creative" and original personalities who could rival the reigning Parisian couturiers as well as the Italian *alta moda* and ready-to-wear creators.

The comparison to Europe, and France in particular, was important. Fashion and the creation, production, and exportation of luxury goods were vital components of France's economy and culture. Consequently, fashion in France has long been a respected craft, with its creators viewed as talented artisans. In a national effort to advance its high-end fashion, or *haute couture*, the French devised governing bodies charged with missions such as protecting original creations. One body, the celebrated *Chambre syndicale de la haute couture*, set forth rules for all its members (such as size of the workshop and the number of original designs each season) but also provided legal support and copyright protection.

The French fashion establishment also fostered the idea of the fashion designer as artist. As early as the eighteenth century, the great *marchande de mode* (or stylist/couturiere) to Queen Marie Antoinette, Rose Bertin, pioneered the idea of a fashion designer as a creative genius and celebrity. So elevated was her status that she was known as the *Ministre de la Mode* in Paris. Over the next two centuries, couturiers from Charles Frederick Worth to Gabrielle "Coco" Chanel to Yves Saint Laurent would follow Bertin's lead and become lauded creators.

There was no such system or culture in the United States. In fact, American designers not only had to fight French fashion dominance, they had to battle manufacturing establishments that undermined them in their own backyard, one example being the New York Dress Institute (NYDI). Formed in 1940 as a joint venture between hundreds of New York City clothing manufacturers and the International Ladies Garment Workers Union (ILGWU), its purpose was to advance the sales of dresses and clothing made in New York by promoting the city as the fashion center of the country. "Facing wartime recession, and aware that the garment industry was the city's single largest employer, Mayor Fiorello LaGuardia was anxious to see the city take advantage of Paris's demise to ensure its own ascent."[5] A specially made label, "New York Creation," was designed and sewn into dresses to identify the products of members. The label was a symbol of patriotism as well as a source of tax revenue—but not a celebration of the designer.

But when the NYDI hired Eleanor Lambert as its publicist, she swiftly and shrewdly suggested that the campaign be shifted to designers, not manufacturers. Lambert, who had worked to promote artists before she moved into fashion, had to wrest control from the very people who had hired her. Although manufacturers were the public faces of apparel companies, Lambert understood that it would be necessary to create a "cult of personality" around designers if New York was to become a fashion epicenter. Lambert implemented her strategy in three steps.[6]

First, she reinterpreted the 10 Best-Dressed Women list that had been started in the 1930s by Mainbocher,[7] a couturier who was born in the United States but began his career in Paris. Upon Mainbocher's return to the United States at the onset of World War II, it was renamed the "International Best-Dressed List." Soon after its reincarnation, women from around the world were vying for inclusion to this increasingly prestigious "club" of style leaders. The "List" was important because it was dominated by American names and, more important, was generated in New York City by American critics closely tied to the local fashion industry. The list is now under the watchful eye of *Vanity Fair* magazine.

Next, Lambert created the Coty Awards in 1942. These prestigious American fashion awards would become the industry's gold standard in its heyday.

Finally, Lambert was responsible for organizing what would become known as New York Press Week in the early 1940s, which, in turn, coincided with the creation of the New York Couture Group. Around 1941 (according to most sources), the highest-quality garment manufacturers in the city, such as Harvey Berin and Maurice Rentner, formed an exclusive offshoot of the NYDI that they called The Couture Group to sponsor New York Press Week. In a condensed time frame and in a centralized location, leading fashion editors from newspapers across the country were brought to New York to see the latest seasonal collections. National press coverage expanded because of the newly coordinated and centralized presentations.

Although manufacturers continued to hold sway on Seventh Avenue for the next two decades, the increased prestige of New York as a style and fashion center led to a shift in the late 1950s and early 1960s. Arnold Scaasi recalled the heady atmosphere in New York on the cusp of change:

> *Everyone was kind of shocked [at the CFDA's inception] because it was like stepping away from another group that was bigger [the Couture Group] and kind of like what the CFDA is today. . . . A great many of the people in that group were people who went to Paris and bought from the couture to make line-for-line copies. . . . We were separating ourselves*

> *from the manufacturers, which was more of a reaction to Eleanor [Lambert] than to the Couture Group, because Eleanor was very much in the forefront of the other group until she formed the CFDA. The main thing was to take the creative designers away [from the manufacturers and the Couture Group] and 'creative' was a very important word at that moment. When she did that, it [the CFDA] really took off.*[8]

BIRTH OF THE CFDA

As Scaasi noted, the person who did more than any other to create and ultimately advance American fashion and the CFDA early on was Eleanor Lambert. "All I did was start it," noted the publicist. "I've always said that getting people together as a community helps further their identity as a whole. We were a group of people of equal qualifications and equal thoughts about moving forward."[9] What is interesting about this quote beyond Lambert's feigned humility is that she places herself alongside the designers she cultivated and represented, referring to all collectively as "we," and lays claim to all having an "equal" ability and mind-set.

A born showwoman, Lambert was fashion's first impresario. It was she who approached Senator Jacob Javits of New York about advancing fashion on a nationally recognized platform.[10] Javits then joined forces with another charismatic political, Senator Claiborne Pell of Rhode Island. Born in New York City, Pell was chairman of the special subcommittee on the arts (which, in turn, was under the Committee on Public Welfare). Following the lead set forth by President John F. Kennedy, the two senators sought to establish the National Council on the Arts, while Lambert pushed to include fashion and have it validated as an acceptable form of American art, alongside painting, music, and dance. However, as the story goes, that would require the involvement of a not-for-profit (i.e., artistic) organization, rather than a commercial industry or business enterprise.

The CFDA would fulfill this "artistic" requirement. In October of 1962, Pell and Javits invited Lambert to appear at an open hearing on the establishment of an arts council. At the senators' urging, Lambert rallied a group of designers to establish the CFDA in order to "further the position of fashion design as a recognized branch of American art and culture" and "to advance its artistic and professional standards."[11] Its charter was filed on December 6, 1962.

The founding members were a small, exclusive group of twenty: Bill Blass, Donald Brooks, Betty Carol, Jane Derby (who

United States Senate

WASHINGTON, D.C.

October 31, 1963

Mrs. Eleanore Lambert Berkson
Eleanore Lambert Company
32 East 57th
New York 22, New York

Dear Eleanore:

It would be interesting to get some good newspaper or magazine material on our leading designers for insertion in the Congressional Record. I hope that these would include Mollie Parnis and Pauline Trigere.

With warm regards,

Sincerely,

Jacob K. Javits, U. S. S.

JKJ/smg

United States Senate

COMMITTEE ON
LABOR AND PUBLIC WELFARE

November 12, 1963

Mrs. Eleanor Lambert
Council of Fashion Designers
of America
32 East 57th Street
New York 22, New York

Dear Eleanor:

Thank you for your letter of October 31 and the enclosed transcript of your testimony before the Arts Subcommittee on the Senate Committee on Labor and Public Welfare in behalf of the arts legislation.

We were very pleased to have your testimony which will be included in the printed record of the hearings.

Your cooperation and support are very much appreciated.

With best wishes,

Sincerely,

Jacob K. Javits, U.S.S.

JKJ:alg

---

famously hired the young Oscar de la Renta), Luis Estévez, David Evins (a leading shoe designer), Rudi Gernreich, Bud Kilpatrick, Helen Lee, Jean Louis, John Moore, Norman Norell, Sylvia Pedlar, Sarmi, Arnold Scaasi, Adele Simpson, Gustave Tassell, Pauline Trigère, Sydney Wragge (who began as an assistant for the late, legendary Claire McCardell), and Ben Zuckerman.

The following month, January 1963, Wragge chaired the first official meeting of the CFDA. He was also elected its president, a post he would hold for two years. In a mere few weeks, the organization had grown more than twofold. New members included Stephanie Cartwright, Ceil Chapman, Jo Copeland, Lilly Daché, Florence Eiseman, Anne Fogarty, James Galanos, Sophie Gimbel, Margaret Jerrold, Mr. John, Mabel Julianelli, David Kidd, Anne Klein, Richard Koret, William Lord, Jose Martin, Vera Maxwell, Marie McCarthy, Vincent Monte-Sano, Mollie Parnis, Sara Ripault, Leo Ritter, Helen Rose, Roxane, Karen Stark, Jacques Tiffeau, John Weitz, and Andrew Woods.

While some of the designers listed above have faded into obscurity, others ascended to the pantheon of fashion history, and their hallmark designs conjure up instantly recognizable images. This CFDA designer collective, including the well-known and the obscure, gave each of these American creators a platform on which to compete with their Europe-based counterparts.

THE EARLY YEARS, 1963–70

One of Lambert's early efforts to widen fashion's appeal was to stage a televised fashion show. Taped on location at the U.S. Pavilion at the 1964 World's Fair site in Queens, the presentation hosted by Nancy White, editor in chief of *Harper's Bazaar*, showcased the work of leading CFDA members. The show aired on WNEW-TV, Metropolitan Broadcast, on Monday, July 6, 1964, at 10 p.m. Not only was it a "tribute" to Senator Javits, it featured a thirty-member Honorary Committee that included the senator's wife, Mrs. Franklin Delano Roosevelt, Jr., and Lambert herself. More modest shows followed, such as one hosted by the Smithsonian Institute in Washington, entitled "The Contemporary Art of American Fashion." Led by Lambert and cochairmen Bill Blass and Donald Brooks, five thematic fashion shows were presented on November 15, 1966.

Most were meant for smaller audiences but were more elaborate and ambitious in scope. In the fall of 1963, the CFDA presented the "American Pageant of Fashion and the Arts" at the Waldorf-Astoria ballroom. The *New York Herald Tribune*[12] reported that a "glittering list of celebrities, social and stage, modeled fashions by the CFDA," and the pageant "benefited both the National Cultural Center and the American Shakespeare Festival and Academy." The prologue was delivered by Helen Hayes in a Ceil Chapman design, while dance (Paul Taylor's *Aureole*), Shakespeare (excerpts from *The Tempest* and *A Midsummer Night's*

Dream), and thematic fashion presentations ("Moments in Fashion") were intermingled throughout the evening. Artwork by the likes of Louise Nevelson served as backdrops. Actors such as Elizabeth Ashley and Robert Redford shared the stage with singer and pianist Bobby Short; the celebrity models included Mia Farrow, Sally Kirkland, Geraldine Stutz, and Betty Furness; and the designs were by Norell, Trigère, Gus Tassell, Jacques Tiffeau, Anne Klein, Donald Brooks, Bill Blass for Maurice Rentner, Rudi Gernreich, Anne Fogarty, Arnold Scaasi, and Luis Estévez.

Similar programming—with the linking of fashion with the arts—continued throughout the 1960s. One the highlights was an evening of ballet and fashion, where on Sunday, September 25, 1966, the CFDA hosted a benefit for the American Ballet Theatre. Entitled "Fashion and Broadway Salute the ABT," the show was staged at the St. James Theater and hosted by Lauren Bacall, who wore Norell. Ballets such as George Balanchine's *Theme and Variations*, Jerome Robbins's *Fancy Free*, and Agnes de Mille's *Skating Scene* from *The Wind in the Mountains* alternated with fashion shows, with titles such as "All Black" and "The High Pastels," which highlighted works by CFDA members. Senator Javits and other attendees enthusiastically praised the event for its professional quality, as well as the beauty of both the dance and the fashion components.

According to a letter from Harold Taylor, president of the board of trustees of American Ballet Theatre, to Lambert,[13] the evening was also a fund-raising success. "You raised a large sum of money," he wrote, "for one of the great ballet companies, and you brought together the fashion industry and the art of dance in ways beneficial to both."

One of the reasons the evening was so successful was the fact that Jacqueline Kennedy was the event's honorary chair. Lambert understood the power of celebrity, and Mrs. Kennedy was one of the most recognized and admired women in the world. But the more subtle power of Kennedy's participation could be found in her role as a champion of the arts and high culture. She and her husband helped to elevate the importance of art and design in America and to accelerate the acceptance of certain fields that might otherwise have been overlooked. Ballet, like fashion, had once seemed an art form unlikely to flourish in this country. A product of the great courts of Europe, from Louis XIV to the tsars of Russia, its elitism could be taken as practically un-American. Yet New York became the classical ballet capital of the world during the 1960s, and dance schools and companies flourished around the country. The desire to promote fashion was part of this cultural upsurge, and Lambert, who had strong connections to art since

her early days as a publicist as well as an uncanny ability to read the zeitgeist, took full advantage of this momentum.

Although it was not part of the CFDA's original mission, the organization began to foster educational programming for the next generation of designers. The sponsor of several prestigious and generous scholarship funds today, the CFDA's original efforts to create educational opportunities happened almost by chance. Lambert recalled one of the first meetings convened by the U.S. Senate for the new Special Subcommittee on the Arts, headed by Nancy Hanks.[14] Lambert had found herself uncharacteristically at a loss for words. As dignitaries from various fields spoke eloquently about the need for public support of art, Lambert fell silent. "Maggie [Agnes] de Mille for example, represented dance and was brilliant," noted Lambert. "I've never heard such an eloquent speech about one artist by another. She wanted the council to pay for a sabbatical for Jerome Robbins, which was approved, and it was during that time that he choreographed the ballets *Dances at a Gathering* and the *Schoenberg/Wuorinen Variations*."[15]

After suffering from such intimidations for most of the day, Lambert was finally asked by Hanks if there wasn't anything the council could do for fashion. Lambert said, "I don't know, but I would like $25,000 to establish a location at the Metropolitan Museum of Art and try to get an American showing of clothing there." Lambert was quickly able to organize one of the CFDA's first important events, which brought together, on Saturday, March 26, 1966, museum specialists, curators, educators, and a few designers for a panel discussion entitled "Fashion and Costume in Relation to the National Council on the Arts."

Blass, Jo Copeland, Mr. John, Sylvia Pedlar, and Mollie Parnis were joined by representatives from institutions that were highly influential in developing fashion studies in the United States. The educators and curators included George Bayless and Ann Keagy of the Parsons School of Design; the Metropolitan Museum of Art's textile curator Jean Mailey and the Costume Institute's Polaire Weissman; Robert "Bob" Riley of the Brooklyn Museum and, later, founder of the Museum at the Fashion Institute of Technology (Weissman and Riley were also "honorary" members of the CFDA); Alice Beer of the Cooper-Hewitt; Alphonse Cavallo, the Museum of Fine Arts, Boston; and representatives from the Dallas Museum of Art, Howard University, the Smithsonian, and the Rhode Island School of Design. The panelists discussed what could be done to further education at institutions outside of New York, such as creating documentaries of leading designers, filming runway shows,

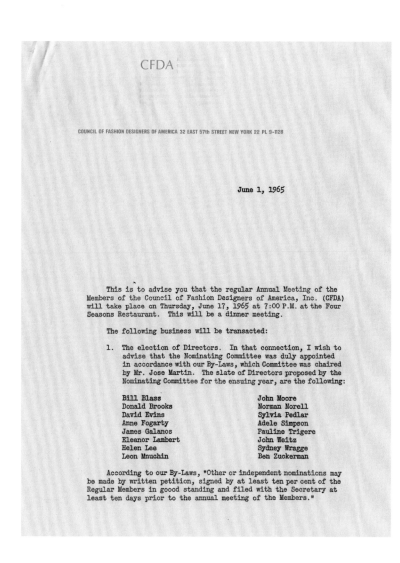
the equivalent of an "artist-in-residence program for fashion designers, a national program for designs to travel and speak at schools, and a government-funded museum tour of the best examples for leading designer collections."[16]

Keagy, the legendary Parsons instructor, expressed strong support for documentaries and fashion history lectures. Riley, the fashion-designer-turned-curator, concurred with Keagy and expressed his belief that design students needed access to historical objects. He stated that "most of the students have never seen really fine clothes, not of yesterday and certainly never the best of today. It is kind of like graduating an art major who has never seen Rembrandt or looked at a Picasso."[17]

This panel discussion laid the groundwork for the first CFDA-sponsored museum exhibition. In 1967, the CFDA was able to match the National Council on the Arts' funds for the Metropolitan Museum of Art's Costume Institute to host a show entitled *The Art of Fashion*, which was on view for ten weeks. It was an unprecedented success. It combined live models in contemporary dress by CFDA members with historical objects mounted on mannequins from the museum's permanent collection, all set within twelve galleries. Joseph Noble, the museum's administrative director, said at the time that it was one the best-attended exhibitions in the Metropolitan's history, drawing 180,093 visitors. Noble formally thanked the CFDA in a letter dated November 13, 1967, for the "gift of $25,000 which helped make this exhibition possible, and . . . for the unswerving

devotion of so many of your members in helping to arrange for the contemporary fashion section."[18]

The exhibition actually had loftier goals. One critic noted that "the purpose of the exhibit is to treat fashion as great design, as an art form rather than a historical document."[19] In the same article, the Metropolitan's director, Thomas P. F. Hoving, stated that "quite a few people think that American designers are leading . . . the world. I'm one of them."

The exhibition concept traveled further afield to the Cincinnati Art Museum. On February 27, 1969, a show in the museum's costume wing was launched with a celebratory, fund-raising dinner. *Art of American Fashion* was so successful that a second version was organized in Cincinnati two years later and then another in Philadelphia in 1970. Lambert told journalist Eric Wilson that the CFDA had "tried to make people throughout the country understand the meaning of fine clothes and the personality of designers. We tried to humanize the idea of high-fashion American clothes."[20]

One of the leading mandates of the CFDA today is to provide educational scholarships for students and funding for bourgeoning designers. Because the first scholarship was not created until 1986, many have assumed the organization had no prior record of such endeavors. There is evidence to the contrary. On September 12, 1968, the CFDA launched a program for disadvantaged youth—the Urban Project. A letter housed in the Lambert/CFDA archives at FIT states that "no problem is more pressing these days than the plight of the underprivileged, under-educated people who live in urban areas." In an effort to help young girls from poorer neighborhoods in the city, Lambert suggested that the CFDA start by choosing about twenty girls "with interest in fashion." Each would take a course of study, about two to three hours every other week for a total of fourteen sessions, in order to "acquaint them with every aspect of our industry."[21] Instruction included museum visits, trips to designs schools and manufacturing centers, individual counseling, and a sewing project. CFDA mentors included Arnold Scaasi, Anne Fogarty, Donald Brooks, Vera Maxwell, and Victor Costa.

Educational outreach was but one example of the many diverse projects that the CFDA undertook in its first decade. The advancement of education, specifically the rise of college degrees for students training to become designers, and the relationship forged between schools and museums, led the way for later scholarship programs sponsored by the CFDA over the coming years.

Along with education, Lambert recognized another important issue: a designer's intellectual property. According to the

archives of the CFDA, Lambert made a presentation in 1975 to the New York State Bar Association concerning the need to protect fashion design. Around the same time, the CFDA led the industry in opposition to legislation that would reduce tariffs on fashion-related imported goods. In letters to U.S. Senators Daniel Patrick Moynihan of New York and Abraham A. Ribicoff of Connecticut, the CFDA noted that lifting those tariffs would have the ability "to destroy American fashion and make it less competitive."[22]

Lambert was an active CFDA member from the organization's inception in 1962 until the early 1990s, and she was an honorary member until her death in 2003. The organization recognized her contributions twice at the CFDA Fashion Awards. In 1988, she received the Lifetime Achievement Award in the cause of fashion, and in 1993 she received the Council's Industry Tribute Award. In 2001, the CFDA created the Eleanor Lambert Award, now known as the Founder's Award, to honor and to celebrate unique contributions by individuals to the world of fashion.

GROWTH OF THE CFDA:
1970–90

In the 1960s and 1970s, the CFDA remained a somewhat insular group that had, in the words of former president Stan Herman, "the feel of an exclusive club."[23] It was also organized in a somewhat laissez-faire manner. Annual meetings were held at the elegant Four Seasons restaurant on East Fifty-second Street (as were celebrity and designer luncheons). The business of the day was discussed, along with plans for regional fashion shows to promote New York designers around the country. Such events were fancy but not costly. According to Lambert, the CFDA was not required (or even asked) to spend much money. The cachet of its designers meant that they could ask for "important locations, and get them," at little or no cost.[24]

The CFDA's offices were based out of Lambert's public relations firm at 32 East Fifty-seventh Street. "The thing was so informal that I called upon people who I thought were leaders and asked them to do the work," explained Lambert. For example, the Council's eagle-eyed secretary and treasurer, David Evins (a leading shoe designer who had worked for Hermès and was one of the first to go from being a ghost designer to the head of his eponymous company), made sure each member paid annual dues of $250.

Although the Lambert archives in the FIT Library's Special Collections is extensive and contains many letters, telegrams, and notes detailing the creation of special events, the day-to-day business and the efforts of many of the CFDA's members, including

its presidents, are less well documented. There is scant record, for example, of Sydney Wragge's tenure from 1963 to 1965. The same can be said for the presidency of Herbert Kasper, 1977–79. Kasper, in a 2007 interview with journalist Rosemary Feitelberg, did recognize the importance of the CFDA. "People are producing and selling clothes all over the world today, and the CFDA has grown at the same level. It's become more important within the framework of the country, and especially New York."[25]

Norman Norell, who was the president for nearly eight years, 1965–73, and a key participant in early CFDA fashion shows, was sparing in his correspondences with Lambert; there was also paucity in his prose. Even Bill Blass, who served as the president from 1980 to 1981, left little documentation and did not mention the organization in his 2002 autobiography, *Bare Blass*. However, according to the board meeting minutes,[26] Blass did head a campaign to "beautify 7th Avenue" by planting trees in newly installed planters and, along with Mary McFadden, he got permission to hang "fashion" banners from lampposts in the fashion district.

The office of the presidency has even been referred to as an "ancillary post or an excuse for a martini."[27] The lack of archival material supports the assessment by many that Lambert was the de facto leader of the CFDA in its first two decades, regardless of who might have been president, of this small, exclusive group.

Mary McFadden credits herself with one major accomplishment during her two years of presidency (1982–83): persuading Lambert to release all the organization's papers to the officers of the CFDA. The organization took control of the documents—and therefore its business dealings—by hiring a secretary. McFadden stated, "We were better able to run it [the CFDA] because now it was in the hands of the members."[28]

The membership understood the need for independent staff to oversee its business. President Perry Ellis made this a key goal and, in 1985, hired the first paid staff member, Executive Director Robert Raymond. In addition, he opened

the CFDA's headquarters. Located at 575 Seventh Avenue, the CFDA finally had its own identity and was no longer confined to designer's showrooms.

Under the leadership of President Oscar de la Renta, the CFDA would change in other ways as well. De la Renta was president from 1973 to 1976, and then again from 1987 to 1989, after taking over for Ellis, who died of complications from AIDS. Furthermore, he was viewed as being the person who filled Lambert's shoes and held considerable sway over the CFDA, even during the years he was not the president. Some have noted that de la Renta also had influence over Carolyne Roehm's tenure as president from 1989 to 1991, as she was his disciple and former employee. He was an integral part of the group that created the CFDA Fashion Awards as well as the first fashion scholarship program.

The highlight of de la Renta's early leadership was the fashion show spectacular, billed as a *Grand Divertissement à Versailles*, held on November 28, 1973. It was not a CFDA event per se, but it was put together by Lambert (featuring some of her clients) and her connections to the curator of the palace, Gerard Van der Kemp, and the socialite Baroness Guy "Marie-Hélène" de Rothschild. The Versailles event was a face-to-face fashion competition between five titans of French haute couture—Yves Saint Laurent, Marc Bohan for Christian Dior, Hubert de Givenchy, Emanuel Ungaro, and Pierre Cardin—and five Americans—Anne Klein, Oscar de la Renta, Bill Blass, Halston, and Stephen Burrows.

While the French poured money into the lavish production—which included dancing by Rudolf Nureyev, a rocket ship for Cardin, floats pulled by live animals, and dancers from the Crazy Horse nude revue—it was the Americans "who stole the show."[29] So elaborate were the French sets that the clothes were almost obliterated. The clean and simple lines of the American fashions were highlighted by a stellar performance from Liza Minnelli, as well as the novel presence of several vivacious African-American models. Journalist Enid Nemy put it succinctly in the title of her article about the event: "Fashion at Versailles: French Were Good, Americans Were Great."[30]

The success of the America contingent was astonishing to many, including its participants. One reason for this was the bickering between the designers, especially a rift between Halston and Anne Klein. Klein, noted Donna Karan (her assistant at the time), was treated "as if she did not belong there" because "she was *sportswear*"[31] and was included only because she was Lambert's client. Another reason was that many elements of the American presentation, from sets to rehearsal time, were not properly executed

(due to translation problems), were deliberately undermined by the French, or were further fraught with infighting among the Americans. Problems aside, the Americans were fresh, and the event recalibrated their own sense of identity. Blass recalled:

I thought I understood the lean, agile, racy glamour of American clothes. Yet, no one was prepared for the shock, the next day, of seeing them on a bare foreign stage . . . and on skinny black girls. . . . But it was the honesty, the pure simplicity, of our presentation—which lasted only thirty-five minutes compared to the two hours for the French— that brought the audience to its feet and made [Marc] Bohan later say: "After we saw the Americans, we looked like idiots."[32]

This flamboyant and whimsical event and many other CFDA fashion presentations were organized quickly with little long-term planning. A tiny but powerful hierarchy supported this blend of grand ideas and slapdash planning. De la Renta confirmed the informality of the CFDA's interworkings: "I operated from my office with my secretary doing all the work and a legal firm doing the accounts, but the designers always played a part in forming its direction."[33] The Lambert archives back up de la Renta's assertion that he relied on his own staff and did much to advance the causes the CFDA supported.

In a number of letters dating to the early 1970s, de la Renta appears to have been especially active in supporting the annual fund-raising dinner for the Metropolitan Museum of Art's Costume Institute. In a letter to members dated November 27, 1973, de la Renta noted that the "CFDA has been asked to be responsible for only 200 of the 500 tickets issued for the evening's dinner and private preview." In a letter from the Met's director, Thomas Hoving, dated March 12, 1974, de la Renta was personally thanked for what can be assumed to have been that year's net of $54,693 (a memorandum dated January 24, 1974, noted that the gross was $77,860, less expenses totaling $23,167).[34]

Furthermore, de la Renta personally oversaw the funding of overtime payments to insure that a documentary film on Cristobal Balenciaga (the subject of the Costume Institute's monographic exhibition) would run each Saturday for the duration of the show. His report, dated March 27, 1973, went before the board of the CFDA, during a meeting held in de la Renta's showroom.

In between his presidential terms, de la Renta advocated the idea that the organization should start its own awards ceremony. Like many people, he felt that the Coty Awards had become too linked commercially to its sponsor. The designer stated to journalist Eric Wilson, "I felt there was a conflict of interest. It was like a little clique headed by Grace Mirabella of *Vogue*, and they kept giving awards every year to the same designers. I strongly felt that we as an industry, we as designers, should be in control. Like the Oscars is [sic] part of the movie industry, I felt this [relationship] should be more formal."[35]

One of the most important developments in the history of the CFDA was the subsequent creation of the organization's own fashion awards to compete with the Coty Awards. A fixture for decades, the first Coty Awards ceremony was held in January 1943, and the winner of the Winnies (the nickname for the womenswear awards) was Norman Norell. The Winnies were awarded only to designers based in America, unlike the Neiman Marcus Fashion Awards (1938–95), which honored designers from around the world.

In their heyday, the Winnies were considered among the most prestigious awards in the field and were viewed as the fashion equivalent "of the Oscars and the Tonys." The Coty Awards ran until 1984, but began to lose importance around 1979. One key reason cited for their demise was the belief that designers could not even be nominated if they did not have a fragrance deal with Coty, and especially not if they had licensed perfumes with competing fragrance companies. Halston cited Coty's blatant overcommercialization of the show. Their demise was further hastened by the rise of the newly created CFDA Fashion Awards in 1980.

Journalist Leonard McCants noted that the CFDA decided to host its own televised awards program, not unlike the Academy Awards. The CFDA opted for a more democratic and informed selection process than had been in place for the Winnies. "Instead of the reported 90-member jury for Coty's 'Winnies,' most of whom, designers complained, never saw all of the collections they voted on, the CFDA's nominating panel includes fifteen fashion journalists and retailers who see every collection. That group will then hand down a list of nominees for the full body to vote on."[36]

The first awards ceremony, in 1980, did not go over well. Blass, the president of the CFDA at the time, set off a firestorm when he declared that all three nominees for women's apparel— Geoffrey Beene, Calvin Klein, and Perry Ellis—would be named cowinners. While the intention was to avoid "the spectacle of prominent designers losing in front of a national television audience," it led to a revolt. Beene rejected the award, noting that "losing, if indeed that might have been the case, is a great part of sportsmanship, but there isn't any sport involved in this. The industry needs a major award for its merit, not its emotion." Halston described the event as "a mess" and a "damn shame."[37]

The setback was short-lived however, because the CFDA Fashion Awards would garner great attention by the end of their first decade. Attendees included Marlene Dietrich, Katharine Hepburn, and 1988 special honoree, First Lady Nancy Reagan. Furthermore, Lambert dropped Coty as a client to orchestrate the new industry awards, which were free of sponsorship or commercial affiliation. After more than forty years, the Coty Awards were discontinued. In 1985, Donald Flannery, the senior vice president of Pfizer, Inc., Coty's parent company, noted that they had fulfilled their mission: the promotion of American fashion design and designers.

The CFDA Fashion Awards would expand and change over the next three decades but retain the promise of giving American designers, as well as select international colleagues, a celebratory platform for recognition. In the 1990s, attendance at the awards ceremony would swell above one thousand. During the early to mid-1990s, the years that the Hearst publishing company sponsored the event, the glamour quotient would also rise. For example, the late, English-born editor in chief of *Harper's Bazaar*, Liz Tilberis, brought Princess Diana to the event in 1995. First Lady Hillary Rodham Clinton was also a guest that evening.

Starting in 2001, Swarovski became the official sponsor of the CFDA Fashion Awards and, in 2011, celebrated its tenth anniversary in that capacity. In recognition of the company's support, the newly named Swarovski Awards (formerly the Perry Ellis Awards), are given to the best new talent in womenswear, menswear, and accessories design. The Swarovski Awards have helped to advance the careers of such notable young designers as Proenza Schouler and Alexander Wang.

In recent years, the structure of the CFDA Fashion Awards has changed. With relocation to a proper stage and theater at Lincoln Center's Alice Tully Hall, its guest list has become smaller and the ceremony more intimate. Additionally, the nominating and voting procedures have been refined. They now involve an industry committee of seven hundred designers, editors, stylists, and retailers. Collectively, these changes make the CFDA Fashion Awards one of the most important and glittering ceremonies in fashion.

FASHION SHOWS AND PHILANTHROPY: 1991–2006

Beginning in the late 1980s and continuing into the 1990s, the CFDA would undertake programs and events beyond its fashion awards that would change it radically. Interestingly, these seismic changes were not premeditated, as the programs had outcomes that far exceeded their original, humble intent. The events were initially viewed as ways to continue support for worthy causes (a designer sample sale called 7th on Sale) and to satisfy the needs of the council's constituency (centralization of New York Fashion Week, known as 7th on Sixth). However, after implementing the wildly successful sale and organizing the ever-expanding fashion week, the CFDA needed a team of sophisticated professionals to oversee its growth.

Officially, the CFDA became a bifurcated organization in 1973, when it created a separate foundation to oversee its philanthropic activities. However, it was not until the 1980s that the CFDA Foundation, Inc., became a truly active, clearly designated, not-for-profit entity mobilizing its membership to raise funds for numerous charitable causes. Founded by Ralph Lauren, the CFDA Foundation now manages Fashion Targets Breast Cancer, which has expanded to eleven countries and has raised $50 million, specifically for education and awareness. More recently, with the CFDA Health Initiative, the foundation began to address the issue of model health. In 1997, the CFDA issued an industry-wide statement and a call for action against the then-prevailing "heroin chic" aesthetic in advertising and runway presentation. Its most high-profile events have been those created to raise funds for HIV/AIDS organizations, including 7th on Sale and *Fête de Famille* at Mortimer's restaurant. Today, AIDS fund-raising continues to support the CFDA/*Vogue* HIV/AIDS Initiative of the New York City AIDS Fund at the New York Community Trust. Under the presidency of Carolyne Roehm, 99 percent of the membership agreed that CFDA should step up its support of HIV and AIDS fund-raising. These changes required great effort and were by no means uniformly supported by the membership. Yet, under new and enlightened leadership, the CFDA bloomed and laid a sturdy foundation for what it has become today.

With the exception of Eleanor Lambert, no other member of the CFDA has made as indelible an imprint on the organization as Stan Herman. For nearly sixteen years, from 1991 to 2006, Herman served as the organization's longest reigning president. (His second closest competitor for the title was Norman Norell, who held the position for eight years.) Herman's quiet but important work for the CFDA began decades before he assumed the mantle of the presidency, shortly after he became a member in 1967. To this day, Herman remains an omnipresent fixture in the organization.

Longevity in the CFDA is by no means Herman's only claim to fame. By 1998, before he was even halfway through his tenure, the organization had grown and changed significantly. As journalist Joyce Wadler noted:

> *Mr. Herman has had his greatest success, however, as an organizer. Since becoming the unpaid president of the Council of Fashion Designers of America nearly eight years ago, Mr. Herman has made it a force in New York. He oversaw the creation of Seventh on Sixth, consolidating fashion shows that had been scattered throughout the city and bringing them to one media-friendly spot in Bryant*

Park. Under his leadership the council has raised $10 million for AIDS research and $5 million for work on breast cancer. [38]

While Herman has made an indelible mark on the fashion community with the CFDA, it is ironic that he has been less celebrated as a designer. He is prodigiously talented as both a creator and a businessman. Winner of three Coty Awards, Herman was labeled the "people's designer." Early in his career, he specialized in stylish yet affordable women's clothing (designed under the label Mr. Mort). More recently, he designed a bevy of practical wear that is worn by millions. Some examples are QVC's top-selling chenille robes, uniforms for companies from McDonald's to Avis to FedEx, and even hospital gowns that do not reveal the patient's behind.

Perhaps the only missing ingredient in Herman's career has been his lack of self-promotion. Gregarious, articulate, and eternally optimistic, he did not initially seek a position as publicly visible as leadership of the CFDA. Yet, four months after his partner of thirty-nine years, Gene Horowitz, passed away, Herman agreed to become its president as "nobody else wanted the job."[39] He stated that "I could have dissolved, I could have afforded to fade away and do nothing, and I didn't want to."[40]

Under Herman's presidency, the CFDA would undergo dramatic alterations of structure. One major change was the great expansion of its scholarship funds and especially of its philanthropic projects. Another was the centralization of the biannual fashion week presentations and dramatic expansion of New York Fashion Week. Third, during his term, there was a change made in the bylaws to allow presidents to serve more than the originally mandated, two-year, nonconsecutive term. He also changed the admissions process from "acceptance by invitation" to a more rigorous and open application and review process. Finally, there was the hiring of executive directors: first was Fern Mallis (1991–2001); then came Peter Arnold (2001–2005); and Steven Kolb began his tenure in 2006.

The pivotal event that recalibrated the CFDA occurred months prior to Herman's ascension as president. In November of 1990, in partnership with *Vogue* magazine, the CFDA launched 7th on Sale. It was a huge "designer sample sale" that raised $4.2 million for the New York City AIDS Fund. Comprised of several mini-specialty stores, the event lasted four days. Merchandise was donated mostly by CFDA members. Major New York retailers participated, thousands volunteered, and the event was attended by more than 15,000 people. Less than two

years later, in September of 1992, 7th on Sale raised $2.6 million for DIFFA (Design Industries Foundation Fighting AIDS) to distribute to San Francisco and Bay Area AIDS organizations.[41] In 1995, the CFDA Foundation and *Vogue* presented 7th on Sale/The Return to New York. Despite its success, the sale was discontinued for a decade. Renamed 7th on Sale Online, the event—billed as "the world's largest sample sale"—relaunched in 2005 and was reprised in 2007. To date, 7th on Sale has raised more than $17,000,000 for AIDS organizations. AIDS has taken many great talents, such as Halston, Carmelo Pomodoro, Bill Robinson, Willi Smith, and Perry Ellis, as well as countless individuals who worked tirelessly and quietly, behind the scenes, to advance American fashion. The CFDA's fund-raising efforts are a fitting tribute to them all.

The success of the first sale was both a blessing and a new hardship for the CFDA. The organization was simply not able, according to Herman, to adequately manage such a sudden, large influx of money. An experienced executive director was needed. That person turned out to be Fern Mallis.

Carolyne Roehm had just stepped down as president, with no successor in place. Furthermore, the CFDA's director (and only paid staffer at the time), Robert Raymond, was not rehired when his contract expired on January 1, 1990. One of the reasons cited for this decision was Raymond's "demand for a 'substantial' salary increase" because he was "largely responsible for many of the council's recent successes."[42] The void left by Roehm and Raymond gave the CFDA a chance to reorganize. Herman and designer Monica Tilley were the members who comprised the search committee for the newly created post of executive director, and they saw that Mallis was their clear choice. She was officially approved by the board and hired in 1991 on her birthday, March 26.

Mallis, a Brooklyn native, was a public relations and special events professional who had worked most closely with interior design professionals and had organized fund-raising events with groups like DIFFA. Although she was not a fashion professional, Mallis did have some experience in the field. Her first job was a brief stint at *Mademoiselle*: Mallis was one of twenty college students chosen to be guest editors. (One of the events organized for the students by the magazine was a trip to Mr. Mort to meet the designer—Stan Herman.) In her ten-year career at the CFDA, Mallis worked on all of its events and programs. Described as a font of ideas, "Fern never thought small, she always thought big" and "it was inspiring to be around her."[43] Of all her successes, Mallis's primary legacy and most important imprint has been the growth of the fashion week shows, 7th on Sixth. She is also responsible for enlisting the prestigious design firm Pentagram to create CFDA's new logo.

At the time Herman became president, one of the most important but contentious issues facing the CFDA's members was where to stage the biannual press week shows. The merit of showing their collections in a central location was hotly debated. The creation of a centralized fashion show locale did as much as any single issue to raise the CFDA's profile, challenge its mission, force its considerable expansion, and lead to its restructuring.

While New York Fashion Week had been an entity for decades prior to Herman's presidency and Mallis's arrival, a centralized location to host the designers' runway collections was not. The shows were held at disparate locations throughout New York City; journalists and buyers were forced to run all over town to attend them. Herman and the CFDA came up with central-izing New York shows for the 1994 spring-summer collections, presented in November 1993. Entitled 7th on Sixth, the name denoted the heart of the garment industry's home on Seventh Avenue and its new fashion week home on Sixth Avenue at Bryant Park.

Both Herman and Mallis recalled the single incident that became the catalyst for a centralized fashion show venue: At the Michael Kors show in 1991, the ceiling had started to cave in. This galvanized what had been ongoing complaints by the press about safety and the locations that fashion shows were using. Mallis called it the "shot from Sarajevo," but noted that crowded lofts also lost electric power (at Isaac Mizrahi's show one season, 1,200 people sat in the dark until backup generators could be brought in) and elevators got stuck at major fashion showroom buildings like 550 Seventh Avenue. It was "like a rave," recalled Mallis.[44]

Deputy Director: Programs and Operations Lisa Smilor noted that there were so many shows spread across such a vast expanse of New York City that attendees were forced to start their day early, yet traffic delayed arrivals so that the last runway presentation "might begin as late as 11 p.m. due to the efforts to get from one place to another."[45] Because of his position as a board member on the Bryant Park Restoration Corporation, Herman helped the CFDA secure a one-year lease at that location. The CFDA put up tents on top of a cavernous underground space housing part of the New York Public Library's holdings, but the park was unsure of its load-bearing capacity. Structural concerns proved unwarranted, however, and the shows remained at Bryant Park, with the exception of one season on a Hudson River pier, until they were relocated to the Lincoln Center complex in 2010.

The creation of 7th on Sixth, as well as the coincidental formation of the Fashion Center Business Improvement District, were undeniably successful and "brought a new sense of vitality to the fashion industry here." The next season's presentation, in April 1994, rose from forty to fifty-nine runway shows in the tents.[46]

Mallis was vital to both the creation and subsequent success of 7th on Sixth, and she was duly praised for her efforts and enthusiasm. However, some felt that the fashion shows distracted the CFDA from its primary mission. Herman noted that some members bluntly told him that 7th on Sixth was "eating up more time" and was not "what we [the CFDA] needed to be doing." The financial demands and emphasis on profit ran contrary to the not-for-profit status of CFDA. The organization, therefore, decided to sell 7th on Sixth to International Management Group, or IMG (now called IMG Fashion), in July 2001. After ten years, Mallis left the CFDA in order to run the shows independently.

As it turns out, 2001 proved to be a pivotal year for the CFDA and for the entire New York fashion industry. The terrorist bombings of the World Trade Center on September 11 forced the cancellation of Fashion Week, as it had been scheduled at the same time. It was in that environment that Peter Arnold replaced Mallis as executive director of the CFDA. *WWD* echoed the sentiments of many when Arnold was appointed, noting that he "was a surprise choice . . . since his background was in law rather than fashion or public relations." Yet Arnold achieved success. In addition to focusing "on the core mission of looking after members and bringing about relationships with young designers," he oversaw the launch of the CFDA/*Vogue* Fashion Fund Award (to assist burgeoning companies) with the help of Anna Wintour and "considerably expanded the organization's Fashion Targets Breast Cancer project."[47]

Steven Kolb, who was named Chief Executive Officer in 2011 and Arnold's successor, views Arnold as an important figure in the CFDA's growth. He was realistic and organized. He "buttoned [the CFDA] up . . . giving it structure and running the organization like a business."[48] For example, Arnold partnered with 7th on Sixth (now called IMG Fashion) on its fashion shows and, by not treating the shows as a purely profit-oriented enter-prise, ensured that they would benefit the designers.[49]

Arnold had never planned on having a long tenure at the CFDA. In an interview shortly after he announced his resigna-tion in the summer of 2005, he stated, "It was never part of my long-term strategy." He openly noted his interest in becoming the business head of a major fashion company. In the same interview, he said he "would use the job [at the CFDA] as some platform

from which I would go to a design house."[50] He is now the president of Cynthia Rowley.

A year later, after the CFDA Board ratified term limits for its
officers, Herman stepped down as president. His official retire-
ment party was christened Stan's Sweet '16.' The large CFDA
crowd that turned out on November 14, 2006, was considered "a
testament to the man's popularity"—there to recognize "the end
of an era." In speeches, Herman was lauded for his unwavering
support of the mission statement—"promoting American fashion
and American designers"—as well as for "steering the CFDA
towards a more democratic organization which embraced new
talent." Federal Express donated a gift of $100,000 to the CFDA
in Herman's name (as Herman had been designing the company's
uniforms for twenty-five years).

The CFDA's new president, Diane von Furstenberg spoke
glowingly of Herman's "loving, caring" nature and shared her
assessment that he is "in love with life and that's why he looks so
good." She also stated: "I look forward to being president. I hope
I can bring it to the next phase. I don't take it lightly. I will need
Stan to watch over me and help me." And Stan Herman remains a
strong presence at the CFDA. "I'm not retiring to Boca Raton," he
has said. "Why would I? It doesn't get any better than this!"[51]

GLOBALIZATION AND
GLAMOUR: 2006 TO NOW

If Stan Herman is a designer familiar to few people outside the
fashion community, the opposite is true of his successor, Diane
von Furstenberg. She is a fashion celebrity with a larger-than-life
persona that resonates with an aura of glamour and earthy sensuality; she is so recognizable that many know her simply as DVF. Yet
von Furstenberg is also remarkably grounded. She is focused on
work, family, and philanthropic efforts—and as Herman noted, the
CFDA could have elected "nobody but Diane" to succeed him.

Even before her first marriage to Prince Egon of
Fürstenberg, von Furstenberg knew she wanted to become a
designer. In 1970, with a $30,000 investment, she began designing
women's clothes. "The minute I knew I was about to be Egon's
wife, I decided to have a career. I wanted to be someone of my
own, and not just a plain little girl who got married beyond her
desserts."[52] This quote conveys von Furstenberg's determination
as well as her colorful way with words.

As fashion has become increasing global, so too has the
reach of the CFDA. The high level of sophistication that von
Furstenberg has brought to the presidency is an invaluable asset.

Now a U.S. citizen, von Furstenberg is multilingual and retains
a strong European sensibility, which has helped expand CFDA
programs outside of the United States. As Kolb has noted, "When
Diane was elected president, she said I could scream at the
Italians in Italian and beg the French in French."[53] For all her
worldliness, von Furstenberg is highly focused on promoting
American talent.

As von Furstenberg was assuming the mantle of president
in 2006, Kolb began his tenure as the newly hired executive
director. His career-long track record in the not-for-profit and
development fields has proven to be the perfect skill set for the
job. Like his predecessor, but unlike most other members of the
organization, Kolb had no professional background in fashion.
After earning a master's degree in Public Administration from
New York University, he began working as a development officer
at the American Cancer Society and later became the senior
associate director of DIFFA and was the founding director of
MTV's Staying Alive Foundation. His initiatives to raise money in
the fight against HIV and to promote AIDS awareness, education,
and prevention utilize traditional fund-raising tools as well as a
"for-profit business approach" to fund-raising.

One of Kolb's most important initiatives has been the establishment of the Business Services Network (BSN), a community of high profile businesses, both in the fashion industry and
outside it, that creates custom programming to meet its members'
needs while providing tangible value to CFDA members. The
idea was von Furstenberg's. She felt that CFDA membership
should come with more than just the prestige of being accepted.
The network creates strategic access, new business development, licensing opportunities, and jobs, with the shared vision

of supporting CFDA members and their businesses. Additional support services for members include a website, health insurance, legal advocacy, business and technical assistance, industry updates, mentoring, and a series of seminars to train young, emerging designers.

Kolb's success stems from his skills and the fact that he understands his job. He clearly articulates that the CFDA is an "artists' guild" akin to those of the Middle Ages. Furthermore, its trade organization status is there to support its members. The CFDA is "about the designers," so Kolb and staff are always on-call. His motto is "1-800-CFDA means we are customer service."[54]

The person who works most closely with Kolb at the CFDA is Lisa Smilor, Deputy Director: Programs and Operations. Of the dozen professionals now working for the organization, Smilor has one of the longest running tenures. Hired in 1996, while the CFDA's first scholarship named for the late designer Perry Ellis was being formalized, Smilor was brought on to spearhead both educational initiatives and programs to support CFDA members, and these programs have grown under her leadership. Many people have noticed her nurturing and supporting role. Diane von Furstenberg has affectionately referred her to as "the Godmother of Fashion."

Under von Furstenberg's leadership, and together with Kolb and Smilor, domestic educational funding has expanded greatly in the past five years. "The CFDA is devoted to supporting and nurturing new and emerging design talent. The CFDA's educational initiatives were established to assist aspiring fashion designers in their high school, collegiate, and postgraduate studies, and the early stages of their careers. The goal of the CFDA's educational initiatives is to ease the transition from student to professional designer."

The CFDA has been organizing educational programs since the 1960s. However, it did not formally establish an annual, ongoing scholarship program until 1986. Its first, named in honor of the late designer Perry Ellis, was set up to benefit fashion students at the Parsons School of Design.

It would be another decade before the CFDA would create its second scholarship, a merit-based grant for full-time students in a four-year program in their junior year. Since its inception, the highly competitive CFDA Scholarship Program has awarded over 135 scholarships totaling more than $500,000, to attendees of the nation's top design colleges and universities.

While it took decades to establish its first funding programs for students, the CFDA has created several more in less than five years. In 2007 alone, it launched the Clara Hancox Scholarship

Fund for menswear design (Hancox was a menswear reporter for the *Daily News Record*, or *DNR*, from 1944 to 1993); the Geoffrey Beene Design Scholar Award for the most exemplary and innovative womenswear student (Beene's foundation donated $5,000,000 for this special award and to support the CFDA Scholarship Program in general); and the CFDA/*Teen Vogue* Scholarship for promising high school students. In 2009, the Liz Claiborne Design Scholarship Award was endowed by Art Ortenberg, the late designer's husband and business partner.

The CFDA continued to extend its philanthropic arm and was quick to respond to world events. In 2001 it organized and enlisted the industry to sell Fashion for America T-shirts, raising $2 million for the Twin Towers Fund. In 2010, funds were sent abroad after the CFDA raised a million dollars for the Clinton Bush Haiti Fund, through the sale of the Peter Arnell–designed "Fashion for Haiti" shirts. One year later, in 2011, the CFDA raised $500,000 for the Japan Society to assist earthquake and tsunami relief efforts.

The CFDA has also been an advocate for the professional needs of the membership. One example is its support for keeping apparel production in New York. Members have participated in rallies, such as "Save the Garment Center" in October of 2009. The CFDA has also partnered with other not-for-profit organizations, such as the Design Trust for Public Space. The CFDA collaborated with designer Yeohlee Teng on the Made in Midtown initiative, which under her leadership sponsored interviews with stakeholders, including the unions and factory owners, as well as feasibility studies of critical fashion production. Support for the project came from such sources as the Diller–von Furstenberg Family Foundation and the CFDA. Along with New York Mayor Michael Bloomberg, the Economic Development Corporation, Newmark Holdings, and Target, the CFDA Fashion Incubator was launched. Its goal is to support designers with subsidized studio space and to encourage mentoring in the heart of the Garment Center.

Another important CFDA initiative was to "restore consumer confidence and boost the industry's economy in the midst of the recession" with the debut of "Fashion's Night Out" (FNO) in September 2009. It was *Vogue* editor in chief Anna Wintour's idea, along with von Furstenberg, to enlist the support of Mayor Bloomberg. Bloomberg has said, "When Anna and Diane ask you to do something, you say yes." More than eight hundred stores across the city's five boroughs stayed open late (until 11 p.m.) and hosted special events with fashion celebrities. CFDA partners *Vogue* magazine, NYC & Company, and the City of New York, did much to publicize the event, which was deemed a huge success.

In addition to revenue raised for businesses, proceeds from the special FNO T-shirt benefited the September 11 Memorial and Museum and the New York City AIDS Fund, and an expanded FNO collection now continues to support the New York City AIDS Fund. FNO is now an ongoing annual event.

The CFDA also performs more traditional trade association work with similar organizations in Paris and Milan, in order to promote design protection internationally. Under von Furstenberg and Kolb, the CFDA is the first American organization to spearhead efforts in Washington to pass the Innovation Design Protection and Piracy Prevention Act. This problem is not new (Parisian couturiers struggled with piracy in the early twentieth century), but the CFDA's efforts to protect a fashion designer's work from being copied without permission is groundbreaking.

Over the past decade, the CFDA has recognized the growing popularity of fashion. To reach an expanding audience and to document both the history of American fashion and the lifestyle of its membership, the CFDA has produced a series of books with the publishing house of Assouline. Titles include: *American Fashion*, *American Fashion Accessories*, *American Fashion Menswear*, *American Fashion Cookbook*, *American Fashion: Designers at Home*, *American Fashion Travel: Designers on the Go*, and *Geoffrey Beene: An American Fashion Rebel*.

The most recent undertaking by the CFDA is the book and exhibition to celebrate its fiftieth anniversary: *Impact*. This project was von Furstenberg's brainchild. Not only did she provide the scope of both the book and the exhibition, she also gave the projects their title. The organizers clearly understood that while the book could present the work of many of the hundreds of CFDA members, past and present, it certainly could not put on view an equal number of garments in a single exhibition. Far fewer objects, less than one hundred in total, were the maximum that could fit in the galleries at the Museum at FIT. With these constraints in mind, von Furstenberg devised what seemed to be the best way to present work by the council's members, a way that would not be based only on quality, financial success, historical significance, or name recognition. Her solution was an exhibition that would highlight CFDA members who have had the most "impact" on fashion. In a meeting in August 2010 with the CFDA and Museum at FIT organizers, von Furstenberg's concept and title were enthusiastically embraced and the efforts to make them a reality began.

Impact is a fitting tribute to the hundreds of members and thousands of constituents who have worked so diligently to create the CFDA, to expand it, and to make it the embodiment of self-advancement and altruism that it has become in only fifty years. While the history of the CFDA is complex, detailed, and rich—and rightfully deserves to be documented—this essay is but one humble effort to illuminate the council's many achievements. The essay, the book, and the exhibition are dedicated to the countless individuals who shared those achievements with all of us.

NOTES

1 Eleanor Lambert Archives, Special Collections, Fashion Institute of Technology, New York.
2 Bill Blass and Cathy Horyn, ed. *Bare Blass*. New York: Harper Collins.
3 Eric Wilson. "Declaration of Independence," *WWD*. June 2000, 14.
4 Eleanor Lambert Archives.
5 Gabriel Montero and Anne Bonacum, ed. *A Stitch in Time: A History of New York's Fashion District*. New York: Fashion Center District Management Association, 2008: 17.
6 John Tiffany. Interview by author via phone, Saturday, April 16, 2011. Museum at FIT, New York.
7 Amy Fine Collins. "The Lady, the List, the Legacy," *Vanity Fair*. April 2004.
8 Wilson. "Declaration of Independence," 14.
9 Ibid.
10 Tiffany interview.
11 Eleanor Lambert Archives.
12 Eleanor Lambert Archives, December 31, 1963, p. 8.
13 Eleanor Lambert Archives, September 29, 1966.
14 Nancy Hanks (1927–83) was called the "mother of a million artists" for her work in building federal financial support for the arts and artists. Her years as chairwoman of the National Endowment for the Arts and of the National Council on the Arts saw great expansion of their programs and budgets. Hanks was named for her distant cousin, the mother of Abraham Lincoln.
15 Wilson. "Declaration of Independence," 16.
16 Eleanor Lambert Archives.
17 Minutes of the discussion, Eleanor Lambert Archives.
18 Eleanor Lambert Archives.
19 Viola Herms Drath, "The Art Influence: What Fashion Owes Art," *The National Observer*. Monday, October 30, 1967, 5.
20 Eric Wilson. "American Independence," *WWD*. June 2000, 16.
21 Eleanor Lambert Archives.
22 Council of Fashion Designers of America Archives, CFDA Headquarters, New York.
23 Stan Herman. Interview by author, Tuesday, March 29, 2011. Museum at FIT, New York.
24 Wilson. "American Independence," 14.
25 Rosemary Feitelberg. "Presidential Reflections," *WWD Supplement*. Tuesday, May 29, 2007, *WWD*. May 2007, 46.
26 Council of Fashion Designers of America Archives, CFDA Headquarters, New York.
27 Ibid.
28 Ibid.
29 Enid Nemy. "Fashion at Versailles: French Were Good, Americans Were Great," *New York Times*. November 30, 1973, 26.
30 Ibid.
31 Donna Karan, quoted in *Bare Blass*, edited by Blass and Horyn, 124.
32 Blass and Horyn, ed. *Bare Blass*, 125.
33 Wilson. "Declaration of Independence," 16.
34 Eleanor Lambert Archives.
35 Ibid.
36 Leonard McCants, "The Eighties," *WWD*. June 2000, 30.
37 Ibid.
38 Joyce Wadler, "Public Lives; Designer Looks Back With Pain and Pride," *New York Times*. September 11, 1998.
39 Stan Herman. Interview by author, Tuesday, March 29, 2011. Museum at FIT, New York.
40 Wadler, "Public Lives; Designer Looks Back With Pain and Pride."
41 Note that *WWD* reported income of $4.5 million and $2.5 million, respectively.
42 Degan Pener. "CFDA Head May Be Fashion Victim," *New York Magazine*. December 24–31, 1990, 17.
43 Lisa Smilor. Interview by author, Wednesday, April 20, 2011. Headquarters of the Council of Fashion Designers of America, New York.
44 Fern Mallis. Interview by author, Tuesday, April 26, 2011. Museum at FIT, New York.
45 Smilor interview.
46 Arthur Friedman. "7th on Sixth, Act II," *WWD*. Monday, April 4, 1994.
47 Marc Karimzadeh. "Peter Arnold Named Varvatos President," *WWD*. Monday, June 20, 2005.
48 Steven Kolb. Interview by author, Wednesday, April 20, 2011. Headquarters of the Council of Fashion Designers of America, New York.
49 Ibid.
50 Karimzadeh. "Peter Arnold Named Varvatos President."
51 Marilyn Kirshner. *Look Online*. November 15, 2006.
52 Joyce Maynard. "The Princess Who Is Everywhere." *The New York Times*, February 16, 1977.
53 Kolb interview.
54 Ibid.

PRESIDENTS

SYDNEY
WRAGGE
1963–1965

MARY
McFADDEN
1982–1983

NORMAN
NORELL
1965–1973

PERRY
ELLIS
1984–1986

OSCAR
DE LA RENTA
1973–1976 & 1987–1989

CAROLYNE
ROEHM
1989–1991

HERBERT
KASPER
1977–1979

STAN
HERMAN
1991–2006

BILL
BLASS
1980–1981

DIANE
VON FURSTENBERG
2006–present

FOUNDING MEMBERS

BILL BLASS		SARMI
DONALD BROOKS	BUD KILPATRICK	ARNOLD SCAASI
BETTY CAROL	HELEN LEE	ADELE SIMPSON
JANE DERBY	JEAN LOUIS	GUSTAVE TASSELL
LUIS ESTEVEZ	JOHN MOORE	PAULINE TRIGERE
DAVID EVINS	NORMAN NORELL	SYDNEY WRAGGE
RUDI GERNRICH	SYLVIA PEDLAR	BEN ZUCKERMAN

SIDNEY
WRAGGE

He watched them on the golf course and came to the conclusion that a man's tailored shirt could be well adapted to their sports needs. Thus was Sydney Wragge on his way toward success in his specialized field. The logical companion to shirts was skirts. And Wragge found himself in the separates business. Then shirts and skirts were sewn together, and the first Wragge dresses were born.

NORMAN
NORELL

Norman Norell demonstrated that clothes designed on Seventh Avenue could rival the most elegant creations from Paris. Norell was sometimes called "the American Balenciaga" because of the perfection of his tailoring. He also used the finest fabrics in the world and made sure the every detail, from button hole to hemline, was beautifully finished. This superb workmanship was all the more remarkable since he made ready-to-wear, not couture. His sequined mermaid dress epitomized glamour.

OSCAR
DE LA RENTA

The fashion industry is, for better or worse, devoted to the generation of illusions: of youth, wealth, and well-being, of the notion that life can be sunny and glamorous around the clock. Oscar de la Renta's exceptional body of work is, in this sense, no exception. Who can look at his fabulously ruffled flamenco dresses without mentally zooming off to a floodlit fiesta by some tropical pool? Who can slip on one of his fur-trimmed double-face suits without fantasizing about hurrying across the Tuileries on a mysterious romantic assignment? But what's wonderful and exceptional about Oscar is that he miraculously embodies and inhabits the fantastic world suggested by his creations. He takes his dominoes very seriously, is a political mediator, a philanthropist, a society dazzler, a patron of the arts, a diplomat, a devoted family man, and a great designer. I regard him as fashion's Renaissance man.

—Anna Wintour

KASPER

After studying in Paris, Kasper returned to New York, and Lord & Taylor bought some of his clothes. One of his dresses would become the department store's all-time best seller. Consequently, the buyer told him that the store wanted to promote him as one of their young American designers. Kasper did a fashion show, appeared on the front page of *WWD*, and became a star overnight. Two years later, he would receive his first of three Coty Awards (three Coty Awards = Hall of Fame status).

"Over a lifetime of designing, I've evolved a philosophy that comes from creating clothes for a particular kind of American woman—who, by the way, I very much admire. This woman is adventurous and vital with a lifestyle that demands she play many different roles throughout the day. It's the confident spirit of this kind of woman that inspires me most."

BILL

BLASS

Having brought the comfort and simplicity of sportswear into the realm of formal dressing, Blass can rightly be credited as one of the creators of a true "American style." His blending of classic fabrics, like cashmere and satin, has made him a favorite among this country's best-dressed women. Labeled the "hardest working man on Seventh Avenue," Blass has cultivated an unforgettable personal and professional style.

MARY
McFADDEN

Mary McFadden was virtually born into textiles: Her early years were spent on a cotton plantation near Memphis, Tennessee. She was educated at Foxcroft, in Middleburg, Virginia; the Traphagan School of Design; Ecole Lubec, in Paris; the New School for Social Research; and Columbia University. From 1962 to1964, Miss McFadden served as director of public relations for Christian Dior in New York. Following a move to South Africa in 1965, she became an editor of Vogue South Africa , while acting as contributing editor to *Vogue*'s U.S. and French editions. Returning to New York in 1970, Miss McFadden continued her association with *Vogue* as special projects editor.

During her extensive travels, Mary McFadden collected unusual African and Chinese silks. Using these textiles, she designed three tunics that attracted the attention of her colleagues at *Vogue*. The tunics were heralded as "a new departure" by the magazine. Henri Bendel bought these first samples.

These and subsequent Mary McFadden designs are unique in the way they float on the body. Quilted jackets and coats are inspired pieces of body sculpture. "Marii" pleated gowns, Miss McFadden's distinctive trademark, are striking for their luminous color palette. The secret to "Marii" pleating was discovered in a satin-back fiber found in Australia. The fiber, when subjected to the heat-transfer process, fell like liquid gold, softly on the body. That was the secret that built my business. If it were not for the workshops in Mumbai, New Delhi, and Lucknow, I could never have achieved such beautiful embroideries.

PERRY
ELLIS

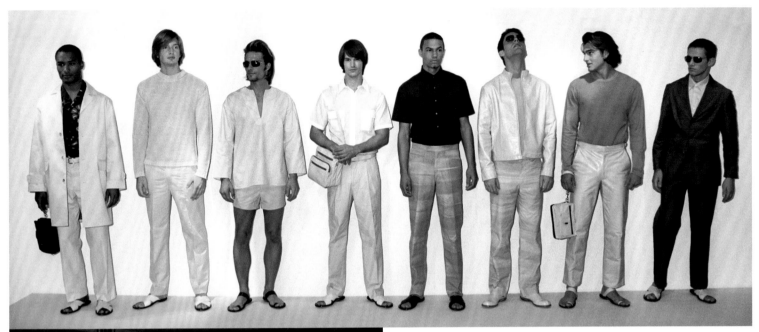

"Always provide the clothes needed for daily life," Perry Ellis once said of fashion. He wasn't the first to present the idea that designer sportswear could be produced for everyday wear, but he was certainly one of its most successful champions.

By the late seventies, his women's line, Portfolio, had become synonymous with clothes that were casually contemporary and totally wearable. "Modern classics" is what he called the knit polos and cable knit that populated his collections. Fashion wasn't supposed to be hard to understand; it was meant to be thoughtful but confident and playful too. If the clothes didn't telegraph that idea properly, he did. Perry's signature was skipping down the runway at the end of his shows.

If Perry helped define contemporary American sportswear as effortless, he was among the first to understand that a fashion brand could be more than mere apparel too. He translated the cachet of his sportswear into shoes, perfume, and accessories. Perry fully understood that a designer's name and the vision it represented were just as powerful as the clothes he or she designed.

More than two decades after his death, Perry Ellis's impact on American sportswear governs everything we do at the brand, from the way we market the collections, to the design and styling of the clothes. I don't skip down the runway, but if I can suffuse the brand with that kind of amiability, then we're keeping Perry's legacy alive.

—John Crocco

CAROLYNE
ROEHM

My passion for designing clothes began when I was a child, with fantasies of glamorous women wearing beautiful gowns that dazzled everyone when they entered a room. That youthful and fanciful vision matured into a desire to create clothes that fit into the prevailing lifestyles. My goal was to make women feel confident, feminine, and sexy. Being a woman made it easier to identify the needs of busy and multifaceted modern women. With my designs, fabrics, colors, and accessories, I tried to instill a sense of capable confidence in a tailored suit worn in the boardroom, and with my evening clothes, my goal was to offer sexy and alluring clothes that fit into the private side of their lives, allowing that very feminine side of their personality to shine.

When I reflect upon my years in the fashion industry I feel the most impact I had was not in design or fashion. The AIDS epidemic was raging when I became president of the CFDA, and it became my mission to mobilize the fashion industry to help fight this horrible disease that was taking the lives of so many of our talented artists. I felt very strongly that it was our industry's responsibility to act, and not just talk or mourn. Fortunately, I gained a powerful ally when Vogue's Anna Winter stepped forward and said she wanted to be involved. We asked Donna Karen and Ralph Lauren to be cochairs of the very first "7th on Sale."

With single-minded leadership, and a huge amount of work from all of the CFDA members, the retail community, and the industry press, I felt when the curtain went up on opening night that it would be the most meaningful IMPACT any of us could make. "7th on Sale" raised $4.5 million, a huge amount of money in those days. What we accomplished then will always remain a powerful example of how a group of talented people can pull together to create a magical event for a good cause.

My varied design career has lasted for more than half a century. During that time I have designed every article of clothing that covers the human body, but the one category that I have made my own is the world of uniform design. My contribution was to take the two-dimensional branding of major corporations and make the uniform an integral part of the brand identity. The employee is no longer uniformed to disappear but is uniformed to extend the brand platform.

Starting with the Avis corporation, I've designed uniforms for TWA, United Airlines, and Eastern Airlines, and have been the designer for FedEx since 1980, a relationship that I still enjoy today. I designed for JetBlue before they even had a name and helped create their brand identity through the clothes. Recently, in designing US Airways, I was challenged to combine two major airlines into one vision; two different cultures brought together by one uniform.

The uniforms for McDonald's set the standard for fast-food dressing over a fifteen-year period. I've clothed almost every casino worker along the legendary Las Vegas Strip as well as the very first mega cruise ships for RCCL. The uniforms for Amtrak's Acela Express were the first designer uniform for rail travel.

My sixteen years as president of the CFDA had as much of an impact on American fashion as any other part of my

design life. Its tenure brought together the power of all of America's talent and prepared a solid foundation for today's vibrant organization. The three hundred thousand customers who have kept me on QVC for eighteen years would make a claim for that impact, as would those who remember the contribution I made in the sixties and seventies with Mr. Mort, the company that revolutionized junior dressing. But it is my contribution to the world of uniforms, and the fact that not a day goes by without my seeing someone in a Stan Herman uniform, that is my calling card to design.

Feel like a
woman,
Wear a dress!

Diane Von Furstenberg

DIANE
VON FURSTENBERG

Once upon a time there was a princess with an idea. The idea was a dress, a dip-dry, cotton jersey dress that wrapped in front and tied at the waist. The princess devised cunning prints in vivid colors and in no time, women all across the land were buying the dresses—five million of them—and wearing them. And even though the princess was a member of the jet set and a glamorous party girl, her customers felt that she must have understood them to have invented something so comfortable and practical and so suited to their everyday adventures and newfound sense of independence.

It was the 70's and en masse, the women of the land had gone to work. Wearing a wrap dress by the princess, the women went on job interviews, they went straight from the office out to dinner, they went around the world. The dress epitomized not only the spirit of women's liberation, but of sexual liberation too: in two minutes flat a woman could be dressed and out the door; she could be undressed in even less time.

Years passed and the princess moved on, until one day her son took for his bride a damsel who cherished the dress that was long forgotten. Under the spell of the 70's, she and her friends searched thrift shops for vintage versions. And so it came to pass that the wrap dress, after a long sleep, was reawakened. The calendars had been turned to the fall of 1997, and all the signs said that the now classic dress would live, happily, ever after.

—Holly Brubach, "Wrap Star," *New York Magazine*, 1997

IM
PA
CT

CFDA
DESIGNERS
A *to* Z

WHAT IS
YOUR BIGGEST
IMPACT
ON AMERICAN
FASHION?

JOSEPH
ABBOUD

Joseph Abboud has said that his clothing is as much about lifestyle as design. Since 1986, after breaking away from Ralph Lauren, he has filled a niche in the fashion world with his creations for men. For the contemporary individual seeking a facade that is as casual, elegant, and as international as the accompanying life, Abboud offers comfort, beauty, and a modernity that is equally suitable in New York, Milan, or Australia. Abboud was the first menswear designer in the United States to revolutionize the concept of American style.

REEM
ACRA

Although she is known for her incredible gowns that regularly appear on the red carpet, Reem Acra is also responsible for shaking up the traditional bridal industry with her trendsetting, embroidered wedding dresses.

Educated in Beirut, New York, and Paris, Acra burst onto the bridal scene in 1994 with a range of wedding gown designs that drew on her Lebanese roots as well as her European and American schooling. Her gowns, which continue to be sought after, feature breathtaking embroideries and stunning silhouettes.

In her first advertising campaigns, the departure from the sweet innocent bridal images into cutting-edge fashion statements galvanized the staid wedding industry, which had become mired in boring, uninspiring images of brides. The Reem Acra bride became synonymous with luxury and opulence.

Today, brides still flock to Reem Acra for a statement that sets them apart from their contemporaries and leaves them with an unforgettable memory of the most important event in their lives.

ADOLFO

"I wonder what people mean exactly when they call themselves designers," said Adolfo, twisting the thimble he wears on his middle finger. "I don't think of myself as a designer. I think I am a dressmaker. I like to make beautiful clothes, to cut them and sew them. I pick up ideas from all over and work them up in my own way. I never want to intimidate or scare the person who is shopping."

—Bernadine Morris, *New York Times*, June 19, 1990

ADRIAN

I believe in a "design continuum" of clothing that is essentially modern, that reflects the changing patterns of living, evolving gradually but continually.

Good design can be directional *and* timeless, functional and innovative in the tradition of American sportswear, and responsive to the needs of a woman equally committed to professional responsibilities and an enduring personal style.

Everyone has a unique interpretation of the world. Mine comes from an upbringing rooted in tradition and sculpted by the constant changing of the new world—nature and nurture. A citizen of the modern world, I stand on the bridge between East and West, between past and future, between luxury and accessibility.

I envision a world where objects made by skilled crafts-people can sit alongside mass manufacturing, where generations of skill are still alive and desired, where thoughtfulness is the greatest virtue, where a considered life is the richest one, where we realize there is another way.

My work is to help make that possible. I work with gold that holds history, diamonds that see the future, and rubies that long for love. There's a story in each stone: I'll leave it for you to find them on your own.

WARIS
AHLUWALIA

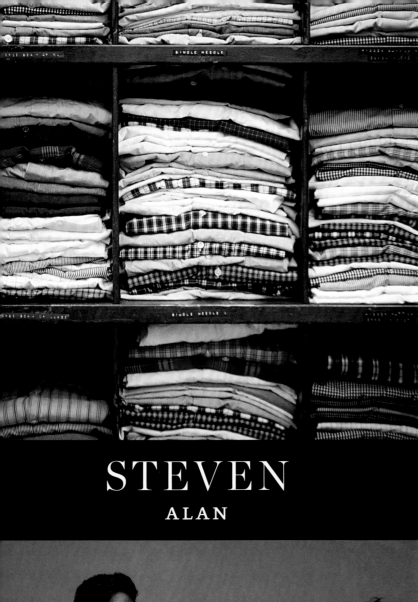

STEVEN
ALAN

Steven Alan's idea of the perfect shirt has always relied on the basic fundamentals of fabric, fit, and finish, proving that comfortable doesn't have to mean sloppy. His now iconic silhouettes and playful detailing have come to define the personality of a generation, infusing modern, urban sensibilities with classic American simplicity.

Immaculately fussy in both tailoring and proportion, yet comfortably unfussy in the final effect, his shirts are "refined but disheveled" and very wearable. His reintroduction of traditional fabrics has created somewhat of a men's shirting revolution that continues to inspire new colors, patterns, and interpretations. These design concepts are combined with a number of innovative production techniques to create shirts that capture the self-conscious "this old thing" look that is both individual and shared. This philosophy was further articulated to include a line of women's shirts that are classic, empowering, and sexy in a particular way.

SIMON
ALCANTARA

I believe my greatest impact on American fashion was ushering back a bold femininity in jewelry after a period in the nineties when American women barely wore any jewelry at all. I began working on really big and bold pieces in the year 1999 as a personal creative project, and my jewelry was chosen for the Fall 2000 Oscar de la Renta fashion show in NYC. Jewelry that striking had not been seen on the runway in years, and it made a huge impact. By September 2000 I had my first cover! It was *Elle* magazine featuring my necklace on Christy Turlington. The tagline read: "The new glamour. Bold feminine chic."

Many other editorial credits and covers followed thereafter, and along with that, other designers also began creating big and bold jewelry and soon this was all you saw on the market. Gone were the tiny, almost imperceptible pendants and earrings, and women were once again adorning themselves to be seen. They looked powerful. This bold femininity persists today.

JEANNE
ALLEN
&
MARC
GRANT

Jeanne-Marc, the venerable San Francisco fashion label owned and designed by Jeanne Allen and Marc Grant, debuted in New York in 1978 with the full-frontal domination of Bonwit Teller's closely watched Fifth Avenue windows. "Will Success Spoil Jeanne-Marc?" was the 50-point headline in Bonwit's full-page *New York Times* ad.

By the late eighties the American collection was being exported to shops in London, Paris, and Tokyo. The Japanese mega-company Itokin took notice and licensed Jeanne-Marc for that island nation. Martex and Fitz and Floyd adapted the trademark Jeanne-Marc design elements and licensed the label for their bedding and tableware collections.

Well before the current obsession with celebrity, *People* magazine featured Allen and Grant in an article along with many of the celebrities who were Jeanne-Marc fans.

CAROLINA
AMATO

I am part of an original core of accessories designers in the CFDA that is probably twenty or so strong. In the early 1980s, we forged into the market with original accessories concepts and ideas at a time when the market consisted of black gloves, gold-plated clip earrings, and metal link belts. Handbags were called pocketbooks and were black or brown, and scarves were square silk prints, period. We primed the fire that led to the explosion of the current accessories business. Great accessories were and are our one and only passion.

Gloves are an expressive and poetic accessory. I love how they function to adorn as well as to protect the hands. I have worked diligently to create a wide variety of ways to reinvent them. I hope that my dedication for more than thirty years in designing an enormous archive of feminine cold weather accessories will be my lasting impact.

RON
ANDERSON
&
DAVID
REES

TENTHOUSANDTHINGS was at the forefront of introducing a new style of fashion jewelry that became known as personal jewelry. At a time when costume jewelry was mostly seen as an extension of American and European fashion houses (think faux Chanel pearls), it introduced a collection based on delicately proportioned necklaces and earrings made from fine materials—sterling silver, gold chain and wire, and semiprecious and precious stone beads and pearls—often in odd natural shapes and always in an intimate proportion.

This was something radical in the eyes of fashion editors, retailers, and high-end customers. TENTHOUSANDTHINGS went on to introduce several innovations: the use of black chain, which turned into a huge trend, wire and chain beading techniques, and artfully crafted compositions using briolettes and rare and unusual stones. As with all jewelry and art movements before them, what was once revolutionary has become the ubiquitous jewelry of today.

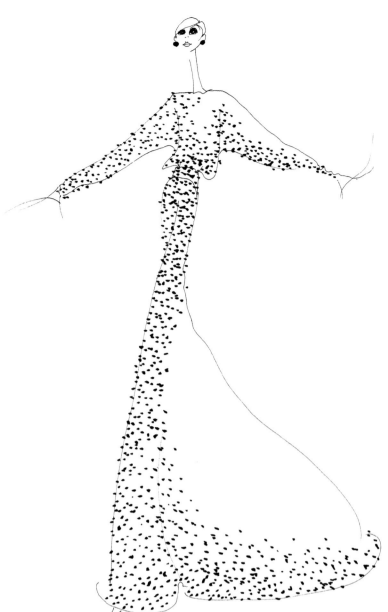

NAK

ARMSTRONG

Nak Armstrong is celebrated for introducing a modern aesthetic to the fine jewelry category through his pioneering of a revolutionary way to wrap-set gemstones in gold chains.

Internationally recognized for innovative departures from standard metalworking, Nak is specifically credited with developing a technique for setting stones in metal netting. This approach allows for a previously impossible movement and agility in jewelry. Adopted today by jewelers worldwide, the effect creates an illusion of delicacy, making pieces appear both fragile and bold. It is this type of challenge that Nak applies to form and design that has left such a mark on the fashion community.

Nak's artistic philosophy is to respect history while creating new paths in technique and design. He uses architecture, sculpture, and fashion influences in his pieces, all of which can be seen in his recently launched eponymous collection, Nak Armstrong.

Aesthetically, Nak's designs have given fine jewelry a youthful, modern edge. Technically, he has forged techniques that have forever expanded the possibilities of working with stones and metals. Overall, he has helped blur the boundaries between accessories, fashion, and design.

JOHN

ANTHONY

"John Anthony is one of the most dedicated and multi-faceted of designers, the minimalist of American fashion."

—1978, Grace Mirabella, editor in chief, *Vogue*

"John is an American designer who understands his craft."

—1981, Ben Brantley, fashion editor, *Women's Wear Daily*

"His shapes are basically simple, but the luxury is inescapable, 'throwaway elegance.'"

—Bernadine Morris, fashion editor, *New York Times*, 1982

LISA
AXELSON

Since 1954, Ann Taylor has understood the evolving needs of modern American women, sharing and identifying with their desire to be strong and feminine, beautiful and stylish, confident and genuine.

For me, it's about the perfect pieces—the foundation of every woman's wardrobe. These are those amazing, go-to pieces you can always count on like a best friend, that work with you, not against you . . . and add style and individuality to all that you do.

BILL
ATKINSON

This trained architect constructed and reinvented individual sportswear pieces, especially through his concentration on new optics of materials—rhinestone-embroidered black/white tweed for an evening coat for instance.

LUBOV & MAX

AZRIA   AZRIA

BCBGMAXAZRIA began in 1989 with a single dream—to create a beautiful dress. More than twenty years later, the BCBGMAXAZRIAGROUP fashion house delivers beautiful dresses, sportswear, outerwear, accessories, and more, to more than 13,500 points of sale worldwide. Since the beginning, Max and Lubov Azria have brought a distinctly European sophistication to American fashion, creating a unique aesthetic and sensibility that are now an inextricable part of American design.

     The acronym BCBG stands for *bon chic, bon genre*, Parisian slang for "good style, good attitude" and an idea that epitomizes the influence of BCBGMAXAZRIA. The brand's collections are at once innovative, wearable, and effortlessly chic. Of all the accolades Max and Lubov have received, their greatest honor is being a part of a woman's life for everyday moments as well as momentous occasions. It is for her that BCBGMAXAZRIA designs, and because of her that it thrives.

MARK
BADGLEY
&
JAMES
MISCHKA

It never interested us to do office clothes.
We're total suckers for glamour.
Glamour always works.

YIGAL
AZROUËL

When I reflect on what my impact has been on the fashion industry as a designer, I feel one of my distinct trademarks is the art of draping. This technique is the foundation and base that transform my creative process from beginning to end. Sketching does provide a point of reference for me, but since I am such a visual designer, my most successful pieces have come from literally sitting in front of a mannequin and physically draping the fabric to form the garment.

As a self-taught drape designer, everything from the initial process through the end result of my work is molded by a very hands-on and old-world technique. I treasure that I can take this process, physically touch and feel the components of the design, be infinitely inspired to create, and still have endless surprises in the fabric being manipulated. I think the designs that I bring to the industry are a direct reflection of this three-dimensional art form made in a modern and constantly evolving way.

JHANE
BARNES

When I entered menswear thirty-five years ago, everything was black, gray, and navy. I wanted to change the way men dressed: the styles, colors, and fabrics. I started with style, introducing one-piece/gusset sleeves and the "sport coat blouson." Later, I designed textiles from the ground up: I bought handlooms and learned to weave, which continues in my studio today. My textile innovations paved the way for fancy fabrics and color in menswear.

I've pushed the limits of textiles with mills all over the world. When I first started, I experimented with weaving and designing novelty yarns with American mills. My next stop was Japan, where I became fascinated with complex woven structures and unusual finishing. Now, with my own mills and factories in China as a result of a new partnership with A.W. Chang, there is no limit to what I can try! I am so excited to continue my innovations as a menswear designer.

JEFFREY
BANKS

I believe that my biggest impact on American fashion has been to look at classic "good taste" clothes in a whole new light. First in menswear, and then womenswear, children's wear, and home furnishings.

In menswear, I first made an impact (in my first year in business) as the youngest Coty Award Winner ever by designing a complete collection of masculine men's furs. A few short years later, I took the top prize for Menswear Designer of the Year. The hallmark of my designs has always been an extravagant and exuberant use of color and pattern. This was very evident in the collection of men's, women's, and children's clothing I designed for Merona Sport. The great success of Merona led to my women's Jeffrey Banks Collection.

An obsession with tartan plaid led to my first bestselling book. This, in turn, led to HSN asking me to design an extensive collection of products for the home, which includes everything from clocks to furniture to bedding. I can impact every facet of my customers' lives, from the clothes they wear to the plates they eat from.

VICTORIA
BARTLETT

VPL has been advocating a new way of wearing underwear since the inception of the brand in 2003 and initiated a currently emerging trend of blurring the boundary between underwear and outerwear. VPL's influence beyond fashion has been seen in the arts, visual culture, music, dance, and ballet.

"VPL brings weightless layerable underthings
and casual wispy overthings
to a generous array of female shapes."
—*New York Times*, 2010

"Victoria Bartlett did those harness-style
bra-tops first, y'all, and don't forget it."
—*New York Magazine*, 2010

JOHN
BARTLETT

When I launched my collection in the early nineties there were not a lot of independent American menswear designers exploring the themes of sexuality and gender, two themes that I focused on as a sociology undergrad at Harvard. I liked to fill a runway with diverse concepts of masculinity and have always enjoyed experimenting with the spectrum of male archetypes from *geeky sexy* (think Forrest Gump) to *rugged/refined* (Brawny paper towel guy anyone?).

    Having been in business now for almost twenty years, I find my "guy," the John Bartlett man, has evolved and grown as I have. Today he is still exploring themes of what it means to be a man, and that includes giving back to society and working on behalf of abused animals, which have no voice of their own. To me, "real men" are kind to animals, and I hope that one day my "IMPACT" will marry my two great loves, fashion and animal welfare advocacy.

DENNIS
BASSO

I believe that my biggest impact on American fashion has been in my work with fur. Many designers begin their careers designing sportswear or cocktail clothes. In 1983, when I showed my first collection, it was exclusively furs, and for the next twenty years furs were the mainstay of my designs.

I think what has made my designs unique has been that I never treated fur in the traditional manner that "furriers" did worldwide. I always looked at fur as if it were a fabric that could have shape and movement. I have continuously experimented and tried new techniques and texture combinations, which have set my furs apart. I believe it is because of this uniqueness that I have had the good fortune to dress some of the most influential, beautiful, and talented women from around the world. I always strive to find a new design approach, not being afraid to mix various furs together, to integrate hand embroidery and fashion fabrics, and to treat fur not only as outerwear but also as ready-to-wear.

Today, many designers have joined the world of fur design, as I have joined their ranks in designing ready-to-wear. But, however diversified my collection becomes, somehow, fur is always the first thing people think of when they think of the Dennis Basso brand.

SHANE
BAUM

Shane Baum's contribution to eyewear has been significant and much imitated. An early proponent of vintage eyewear, Shane is best known for layering complex combinations of colors and employing intricate details that were not technologically possible during the majority of the twentieth century, bringing the past into the future. His signature collection, entitled Leisure Society by Shane Baum, employs state-of-the-art CNC (computerized numeric control) machining on block titanium. With more than six hours of elaborate engraving, the frames are subsequently plated in 12-, 18-, and 24-karat gold, making them some of the most luxurious eyewear ever created. Despite the proprietary technologies, the eyeglasses have a decidedly mid-century feel with complex Victorian and baroque embellishments.

BRADLEY
BAYOU

HALSTON TRIBUTE: While Bradley was the creative director for Halston, he restored the brand to its original stature: once again hanging in Bergdorf Goodman and on the backs of A-list celebrities. As a tribute to Halston, Bradley channeled the Studio 54 days and designed fabric rich with Andy Warhol's quotes in a classic Halston silhouette. Bradley had just finished showing the new Fall 2004 line, styled by Rachel Zoe, when he met up with Mercedes Scelba-Shorte, the finalist from *America's Next Top Model* season 2, to take this image. It was an exciting moment as the Halston label hadn't been this popular in more than a decade! The Berlin Museum of Modern Art requested the dresses, for an exhibit showcasing American fashion designers and art, where they made their appearance alongside this image of Bradley and Mercedes.

OPRAH: Bradley dressed Oprah Winfrey to receive the first Bob Hope Humanitarian Award at the 2002 Emmy Awards. This was an important moment in history as well as for Oprah and Bradley. Oprah looked amazing and was on the covers of *People*, *Us Weekly*, and *In Touch Weekly*. She also made *People*'s Best-Dressed List and was picked as number twenty-nine for *InStyle*'s 100 Best Dresses of the Decade. This was a pivotal moment in fashion for Oprah as the beginning of her journey into couture and red carpet events.

VICKI
BEAMON
&
KAREN
ERICKSON

Our fantastic runway collaborations and our enduring signature pieces created for everyone from Madonna in 1986 to Lady Gaga in 2011 are our legacy!

GEOFFREY
BEENE

One of America's true design pioneers, Geoffrey Beene challenged the American fashion establishment by creating haute ready-to-wear for women; body-centric designs "using seams, geometry, and hardware to define and insinuate" the female form. Winner of eight Coty Awards and three CFDA Awards, Beene was also one of the first American designers to show his collections in Europe.

Beene's designs might well be memorialized in a time capsule as "visionary, witty, irreverent, iconic, and timeless." He left his distinctive imprint on four decades of popular culture by "reinventing the connection between clothes and lifestyle many times over." He embraced synthetic fabrics before others and preferred dancers to models for show-casing the enhanced body movement and comfort to be found in the aesthetics of his collections. From his early collection of constructed designs to his famous eveningwear of sequined football jerseys and ballroom gray flannel, "Beene's essentialist view of fashion lifted it from the realm of the frivolous: The more you learn about clothes, he observed, the more you realize what has to be left off." He was, in his own words, "a body designer rather than an antibody designer" later in his career.

Today Geoffrey Beene, LLC, is a fashion empire comprised of men's ready-to-wear and men's and women's accessories and fragrance. Beene's futurist vision lives on through the Geoffrey Beene Foundation, which has transformed this iconic brand into a philanthropic powerhouse that supports research innovation and out-of-the-box solutions to a host of medical and societal issues.

SUSAN
BENNIS
&
WARREN
EDWARDS

SUSANBENNISWARRENEDWARDS is a collaborative creative partnership between designers Susan Bennis and Warren Edwards.

SBWE has consistently stood for advanced styling, quality hand-craftsmanship, and an unabashed sense of luxury. Innovative design and marketing are hallmarks of SBWE's fashion leadership. Creating and developing four major collections per year out of their own retail environment, SBWE's unique designs combine the unexpected and the sensual. Their work incorporates exotic leathers, luxury materials, hand embroideries, intriguing themes, and explosive color. SBWE's award-winning advertising campaigns have created powerful, unique images emphasizing the individual products and artistic details.

In acknowledgment of their significant work, the Costume Institute of the Metropolitan Museum of Art selected a representative group of fifty styles designed by SBWE to be housed in the permanent collection. The original design sketches were also included along with this group. The Metropolitan Museum has reproduced selected styles from the SBWE collection as Christmas ornaments available at the Met store. At the time of the collection's inclusion, Diana Vreeland, special consultant to the Costume Institute, lauded that SBWE's designs allowed one to have "the smartest, prettiest feet for any occasion."

ALVIN
BELL

As a fashion designer, I have always been about dressing *global women*.

My love, passion, and style have been to achieve one singular goal: I want the consumer to look and feel like a movie star. Women have always told me that they keep my clothes in their closet for years and never throw them out. I love that!

The real deal for me is to be remembered not just for fashion, but for art, too. There is something about the unknown that is exciting. And then there is the sparkle of feeling and hearing your own heart racing with joy from a new piece of wonder. It's the sublime delight of being dressed like an alchemist in a dark suit, black sunglasses, and a scarf transforming mystic visions into art.

DIANNE

BENSON

Now, in the twenty-first century, the two worlds of art and fashion seem almost interchangeable—seamlessly blended, you might say. This was not always the case—far from it. There was actually a running debate during the Dianne B days of the seventies and eighties by magazines such as *Artforum* questioning whether or not to accept pages of fashion ads—were they "artistic" enough?

Everything has changed, but back then when Dianne B presented her version of fashion exhibition and advertising, it was seen through the eyes of artists, many of whom are today's blue-chip art stars like Robert Mapplethorpe, David Wojnarowicz, and Cindy Sherman. Not only did she incorporate their art into her advertising, Dianne pioneered SoHo as a fashion destination. Her postmodern Dianne B store sold her own art-influenced collection, along with designer/artists such as Issey Miyake and Jean-Charles de Castelbajac. In 1983 she opened the all-concrete, vast, and minimal Comme des Garçons store—the first of its kind—when there were only galleries and bona fide artist's studios in SoHo.

CHRIS
BENZ

The most important impact Chris Benz has had on American fashion is his specific use of color as an integral design element in modern designer sportswear.

His bold, exuberant collections convey a sense of history as well as progress and a keen understanding of the emotional, vibrant aspects of how women want to dress. After his debut collection, featuring fluffy mohair jackets and colorful double-knit separates, the *New York Times* dubbed the eccentric spirit of the CHRIS BENZ collection "the best example of the heightened level of sophistication that is expected of new designers today."

A constant and continual voice in fashion, Chris's innate sense of color has established him as a strong element of modern American fashion. *Glamour* says, "He's bringing his super loud color combinations to closets everywhere. The looks are neither Palm Beach nor grungy hippie: even a long skirt is never without a tailored counterpart, such as a button-front jacket."

Propelling American fashion forward, through color and casual elegance, is where the CHRIS BENZ philosophy firmly lies, and for which he has become most recognized and regarded.

MAGDA
BERLINER

Designer Magda Berliner has been producing her namesake collection since 2000. Launched by an editorial in *Vogue Italia*, Berliner was prodded to prove her talents beyond a few leather bits. . . . Well-received by retailers such as Barneys New York, Louis Boston, American Rag, Japan, and Joyce Hong Kong, among others, Berliner's business has held steady as an "in the know" name that caters to indie fashionistas.

In Spring 2002 Berliner offered one-of-a-kind dresses composed of vintage lace and crochet "ribbons" she had collected. Each garment is hand-assembled by Berliner herself and is still a bestseller each season with devotees coveting numerous pieces as heirlooms. Thus, Berliner's impact could be keeping romance alive embodied in a little white frock.

ALEXIS
BITTAR

Over the past two decades, Alexis Bittar has revolutionized the way fashion perceives plastics. Bittar brought a bold sense of reflective light and color to jewelry at a time when minimalism was at its height. Early on in his design career, Bittar developed a strong interest in the idea of fusing the Bakelite and Lalique techniques together; using Lucite he was able to bring this concept to fruition. To this day, Bittar hand-carves and hand-paints Lucite at his headquarters in Brooklyn. Bittar's innovative use of this extremely malleable material has propelled him to the forefront of the fashion jewelry industry. His designs often walk a fine line between fashion and art, and are considered among many circles to be wearable art instead of high-fashion jewelry. Bittar's unique exploration of Lucite has garnered him a position of high-esteem among the fashion elite and allows him to consistently stand out in an increasingly competitive market.

SULLY
BONNELLY

My career in the industry is a testament to what a foreign-born naturalized U.S. citizen can achieve given the opportunities in education, apprenticeships, mentoring, and entrepreneurial incentives offered by life in the United States, and especially in New York City.

Born in Santo Domingo, the Dominican Republic, I came to New York City in 1980 to study at Parsons School of Design. After graduating I immediately began working as Oscar de la Renta's assistant. From there, after stints in the ateliers of Bill Blass and Eli Tahari, I started my own label, in the niche market of women's ready-to-wear, day and evening, priced at under $200 retail. And this, I believe, is my achievement and contribution to American fashion; e.g., designing and marketing high-style clothing at affordable prices, with a well-made and tailored garment appealing to women of any means. This large audience consists of women of a broad age spectrum who want to look in trend without being followers.

MONICA
BOTKIER

My biggest impact on American fashion would be the birth of the contemporary handbag category, which was virtually nonexistent until the Trigger Bag in 2003. I started Botkier because of a specific need. Simply put, I wanted a functional designer bag for a price I could feel comfortable with, around $500 to $600. This idea was revolutionary at a time when designer bags were starting at one thousand dollars and the next step down was a huge distance. There was nothing in between that would satisfy fashion-forward taste and quality with a reasonable price. The Trigger Bag promptly became known as "the bag that launched an industry." Prior to the Trigger, there had never been a young-designer option for a luxury handbag.

MARC
BOUWER

Celebrity: Long before red carpet dressing was a sport, Marc Bouwer attracted starlets the old-fashioned way—he earned their respect with his unprecedented American design by draping fresh, sexy looks in technologically advanced fabrics. Fashion legend Kal Ruttenstein noted: "Marc was doing red carpet dressing, even before it was in style." The parade of celebrities photographed in his gowns provide a snapshot of our glamour-driven, syndicated society of awards shows, film and television premieres, concerts, and sporting events.

f you start with the same Michael Kors turtle-neck, but the trousers are in wool gabardine, a little softer, pleated in front, and slightly ta-pered, like Barry I. Brick-en's, this page—the line is a little easier, the ori-entation a little more ''dressed.''... The long and short of how the silhouette changes with a change of top, opposite. Esca-da's full-length, soft-shouldered, generously cut wool coat, near right, in creamy yellow. Barry I. Bricken trousers, about $145. Peter El-liot, NYC; R.T.W., Ltd., Charleston SC; Mark Shale, Chicago; Hall's, Kansas City MO; L'Elite, Houston; At Ease, Los Angeles. Escada coat, about $698. Mid-August at Bergdorf Goodman; Nan Duskin; Gidding-Jenny, Cin-cinatti OH & Indianapolis IN; Hixons, Milwaukee WI; Bal-liet's; Auer's, Denver CO. ...For the trimness, the finish of a suit, far right, Arthur Chap-nik's taupe wool jacket, just below the waist, lightly fitted, with the season's short-coat look. Jacket, about $285. Late September at Bullock's. De-tails, more stores, last pages.

216   Paul Lange

BARRY
BRICKEN

My career began in 1969 with Trousers By Barry, luxury men's trousers manufactured in America. I pioneered high-fashion men's trousers, introducing fine Italian and English fabrics. After this initial success, I launched a line of women's trousers under the Barry Bricken label, and the volume catapulted from $7 million to more than $20 million. By 1985 my women's business had grown to 70 percent of the total volume of the company, and I decided to expand the women's business to a full collection and open retail outlets.

I think the single best achievement that set me apart from the rest of the fashion industry is the fact that I am synonymous with the best-fitting men's and women's trouser in the market. Today after forty-two years I still have the reputation for making the finest-fitting quality women's trousers with consistency, color, texture, and subtle details.

TOM
BRIGANCE

The designer, known professionally as Brigance, initially won acclaim for his beach outfits, which he feminized with ruffles and frills and made sophisticated with fabrics like gray flannel and black velvet. The Duchess of Windsor was one of his earliest admirers, buying half a dozen outfits from his first beachwear collection in 1939.

—Anne-Marie Schiro, *New York Times*, October 18, 1990

DONALD
BROOKS

Brooks's clothes were known for their clean lines, often surprising colors, and for their distinctive fabrics, most of which he himself designed. There is a boldness about a Brooks design that makes an impact and makes his contemporary dresses for the stage particularly successful.

—Anne-Marie Schiro, *New York Times*, October 18, 1990

THOM
BROWNE

I am trying to introduce
tailored clothing to a new audience.

Dana Buchman launched in September 1987 and enjoyed tremendous success for more than two decades. The brand was the anchor of the bridge department in specialty and department stores across the country, with Saks, Neiman Marcus, Bloomingdales, and Dayton Hudson among its biggest customers.

Designing for the consumer—not the press, not the celebrities, not the store management—was the top priority. Dana Buchman, the woman behind the brand, traveled around the country each year to introduce the new collection to women at in-store fashion shows. Her customers were her inspiration, and her personal connection with the women she dressed fueled her line for more than twenty years.

DANA
BUCHMAN

JASON
BUNIN

Michigan-bred Jason Bunin is designer menswear's best-kept secret. When he first launched his eponymous collection in 1998, menswear had become a sea of khaki, navy, and gray. Bunin ushered in a new era of expression. His mantra: *"Men should wear color. Not be afraid of it."*

Jason designs clothes that incorporate unique details, luxurious fabrics, and some of the strongest color stories in the market. In 1999 no other menswear designers were creating clothes with treatments that each man could personalize and make his own. Jason brought in such fresh details including short-sleeve shirts with adjustable sleeve openings; RiRi zippers in unusual locations on garments designed to expose, or hide, just the right amount of skin; and sunglasses that had patterns printed on the lenses. Commonplace today. Not so then.

ANDREW
BUCKLER

The biggest impact of Buckler on American men's fashion has been the fit—Buckler made it expectable to wear clothes that actually *fit* and followed the contours of the body. We started with a jean and throughout the years created a whole wardrobe, melding roguish American icons with the English bloke aesthetic—and will continue to.

TORY
BURCH

"As her business has grown, Burch has continued to address
the myriad needs of her clients' lifestyle. It's hard to believe that
just five years ago, we bought the collection from a small rack of
clothes that she showed us in the den of her apartment."

—Jim Gold, CEO of Bergdorf Goodman, 2010

With a singular retail concept and vision, Tory Burch launched a collection in 2004 with almost ten categories, a boutique in New York City, and an e-commerce site. Unprecedented. There are now forty-five Tory Burch boutiques worldwide. Her goal was and is to offer customers a designer aesthetic at an accessible price.

Tory became synonymous with the Reva ballet flat (named after her constant inspiration, her mother) and the tunic, inspired by a caftan she found in a flea market. She and her design team strike a balance between staying true to the collection's core of classic American sportswear and evolving. In 2008, her peers acknowledged her with the CFDA Accessory Designer of the Year Award.

Tory quickly embraced the online experience and social media. *ToryBurch.com* is the company's largest sales venue and features a blog with original editorial content often picked up by outside media outlets. Meanwhile, her Twitter dialogues with fans are famous for leading to new product categories (think travel socks!).

In 2009, she launched the Tory Burch Foundation to help female entrepreneurs start and sustain their businesses through microfinancing and mentorship. Tory's long-term goal is to grow the foundation in tandem with her company.

STEPHEN
BURROWS

My biggest impact on the American fashion industry has to have been my participation in the Grand Divertissement à Versailles in 1973, which I was invited to, along with four other cutting-edge American designers, by the French designers. From when I was being honored at the Fashion Walk of Fame, the following statement best describes what I feel was, is, and always will be my impact: "I am known for fluid body-conscious clothes in bright colors which stretch over the body like a rainbow." My boutique in Henri Bendel, Stephen Burrows' World, sold my now famous matte jersey dress with a rippled "lettuce" edging, which has been copied as a finish ever since the day I debuted it in my collection in 1972. Other trademarks include decorative zigzag stitching, my use of color blocking, my innate love of rayon matte jersey, and innovative styles in suede and leather. So what do you wear under a Stephen Burrows matte jersey dress? To quote my muse, Pat Cleveland, when asked just that, "a fragrance!"

ANTHONY
CAMARGO

I have always believed that true beauty is simplicity. I call this simple elegance. When creating Anthony Nak, my goal was not to be a starving artist, but to demystify the industry and become a part of history.

I would like to be remembered for breaking the barriers and creating new techniques to pave the way for a new generation of designers who have been and are inspired by my past work. I live by the rule of simple elegance, that simplicity is the most elegant way.

Today my work reflects this belief more than ever. My current goal is to make a global impact on our society and all the worlds' cultures by bringing to the most affluent and critical of customers the view of less traditional materials as fine materials, to open yet another door of change in how jewelry is viewed. When the smartest and chicest women of our time understand and share in educating our youth, only then will what is the norm be changed.

KEVIN
CARRIGAN

I think that challenge is what drives and inspires me. I work on products that span multiple categories, tiers of businesses, and price ranges globally. I am responsible for the design of the men's and women's ck Calvin Klein bridge apparel line as well as the accessible Calvin Klein lifestyle sportswear offering. This also includes Calvin Klein Jeans and the recently introduced line of ck one apparel, which takes its inspiration from the iconic, unisex fragrance of the same name.

Working for a house like Calvin Klein comes with some inherent design codes based upon the legendary brand's aesthetic, which is grounded in minimalism, architecture, and modernity. As a designer I am very proud of the consistent development work we do with innovative fabrics and advanced fibers to keep our designs modern, interesting, high-quality, and competitive. We use very pure, noble yarns and fabrics juxtaposed with updated materials, techniques, and proportions in our sportswear, suiting, dresses, outerwear, performancewear, and jeanswear lines.

I constantly push for a balance between classicism and modernity to create sexy, current clothes that address how people want to live and dress in today's world, and if I can continue to deliver upon that, I feel that my impact will be realized and appreciated.

OLEG
CASSINI

Cassini had the longest career of any designer in America, covering seven decades. He achieved perhaps his greatest fame as the official wardrobe designer for Jacqueline Kennedy when she was First Lady; he also designed clothes for Joan Fontaine, Joan Crawford, and other Hollywood stars and women of great wealth. But throughout his career he also saw to it that his name appeared on ready-to-wear fashions that were affordable to average women.

—Richard Severo and Ruth La Ferla, *New York Times*, March 19, 2006

LILIANA
CASABAL

My work as founder and designer of Morgane Le Fay can be characterized as an incredible and continuing journey in search of a new definition of beauty. In my thirty years of working in the fashion industry, I have discovered that in addition to "style," design can deliver a sense of healing and happiness. My greatest achievement comes in creating that life-altering feeling for the people who wear my designs.

Through my work, I have found beauty in many forms, and I am very grateful for this. In all aspects of my work—from my initial concepts to the everyday workings of the company and my fantastic team—I take inspiration from the joy and possibility my clothes seem to give to my customers, and I passionately continue both my search for and an expansion of the concept of beauty.

EDMUNDO
CASTILLO

THE LIGHT SANDAL

I wanted to create a shoe that belonged to the twenty-first century, innovative yet timeless in design and fully ornamented by light. In the past, light has been used on heels or in hard parts of the shoe but never in a flexible part such as the upper.

The Light Sandal was designed in collaboration with Oryon Technologies, creators of the ELastolite used in the *Tron: Legacy* movie, an illuminator that is flexible, waterproof, and used for safety in working apparel and first applied in the Motorola Razr cell phone to light the keypad.

The sandal can be charged by plugging a cable into the wedge where the batteries are, and when fully charged, its light can last up to five hours at full luminance or in blinking mode for up to ten hours.

SALVATORE J.
CESARANI

Throughout my forty-year career in American fashion, I have made several unique and significant contributions. In 1978, I was one of just a handful of trailblazing designers who catapulted menswear onto the global stage through the launch of the first men's fashion shows for buyers and the press. Never before had menswear had such a platform for garnering domestic and international attention.

Also in the seventies, when the country was wearing leisure suits, I conceived a softly constructed blazer and trouser—the "sports suit"—consisting of sportswear separates newly sized in small, medium, and large. "The Cesarani collection is really sports clothing refined to the nth degree," said Rita Hamilton in the August 11, 1975, issue of *DNR* magazine.

"His signature is evident in the way he perfectly coordinates his outfits.... His clothes have a cinematic quality that draws attention to every pattern and color," according to the February 16, 1998 issue of *DNR* magazine.

RICHARD
CHAI

My contribution to American fashion is designing clothes to express the spirit of a new generation. Each collection is about questioning the existing conventions of traditional fashion by proposing new ways of dressing and layering that are at once nonchalant and sophisticated. This aesthetic is ungoverned by notions of masculinity or femininity; it is instead drawn from the spirit of individuality.

JULIE
CHAIKEN

As the founder and creator of one of the most recognizable clothing brands in American contemporary women's fashion, Julie Chaiken has impacted the fashion world by creating the perfect-fitting pant. Her fiercely loyal client base returns each season eager for the latest styles. Whether wide and flared, skinny and cropped, or straight and long, each line delivers that impeccable fit and fashion-forward style.

    Since the mid-nineties, Chaiken and Capone continuously delivers collections of exceptional quality and excellent design, ensuring that every American woman has the perfect-fitting pant.

AMY
CHAN

The impact of Amy 8 Chan in fashion was initially in the pioneering of *utility chic* in 1993 and the subsequent development of the unique "Techno Luxe: Industrial Tile as Luxury" mosaic tiling process.

    Amy 8 Chan was one of the first to take inspiration from utilitarian work wear, vintage, military, and nontraditional fabrics and reinvent them as a unique clothing accessories and jewelry collection while evolving the concept of accessories as clothing and clothing as accessories. This vision extended to the reinterpretation of a forgotten fifties-era industrial process into the recognized signature mosaic tile used in the Amy 8 Chan accessory collections.

"In an era where so many of our textiles have lost their connection to historical craft, it is our goal to reclaim a history where products were made by hand, by skilled artisans who played an esteemed role in their communities and passed on their knowledge from generation to generation," is the mission statement behind Natalie Chanin's Florence, Alabama–based company, Alabama Chanin. American fashion has been impacted by the company philosophy of "slow design." The term embodies a way of working that embraces the long-term view over the short-term gain and uses age-old traditions to build products that celebrate strong design principles for modern living. Alabama Chanin has been a great example of a fashionable, sustainable company, one that creates beauty and meaning without producing excess waste or destroying natural resources. Alabama Chanin has shown that sustainable garments do not have to be unflattering or uncomfortable; they can be wearable pieces of art. The production process is simple, yet unusual for the fashion industry. Nothing is made until an order is confirmed; all the manufacturing is done in-house; and the garments are produced completely by hand. Alabama Chanin has gracefully combined slow design, sustainability, and lean-method manufacturing through beautiful couture garments that have impacted and influenced the fashion industry for a decade.

NATALIE
CHANIN

GEORGINA & KEREN
CHAPMAN CRAIG

Marchesa was established in 2004 by Georgina Chapman and Keren Craig as an eveningwear house dedicated to creating one-of-a-kind gowns inspired by the designers' muse and house namesake, the noted eccentric European style icon Marchesa Luisa Casati. Chapman and Craig have since worked to successfully establish a unique position in the market by translating their love of dramatic gowns into a flourishing business, creating what *Women's Wear Daily* has called "dresses to take your breath away."

Dismissing the notion of minimalism in favor of romantic and feminine motifs, Chapman and Craig's inspired, fantasy-like collections have reinvigorated glamour on both the runway and red carpet. Through their acute attention to detail, the designers have emphasized the importance of couture-level craftsmanship in American fashion, creating all of their collections by hand in their New York atelier. Distinguished by meticulous embroidery, striking silhouettes, and studied embellishment, each one of Marchesa's intricate designs truly stands as a wearable piece of art.

RON
CHERESKIN

One key influence I have had on fashion was the cotton sweater, which really did not exist until I brought it to the forefront of fashion. At first, the stores thought it was a crazy idea, since the consumer was limited to wool sweaters. It took about one week after the first Chereskin cotton sweaters hit the retail environment for us to know fashion had changed.

Color was my next big influence, especially introducing pastels to men, which became a major craze for many years and continues today. American spectator activewear was a key element of my early sportswear concepts—bringing designed fleece and ribbed terry cloth to fashion.

I feel there are many more impact concepts I accomplished in American fashion—including using two guys who had children in a very revolutionary ad concept—but in short, I was part of creating the original footprint for casual American sportswear for men that continues to flourish and grow in fashion today.

WENLAN
CHIA

Twinkle is the brainchild of New York City–based designer Wenlan Chia, displaying her affinity for knitwear, love of art, and prolific imagination. Beginning in 2000 as a collection of colorful, exuberant chunky knits, Twinkle has blossomed into ready-to-wear, accessories, jewelry, home furnishings, and yarn.

Twinkle by Wenlan made its runway debut in February 2002. The first collection received praise by both the *New York Times*, which gave it "kudos," and *Women's Wear Daily*, which called it a "bright spot" of fashion week. In 2005, she was selected as one of "Spring's Leading Ladies"—a group of five notable designers—by *Vogue* magazine. Having been recognized for her achievements, Wenlan was inducted to the CFDA in 2006.

DAVID
CHU

American fashion has been celebrated for an ease that is functional and stylish. Its best practitioners tap into aspirational lifestyles, be it one of luxury or of sport. David Chu, creator of the megabrand Nautica, counts among them.

Chu's influence runs deep in consumer consciousness and industry alike. His unique design philosophy, which unites adventure, action, and classicism, blurred the lines between outerwear and sportswear. Chu taught us that the rugged could be elegant, a concept that carries on to this day. So enduring is Chu's legacy that few today can remember there ever was a distinction. Anyone who came of age in the past three decades will instantly recognize the spirited, iconic, color blocked sailing jackets and sweaters of his design. His design reach encompassed a lifestyle empire that extended from fragrance and footwear to watches and home furnishings.

Then there's Chu, master brand builder. From the brilliant "floater" key chains that came with the first jackets to the yacht decking on the floors of Nautica shops to the casually heroic advertising campaigns, Chu's attention to detail created the ultimate American dream of a good life, open and free, always by the sea. As one of the first Asian-American designers to rise to prominence, Chu's life story, intertwined with Nautica, remains an authentic tale that inspires not only the budding designer to pick up a pencil and sketch, but anyone to chart their own dreams.

EVA
CHUN

Harper's
BAZAAR
SEPTEMBER $ 3.00

Pure Simplicity

09

0 754724 7

"It's all about throwing a curve" is how Suzy Menkes described Eva Chun's 1991 Spring/Summer collection. And she was right. Trained as a Chinese watercolorist and calligrapher, Eva's work is informed and driven by the form and discipline of those arts. Eva used top stitches and intricate seams to accentuate and flatter the lines of the body with grace and ease. At a time when so many women were dressing over the top, her statement was more subtle. Eva designed pared-down slips that were cut on the bias and perfectly fitted simple tank dresses that women could wear day to evening. Her bias-cut silk charmeuse dress, worn by Linda Evangelista and photographed by Steven Meisel for the February 1994 American *Vogue*, perfectly captured Eva's vision of timeless, luxurious, and feminine design.

DOO-RI
CHUNG

Doo-Ri's biggest impact on American fashion is her tactile approach to design, as she has always been drawn to draping fabric, in particular jersey. The process of draping allows her to combine something that is very personal with every piece she does. Eric Wilson, a fashion critic of the *New York Times*, has stated that "Her work is a technical marvel, feats of jersey engineering that turn dress hems into suspended necklines and skirts into curtains rising on a stage." Doo-Ri continues to push herself each season to create beautiful, functional pieces that women can incorporate into their everyday lives. *WWD* has noted, "From the get-go, Doo-Ri Chung has played by her own rules when it comes to draping and working jersey—pushing a tough glam mood one season, simple and girlish another, all the while moving toward something a little edgier than where she started." She loves subtle glamour that is still chic and grown-up, but never overdone. Fashion critic Lisa Marsh described this as "Doo-Ri Chung has a way with fabric, particularly when it comes to draping. There are few designers working in New York today that are as adept with making fabric, silk jersey in particular, lay as well as she can."

LIZ
CLAIBORNE

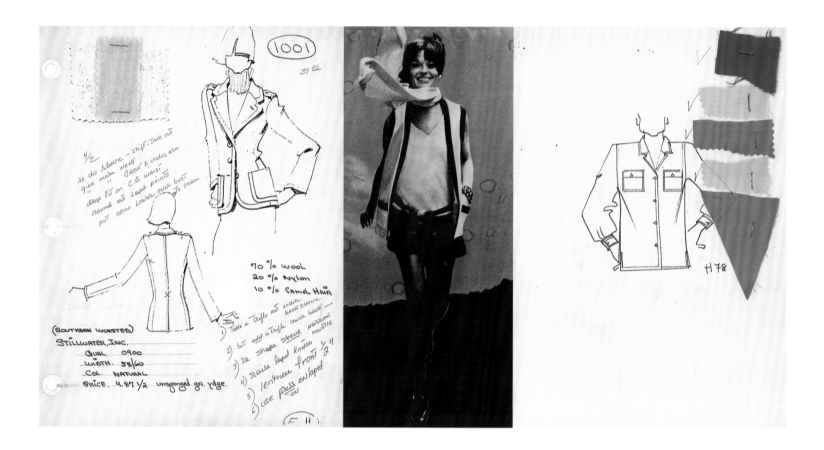

"Liz Claiborne is one of the all-time greats, not just in the apparel industry, but in the history of the stock market." So spoke Brenda Gall, senior industry specialist at Merrill Lynch.

Ms. Gall was acclaiming a woman who had been trained as an apparel designer. But she was also acclaiming Liz Claiborne as the organizer and leader of a powerful company. Liz Claiborne had developed the formidable skill of organizing disparate elements to create a rational and beautiful outcome. That was how she approached the design of apparel and the design of our company.

She participated in the design of an organization dedicated to specific objectives, many of them immaterial: pleasure in respectful interrelationships; dedication to learning and relearning skills; continued self-examination; and simply put, organizational civility.

The story of our phenomenal growth has been told many times. First, Liz hired a number of young design aspirants to sketch, to track down buttons, to check color matching, and to bring us to a point where she then hired an assistant designer. She was still in control, but that control was slipping as she began to remove herself from the actual designing of clothes. Bob Abajian, her assistant in the late eighties, once described a line presentation for a company video: "There our clothes were, hung on racks and special fixtures [at

Macy's in Paramus, N.J.], and it looked as though the entire line was painted with one brush."

As divisions were added, designers were added. Liz designed less and supervised more. "The further one is removed from the actual touching, draping, fittings, the less of oneself is in the product," she said. "That is obvious."

We left the company in 1989. Liz Claiborne, Inc. had matured and was now to be "organized" under new management. Jerome Chazen, experienced in aggressive selling, and a board of directors that was to become increasingly traditional and supportive of the chairman, sat in judgment of the performance and direction of the company. It constantly amazes me how a group of highly successful executives can officiate, year after year, to the detriment of a once-great company.

But Liz, the designer, was far from forgotten. Her most gratifying distinction took place in 1991. She received an honorary doctorate degree from the Rhode Island School of Design.

Somehow she remains iconic. Her style, her dignity, her humility—all of these fashioned the person. She remains a historically great designer—of apparel, of her company, of herself.

—Art Ortenberg, Liz Claiborne's husband

PATRICIA
CLYNE

In essence, Patricia Clyne was a company that spearheaded a way of dressing for a generation of women entering the work force ... The future execs ... The future leaders ... Not quite able to buy designer prices and not wanting to look quite that "done" ... Absolutely not interested in anything "Moderate." Modern, edgy, and feminine—Patricia Clyne, the label.

ANNE
COLE

The Anne Cole Collection sustained the
designer swimwear ideal; the swimsuits were
beautiful, feminine, and quietly sensual. Anne
Cole's sensibility was traditional elegance,
and her swimsuits often recalled the 1930s
beach scene as well as the most elegant
sportswear of Patou.

—Bernadine Morris, *New York Times*, August 11, 1987

KENNETH
COLE

For the future of our children...
Support the American Foundation for AIDS Research. We do.

SEND CONTRIBUTIONS TO: AMERICAN FOUNDATION FOR AIDS RESEARCH, BOX C, NEW YORK, NEW YORK 10116

Models:
Ariane
Christie Brinkley
Kelly Emberg
Cindy Harrell
Beverly Johnson
Andie MacDowell
Paulina
Julianne Phillips
Joan Severance

Photographer:
Annie Leibovitz

Sponsor:
Kenneth Cole

"What you stand for is more important than what you stand in."

—Kenneth Cole

THE MESSAGE IS THE MEDIUM

The decision to commit many of my personal and professional resources to social and community initiatives just seemed to happen. I used to occasionally struggle to justify giving so much of myself to something often perceived as being questionably relevant, that being the business of fashion, aka "my day job." However, I realized early into my journey that if I could make what I did more meaningful than it was, if I could in effect address not only what people looked like on the outside but who they were on the inside, then my efforts might in fact become even more rewarding. Our early years of AIDS advocacy refocused my business priorities, and in 1986 after our first ad promoting AIDS awareness, I suddenly realized what an effect our commitment, personal and financial, could have on the larger community. From that day forward I have always used my voice to distinguish myself from the competition and to raise awareness about important social issues. Our provocative advertising aims to make people think—to start a dialogue and shake things up a little, even if it means going where no company has gone before. Doing what we do requires a certain amount of risk taking, to push things one step further. We've taken many steps, and a few missteps, as we've worked the message into our medium. What started organically as a personal effort and a contribution to the community, as well as a business strategy, has also become our company's trademark.

It is a woman's right to choose.
After all, she's the one carrying it. -Kenneth Cole

It's the media's right to print what they see fit.
It's our right not to buy it.
—Kenneth Cole

LIZ
COLLINS

In 2000, I launched my first collection in New York and rapidly gained notoriety as a designer doing groundbreaking work in fashion knitwear. I developed a special technique called knit-grafting on manual knitting machines and used it to shape, embellish, and construct fabrics and garments in an endless variety of ways. The technique became the cornerstone of my collections, and it manifested in inventive and unusual combinations of materials, distinct design features like scalloped seams, and a fully integrated, concurrent fabric and garment construction process.

I challenged basic knitting technology to go to the limits and found an inexhaustible vocabulary of structures, patterns, and forms through this multifaceted medium. The market had never seen knitwear like this, made by hand, and it was promptly picked up by Barneys and Kirna Zabete, among other important stores, and received a substantial amount of media coverage as my brand emerged.

MICHAEL & NICOLE

COLOVOS   COLOVOS

Nicole and Michael Colovos, creative directors of Helmut Lang since 2006, have become pioneers in elevating the contemporary marketplace. By bringing their philosophy to conceptually design-minded collections that are accessible, the design duo continues to inspire the industry with creativity and innovation. Their emphasis on construction and strong but subtle detail is apparent through the use of their signature combinations of hard and soft fabrics, draped jersey, and angular hems.

SEAN
COMBS

FASHIONTAINMENT: The combination of entertainment with fashion is uniquely Sean John and has made a lasting impact on American menswear.

In 1998, Sean John launched with a collection of denim, velour sweat suits, and baseball caps with the company tagline, "The Future of Fashion." Sean "Diddy" Combs's talent as a performer and producer gave him the unique ability to transform the runway experience into entertainment. He was one of the first designers to use large-format screens on the runway with dramatic films as the shows' backdrops. In 2004 the CFDA awarded him Menswear Designer of the Year. To celebrate its tenth anniversary, Sean John returned to the runway with a spectacular show documented by MTV in a prime-time feature, *If I Were King*.

Vogue's editor in chief Anna Wintour has said Combs "understands publicity, and how to attract the media." She later added, "He's a showman."

RACHEL
COMEY

As the editor of a website that draws in more than 1.3 million female readers a month, I have become very intimate with what young women want to wear and the kinds of designers that inspire them—Rachel Comey leads that pack. She has always had this perspective of being evolved, and perhaps much more established than she may have been in reality in the early years. I believe this is because her vision has always been 100 percent sincere, unwavering, and also very BIG—mindfully deep and broad and carefully textured as if the blueprint of her design mission is something she's been crafting for many years, not just the past decade. She seems to intuitively know what young women want to wear, and plays to that aspirational aspect. A woman feels unmistakably cool and confident in something she has designed, whether it be a pair of her now famous ankle boots or one of her many seriously breathtaking patterned day dresses. Her original textiles have become a hallmark of her brand. That along with her attention to detail—craftsmanship, fabrics, and fit and silhouette—has made it possible to recognize a Rachel Comey design. If I could, I would bet the fashion farm that she is on her way to becoming one of the most recognized and respected American designers of our time.

—Christene Barberich, editor in chief, *Refinery29.com*

ROBERT
COMSTOCK

Leather outerwear, the backbone of his collections, is no longer the European specialty item it once was. Denim jackets and chambray shirts are by now as generic as stadium coats and crew-neck sweaters. If Ralph Lauren is responsible for refining western apparel for the well-heeled, Comstock might be credited with elaborating on it.

—Frances Rogers, *New York Times Magazine*, "Selling True Grit," October 8, 1989

KATHRYN
CONOVER

Through my early years, I lived and breathed sportswear, finding dresses uninspiring and mostly staid. My career took its formative turn when a love interest questioned why I shunned the most universal mode of female apparel. What began as an attempt to answer a simple question moved into a personal and professional obsession.

Thus began my lifelong love affair with the dress and an ever-evolving quest for the most perfectly relevant and exquisite exemplar, in all its various incarnations. I formed my career around finding a newly compelling expression of femininity for the evolving modern woman.

My dress imprint has always been characterized by a distinctly feminine sensibility embodied within the modality of modern fashion and modern life. Draping and fabric manipulation within a strong silhouette and clean lines are signature.

And, while I've long since lost touch with that curious love interest, every day I'm still rediscovering, flirting with, and newly falling for my greatest love affair of all, the dress.

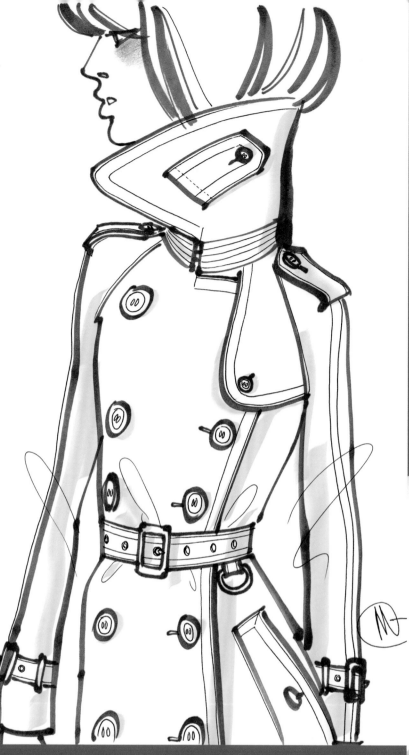

MARIA
CORNEJO

Timelessness is the essence of Zero + Maria Cornejo and of the women who love the clothes we make. What started off as an intellectual, abstract point of view, Zero + Maria Cornejo has become quite universal for all women—using volume, tailoring, draping, and as few seams as possible to create clothes that flatter all bodies. I believe that clothes have a life—the bubble dress, draping, and off-kilter alignments are some of the principal elements that I've enjoyed seeing evolve. Women want clothes that make them feel good, they love, they will want to wear time and time again, and that translate into the various aspects of their modern lives.

MARTIN
COOPER

As the former vice president of design-outerwear for Burberry, Martin steered the helm of the venerable British brand's calling card, the most iconic, recognizable, and emulated item in the fashion lexicon for which Burberry is famous: the trench coat. Cooper extrapolated on the innovation of the trench to create entire wardrobes of outerwear spanning from day to evening to sport in order to meet the needs of the customers' ever-evolving lifestyles. His outerwear for Burberry has been a longtime favorite of the British royal family, U.S. presidents, and Hollywood celebrities.

ANNA
CORINNA
&
DANA
FOLEY

We started at the flea market. Dana was making the clothes she wished she could find AND afford.... I was buying the vintage treasures I could never pass up. She liked my eye, and I loved her clothes. One day Dana came to my booth and said, "We should get out of the rain." We developed a cult following, we opened a store on the Lower East Side, we filled it with amazing designs. The clothes were made by Dana, right in her building on Avenue A. I curated vintage I had amassed from all over the world. Immediately, people fell in love. New, totally original designs and fabulous vintage—it was a rather novel concept at the time. It truly had the feel of someone's closet you would covet. We were making rtw, making great bags, and still finding vintage. Each piece was a statement. Britney, the Bush twins, Heidi Klum, Anna Sui, even Ralph Lauren and his gorgeous son came in to our store. The *New York Times* put us on the cover of their small business section—two full pages about our stores in New York and Los Angeles, our own online shop, sales every day. Fergie, Carrie Underwood, Drew Barrymore, all amazing and beautiful, all devotees. We can't travel across town without seeing our bags on all the cool girls.... Kim France said, "Dana Foley and Anna Corinna seem to have a dead-on instinct for what we all want to look like."

Totally innocent and naive, we entered into the arena.... A bumpy road for sure—but what a trip!

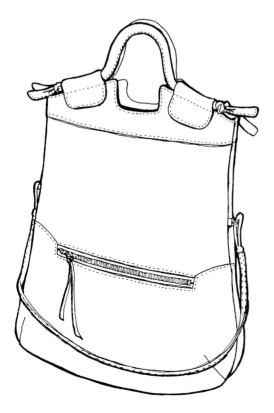

ESTEBAN
CORTAZAR

"Beauty will be convulsive or it will not be."

—André Breton

I believe that is the perfect way to epitomize the soul of the house of Emanuel Ungaro—a maison with codes of maximalist-grandeur and bold beauty, a house that gave me the chance to play with magic and history in this surreal and fantastic world of Paris fashion. The house's aesthetic infrastructure is color and print, and that is my foundation and passion as a designer. Therefore, to have the potential to create within realms of clashing colors and motifs was utopia. My idea was to decode what was established and ignite an evolution of a new aesthetic that would speak of the now but always remain true to the fashionable Ungaro demimondaine.

FRANCISCO
COSTA

"The designer Francisco Costa is making a fine job of creating a twenty-first-century image of Calvin Klein. His skill is to make coats and dresses appear simple—a compass twirl of shoulders above straight-line hips and simple colors like black and white, with a dash of cobalt blue."

—Suzy Menkes, *International Herald Tribune*, February 20, 2010

"Francisco Costa, the current king of pared-down chic, delivered a collection worthy of that title. . . . His presentation epitomized minimalist sophistication."

—Melissa Whitworth, *Daily Telegraph*, February 18, 2010

"None of Mr. Costa's designs looked like those of anyone else, and some of his fabrics seemed to be utterly new inventions, with fuzzy or furry textures. . . ."

—Eric Wilson, *New York Times*, "On the Runway," February 17, 2010

As a designer, one of the biggest challenges is editing. Through a rigorous study in minimalism, I have adopted a process of reduction that involves stripping an idea down to its very essence, making room to understand and fully celebrate its pure form.

I am driven by that quest for honesty, harmony, perfection, and purity; creating balance out of imbalance through shape, fabric, proportion, and color. By eliminating and paring down, I am able to design clothes that can be worn with a sense of ease and effortlessness.

I strive for modernity and clean lines in my work to cultivate that sense of freedom. My goal and my challenge are to design innovative yet timeless pieces—ultimately creating a lasting, powerful statement.

VICTOR
COSTA

I was trained at an early age to attend the haute couture shows in Paris, as the designer for the legendary firm Suzy Perette in New York. In those days, there was no designer ready-to-wear, and the great fashion houses of Paris accepted payment, termed a "caution," from American garment manufacturers to legally interpret their clothes. My job was to observe every nuance of construction of the items shown at Valentino, Dior, Givenchy. I was dubbed "King of the Copycats" by *WWD* publisher John Fairchild in his book *Chic Savages*.

When Christian Dior in Paris asked me to create a ready-to-wear line for them in the 1990s, I was honored and sat in the front row of the great master Gianfranco Ferré's Dior shows, ready to interpret the designs for the American market. My career had come full circle.

The greatest thrill, however, was my boutique at Bergdorf Goodman on the sixth floor, with its gleaming marble floors and rows and rows of Victor Costa ball gowns, dresses, and cocktail suits. My most famous dress is the crumbcatcher, a pleated confection of taffeta; to my delight, Brooke Shields wore the dress when accepting Harvard's Teenager of the Century Award!

JEFFREY
COSTELLO
&
ROBERT
TAGLIAPIETRA

We started Costello Tagliapietra with the belief in the artisanal and in the process of design being just as important as the business.

We are carving a niche in New York fashion nodding to the past with respect to the heritage before us while creating dresses that are elegant and timeless but also right for the needs of our time.

The dressmaker details we have implemented since 2005 are a direct response to the mass production techniques we witnessed being used in the ready-to-wear market. We wanted to do something that honored the past and connected to people in a very personal way; much like an heirloom passed down for generations, we see our dresses that way and produce them with vintage techniques with that goal in mind.

ERICA
COURTNEY

Erica Courtney, a creative genius, has continued to transform her conceptions while holding true to her design ethos of rock-and-roll chic meets red carpet glam. Starting with Swarovski crystals in the disco era, Erica later launched a sterling silver trend with her iconic hearts and crosses. Next came her extraordinary Tahitian pearl and diamond designs, which directed her to the stunning micro-pave settings that are ubiquitous on the red carpet. Erica's signature look of micro-pave diamonds swirling around unique and rare colored gemstones has brought her everlasting recognition and the tagline "Drop Dead Gorgeous." Erica dominates each trend with her own exuberant design thumbprint and vivacious personal style so that every jewel can be easily recognized as quintessential Erica Courtney.

—Cindy Edelstein, jewelry industry expert

STEVEN
COX
&
DANIEL
SILVER

We believe what sets Duckie Brown apart—and what will be the label's lasting impact on American fashion—is the color, tailoring, and humor that is the DNA of every collection. Tim Blanks on *Style.com* writes:

"It was quite literally vintage Duckie Brown in the revisiting of the long over longer proportion, the drop crotch pant (here as juicily colored sweats) and the almost feminine bias cutting which produced for instance a shirt in cyclamen chiffon that tied to one side."

PHILIP
CRANGI

What is most important to me is to create that piece of jewelry you have been looking for your whole life—the piece that best helps you tell your personal story; the piece that makes you feel like the best possible version of yourself.

LILLY
DACHÉ

Lilly Daché was one of the world's most successful milliners. Working in New York, she utilized techniques learned in her native France. Her hats were characterized by bold, sculptural shapes, which required complex blocking. Many were also decorated with seductive veils and trimmings. Most famous during the 1930s and 1940s, when a chic hat was at least as important as a stylish dress, Daché was a milliner extraordinaire.

ROBERT
DANES

bias architecture. That I began working in the bias was happenstance—my partner, Rachel, suggested I try it for a dress I had been working on, and I was immediately enthralled by the fluidity and femininity of fabric draped on the bias. It was also the challenge of draping and constructing clothes on the bias that appealed to me coming from men's tailoring as I had; the typical princess line patterns and shirtwaists had always seemed a bit flat and uninspiring. But what Rachel and I learned quickly was that bias was very easy to do badly, as we saw all too often in fashion all around us and in our own initial forays—seams puckering all over the place and even women with more perfect bodies appearing hippy and lumpy. So I figured out ways to construct and drape that avoided those problems and began to try to create a new modern language of construction and drape.

DONALD
DEAL

Fashion for me is a delicate balance between who we want to be and who we project ourselves to be. I have always had fun with color, color blocking, blending, and mixing. I have worked in a range of mediums but find my true passion lies not only in the art of creating fashion but also in the luxury of the raw materials used to support my vision of fashion. The great thing is that it changes all the time, and yet looking back on my twenty years as a designer, I do find many common links from the past to today. I guess it's true that "the more things change, the more they stay the same." I personally believe that they just get better! That is truly the case with "American" fashion . It just gets better!

LOUIS
DELL'OLIO

Sportswear, as a category, was conceived and created in America. It is the strongest root of "American Fashion." Europe may have adapted this look, but at its heart, it is wholly and distinctly American. As design director for all the Anne Klein Companies, my vision and goal was to bring this American sportswear to the luxury market, crystallizing it as a luxury brand and then translating the essence of that look to a secondary line and its many divisions. We called that A.K. line "Bridge"; we coined the term. It was exactly that—a bridge between Luxe and Affordable. What seems commonplace today, was groundbreaking then. An innovation and a first that was to become a trailblazer and a talisman for many to follow. I built, nurtured, and guided the Anne Klein brand to its pinnacle. My impact, my stamp, stays entirely in American sportswear, bringing it, as *Vogue* stated, to "the Everywoman." I was never a "society designer," nor was I ever an "enfante terrible." I always remain, to use *Women's Wear Daily*'s term, "a money in the bank guy."

For me, American sportswear is American fashion, and that is my signature.

LYN
DEVON

I would love to be remembered for creating ever-playful and ever-polished American luxury clothing. Sharp and fine, bold and graphic, confident and effortless clothing to last a woman a lifetime.

GIORGIO
DI SANT'ANGELO

Di Sant'Angelo exemplified the individual designer. He rose to prominence during the late 1960s when exuberant youth styles dominated. Inspired by non-western dress and hippie antifashion, di Sant'Angelo's clothes were an eclectic mix of vibrant fabrics, rich ornamentation, and ease of cut. Freeing the body was a prime focus. Leotards, bandeaux, and tube dresses made of stretch fabrics covered with layers of filmy chiffon became his leitmotif.

HENRY
DUARTE

I was inducted into the CFDA in the early 2000s. I have been a fashion designer since the mid-eighties, and what I am probably best known for is being a denim, leather, and rock-and-roll designer. I have worked with many interesting and very diverse artists in the music and film industry over the years, from A-list actresses like Gwyneth Paltrow to hard-core musicians like Metallica, but the ones I feel best exemplify my work are in the photos here.

Lenny Kravitz—I worked closely with him in 1993 on the *Are You Gonna Go My Way* CD and world tour. The early nineties were about grunge, so we wanted to take his look up. One of the most dramatic pieces I've ever made, which I think Lenny made iconic, was a long red suede sleeveless vest over red pants for the "Are You Gonna Go My Way" single video.

Bob Dylan—I made his western-inspired suit for the Grammy Awards, first-time winner. I did quite a bit of his tour wardrobe in the nineties.

Lace-front black leather pants and a deerskin shirt are two more items I was well known for. I've made these two pieces for many people, but I feel there is one guy who wore them best, the late Michael Hutchence. "Elegantly Wasted" himself, the man is missed.

Lace-front denim jeans—these started me as a denim designer. Kate Hudson really understood how to wear these. She had just married Chris Robinson and was in the film *Almost Famous*, in which she just shone. I think it's her best film. I also did these pants in stripes, which looked great on both pro surfer Donovan Frankenreiter and Carmen Kass (*Brit Vogue*). This pant leads to my denim career, which leads to the J Brand collaboration—a group of black rock-and-roll skinny jeans with David Bowie names.

KEANAN
DUFFTY

Believing you've had a "big impact" is a bit audacious. I'd prefer to say my contribution to American fashion has been to bring British rebel style to the American runway and retail. I was one of the first British designers to be based in New York and to create a mass fashion collection for Target with a rock icon, David Bowie.

STEPHEN
DWECK

Big, bold, beautiful, brazen, gutsy, colorful, artistic jewelry. When I started designing my first collection in 1981, jewelry of that nature didn't exist. I introduced my brand at Bergdorf Goodman and soon after collaborated with Geoffrey Beene.

The nine-year relationship included accessorizing his couture collections both behind the scene on the runways and for editorial. The best moments came from him designing dresses to work with the jewelry and then selling both to specialty stores as an ensemble.

My radical new approach to jewelry design was the beginning of "Artisan Jewelry." This meant creating for the whimsical needs of fashion and giving the collector a natural alternative to gold and all previous interpretation of jewelry. Jewelry that could be worn, collected, and would weather the cycles of fashion. Jewelry meant to stand on its own artistic merit.

My motto has always been: The rocks of the world meet Brooklyn. Since the early eighties, our jewelry has been made at the Brooklyn studio with precious metals and the most beautiful and unusual gems and minerals. Mixing the two has always been quintessential Dweck. I don't know how to describe myself—a specialty jeweler, mineralist, or fashion accessory designer? I am an amalgamation of all three.

My mission continues as it began: to bring beautiful and unique jewelry worn in the most interesting ways to the most beautiful and unique women.

HENRY
DUNAY

Henry Dunay's designs are recognizable for his boldness and beauty, a combination of rare large gemstones, and imagination of sensual erotic elegant shapes with magical accents that create pieces of "wearable art."

Dunay is an American pioneer who started creating collections with textures that would continuously build through the years from earrings to cuff links. His textures turned into his recognizable brand, and therefore "longevity with worldwide recognition."

MARC
ECKO

My name is Marc Ecko. I am an artist.

My impact on popular culture has been to legitimize what some may have dismissed as pure trend or not fashion: American street style. I have grown my business and my aesthetic from the ground up. I started by painting T-shirts in a garage when I was a teenager. That seedling of hard work and inspiration has grown into a platform empowering me to travel the globe and extend my vision into tailored suiting, home furnishings, fragrance, video games, publishing, and electronics.

In classic American form, I have managed to create something from nothing more than persistence and an unapologetic belief in myself. I am hopeful that my work has given volume to voices that want to forge their own American dream, one that is relentlessly daring to be defined by the past.

One,
+ME

MARK
EISEN

Mark Eisen is globally recognized for his unique definition of modernism, visible in the spare, long, and lean lines of his fashion collections. Launched in the late eighties by Barneys New York and Bergdorf Goodman, his clean, sleek silhouettes were a respite from the grunge look that began to dominate fashion at that time. Mesmerized by line and proportion, he believed in the realism and functionality of clothing. Considered one of the minimalist American fashion movement leaders, Eisen's collections epitomized the monastic, intellectual mood of late-nineties and new-millennium fashion, albeit with his sophisticated, sexy slant. A refined tailor and master knit specialist, he had a history of combining technical advancements with luxury, detail, and practicality. Eisen's signature style defined modern American sportswear—a mix of feminine sensuality, strength, and modernity.

LIBBY
EDELMAN

&

SAM
EDELMAN

Sam Edelman was created only seven years ago, and since that time, designer Sam Edelman has succeeded in doing what century-old fashion houses still strive for: to conceive and execute the design of a product that blurs the line between high and commercial fashion by defining the trend of a season. The Sam Edelman gladiator sandal has undoubtedly made an indelible mark in the industry and on the feet of fashionable women everywhere. The ankle-banding sandal was a trend that graced the streets of St. Tropez and Capri as a chic alternative to thong beach sandals. Through Sam's creative vision and innate understanding of fashion, a European vacation trend has now become an American fashion staple. Ask any woman from age 16 to 60 if there's one pair of shoes she needs in her closet—THE pair of shoes that she cannot live without. When Sam Edelman was awarded "Brand of the Year" in 2009 by *Footwear News*, an influential retailer perfectly summarized the gladiator's significance in the November 30th issue of *FN*, saying, "[Sam Edelman,] particularly its signature gladiator sandals, ranks as one of the store's hottest brands" and that "A woman who is carrying an [Hermès] Birkin bag will also wear a Sam Edelman shoe."

LUIS
ESTÉVEZ

Frequent use was made of stark black and white and of full, rustling skirts, or narrow lines with floating back panels. Estévez also introduced less fitting clothes in the form of barrel-shaped ottoman coats and dresses in two versions; one with a narrow skirt, the other with a puffball skirt. Evening jumpsuits were late 1960s innovations, as was a foray into menswear which featured horizontally tucked evening shirts. He was fond of designing around a strong theme, as in his ethnic-African inspired collection of 1959, featuring oversize tiger and zebra stripe prints. Estévez was also known for his imaginative use of accessories and designed swimwear and furs on a freelance basis for other companies.

MELINDA
ENG

Melinda Eng's designs combine timeless elegance and sophistication with a modern sensibility.

Since she founded her business in 1993, Melinda has always designed for modern women who appreciate beautifully crafted eveningwear.

Melinda is known for her intricate draping, and her attention to detail is reflected in all her designs. Her elegant collections have attracted celebrities like Helen Mirren, Sharon Stone, and Oprah Winfrey season after season.

DAVID

EVINS

Apart from being very successful in his fashion shoe business, David Evins was instrumental in guiding the fate of the CFDA through his early board functions.

Evins worked to make women's shoes lighter and more comfortable. The result was a handmade shoe called "6 ounces," which sold for up to $175 at a time when quality women's shoes cost about $45 a pair.

His designs and manufacturing processes were widely imitated, and he became a favorite among Broadway and Hollywood stars. He designed the "chunky pump" worn by Judy Garland, Marilyn Monroe's "subway sandals," and the shoes worn by Ava Gardner in the film *The Barefoot Contessa*. He made shoes for every First Lady from Mamie Eisenhower to Nancy Reagan.

—Ian Fisher, *New York Times*, David E. Evins, 85,
"A Designer of Shoes for Ex-First Ladies," December 29, 1991

STEVE
FABRIKANT

In the mid-eighties an editor defined my knitwear as modern. It was easier for me to design than to coin my design style. I was designing modern knitwear recognized for its distinctive lines, hardware detailing, and use of color. In a world of fabrics, the knit defined ease in modern and faster times. No fuss.

One of the first stores I sold to was Martha's. I remember taking those seven or eight pieces by bus from Thirty-ninth Street in the heart of the Garment Center. I walked out with an order and, wow, to be in the company of Montana and Blass; Martha had her own eclectic mix. A few months later, Phyllis George, formerly of Miss America fame and hostess of CBS's counterpart to the NBC's *Today* show, wore one of my navy and pink suits on the show unbeknownst to me.

Dressing yourself at four in the morning, needing to look great in front of millions, I define that as modern knitwear.

CARLOS
FALCHI

Since his costume designs for Herbie Hancock, Miles Davis, Mick Jagger, Elvis Presley, and Tina Turner in the late 1960s, Carlos Falchi has been a pioneer in the fashion industry. Among his countless contributions to American accessory fashion and design, the Buffalo Satchel has arguably been his greatest. Heralded by *Women's Wear Daily* as, "the most copied bag of the industry," in 1980, the Buffalo Satchel was a representation of the modern working woman. It was originally constructed of buffalo leather, but quickly evolved into multi-exotic skins such as python, caiman, anaconda, and alligator. Carlos's deconstruction of handbags to create a flexible, durable, and fashion-forward product has set him apart from his peers. In 1983, Carlos won a Coty Award for the Buffalo Satchel. His innovative approaches have been acclaimed by fashion visionaries such as Geraldine Stutz, president of Henri Bendel, who gave Carlos his first retail department; Patricia Field, who used Carlos's accessories in many *Sex and the City* episodes; and an impressive score of designers with whom he's collaborated, including Donna Karan, Michael Kors, Marc Jacobs, Yves Saint Laurent, Vera Wang, Oscar de la Renta, Catherine Malandrino, and Geoffrey Beene. He is a favorite of A-list celebrities such as Cher, Brooke Shields, Eva Longoria, Michelle Trachtenberg, Kim Cattrall, Heidi Klum, Madonna, and Blake Lively. Continually taking an artistic approach to design, Carlos maintains his position as a prominent and creative influence in America's fashion industry.

ERIN
FETHERSTON

As a designer I have fully embraced the concept of collaboration to define and enhance my individual artistic vision. Since the advent of my career, I have partnered with visionaries on multimedia projects ranging from photographic exhibitions to short films that showcased my clothes and illustrated my creative universe. My debut collaboration was the short film *Wendybird*, directed by legendary photographer Ellen von Unwerth, starring actress Kirsten Dunst wearing my Winter 2006 collection. This commenced a series of photographic and film projects that drew upon the talents of Zooey Deschanel, Sarah Sophie Flicker, Karen Elson, and other inspirational women who served as muses. Eventually, the collaborations extended beyond media and led to partnerships with larger retailers like Target and Juicy Couture. This was the perfect combination of my role as a designer and the collaborative work that had become part of my creative process. The traditional fashion narrative focused on the lone designer as an uninterrupted creative entity, but venturing beyond this myth has allowed me to be more creative, inspired, and grateful for my role in the world of fashion.

ANDREW
FEZZA

Where did *metallic gunmetal, Mediterranean blue*, and *iridescent fabrics* fit into men's fashion? How many American men's closets had stamped, embossed leather pants bumping hips with *corded lamb suede* and rubbing elbows with *silk jersey tees*?

Before twenty-something Andrew Fezza burst onto the menswear scene, they didn't. As the youngest member of the fashion-forward Designers' Collective, Fezza gave the menswear industry a kick in the pants and young men across America a newfound sense of fashion. Fezza earned instant recognition as a major trend-setter with his "nothing short of fabulous" leatherwear, "among the most advanced in the American market today," and then developed his trademark look into a full-scale collection of signature men's sportswear.

CHERYL
FINNEGAN

Cheryl Finnegan created her jewelry line, Virgins, Saints & Angels, out of her belief that every woman can use some enlightenment in her life. Designed and handcrafted in Mexico, using relics and symbols such as angels, saints, and goddesses to create inspirational jewelry that showcases the nature of the divine.

Virgins, Saints & Angels has a style that is unmistakable and is a reflection of the designer herself—an Irish American who moved to Mexico, became inspired by Mexican culture and art, and translated it into her personal style, which she often refers to as "Celtic meets Gothic Mexico."

Finnegan has brought Mexican artisan jewelry, and its icons, to the fashion world. Each piece of jewelry becomes infused with the spirit of the person who wears it. Finnegan's designs have been seen on a wide variety of style-setters, from rock 'n' roll to country, hip-hop to punk, politicians to athletes. The common thread among all VSA wearers is that they want to make a confident statement inspired by fashion, art, beauty, or symbolism.

EILEEN
FISHER

In these modern and sometimes overscheduled times, I want EILEEN FISHER to be known for clothes you don't have to think too much about. You put them on and know that they will give you the comfort, ease, and elegance to move with confidence through your day.

ANNE
FOGARTY

"She changed the course
of junior dressing," said Cathy
di Montezemolo, who covered
young fashions for *Vogue*
magazine during that era.
"She didn't talk down to young
people and she bred a
whole host of imitators."

—Bernadine Morris, *New York Times*,
January 16, 1980

TOM
FORD

Just as Flaubert knew Madame Bovary so Tom Ford knows
the women for whom he designs: sexy, confident,
and often flirtatiously androgynous. This is a creature of
his own invention and one, it has become clear, that many
of us long to be. When I think back to the early nineties, when
he first arrived on my radar screen, fashion was buried
deep in the shapeless layers of the horrible grunge look. But
along came Tom with his low-cut velvet hipsters and his
slinky jersey dresses, and grunge was sent scurrying off back
to Seattle. Women woke up to the fact that a little glamour
was missing from their lives—and Tom's clothes, always
sexually empowering, captured their imaginations.

—Anna Wintour

R. SCOTT
FRENCH

I would hope my impact on American fashion would be twofold, with clothing and with technology. I've always designed my collections with constant thought of the customer and have always been careful to do pieces that made a statement, but never one big enough to obscure the persona of the wearer. As a result, several of my pieces have stayed with me since season one, relatively unchanged in silhouette, but only tweaked in detail. The best example is my "Squishy Coat" (long story on the name!), which has been in my collection since my very first season, and again this season, twenty collections later, it was my number one selling item. It is a testament to the fact that in menswear, if an item is classic enough not to alienate, but new enough to generate interest, it can have serious shelf life.

On the technology front, my efforts with the website I cofounded, TheFashionList.com, will hopefully be seen as my second major impact on the world of fashion. It's an example of using the full range of what is available technologically to truly make life easier, the world a bit smaller, and the individual more organized.

JAMES
GALANOS

At a time when every designer worth his needle is working with chiffon, Galanos proves he is a master of the genre. He drapes chiffon. He pleats it, layers it, uses flower prints and fabrics with metallic glints. As tailored as a shirtwaist dress or as seductive as a sarong, he gives chiffon a high style all his own.

—Bernadine Morris, *New York Times*, February 28, 1989

ROBERT
GELLER

I believe the biggest impact the Robert Geller collection has made on American fashion is to offer a new perspective on menswear. The clothes blend a classical European tradition with the rough-and-tumble youthfulness of American sportswear. While the seasonal collections are often a nod to the romance of history, I am passionate about creating modern clothes that provide something unexpected—a never-before-used fabric, a twist on a menswear staple, an unorthodox silhouette, or an unusual approach to accessories. It's a new way of looking at the way men dress themselves. I hope it encourages a generation of guys to express their personality through clothes that are different and elegant without necessarily screaming "look at me."

JENNIFER
GEORGE

I left Seventh Avenue in the late nineties. As an American designer, sportswear was what I related to, what I designed, and what I wore. I loved jersey separates, colorful coats, and great white shirts. There was nothing decorative about my work. A button worked. A zipper zipped. Function inspired form.

I think perhaps "The Great White Shirt" is still the thing I'm known best for. However, if I had to pick the thing I'm most proud of, it would be the blurb that sat on the seats at my Fall 1997 show.

Instead of the typical inspiration statement—one that cites a Hollywood icon or the light in the Hamptons—I wrote about my emotional state at the time. I was getting divorced, and my rage was apparent both on the runway and off. So much so, that after the show, editors and buyers raced backstage to see if I was okay. It was a turning point for me. I shuttered my doors after my 1998 Spring show and turned to words, instead of fabric, to express myself.

GERI
GERARD

My contribution to the fashion industry will be to have created beautiful evening clothes. I've always loved to drape my ideas on a mannequin and found myself to always be inspired by the way working with fabrics creates new silhouettes. Maybe that comes from the time I spent working in Paris when I was just out of school. Even though I consider my style to be American, the French certainly have influenced us all in some way. Presentation and all the fine details are just as important as the product itself.

I have always enjoyed experimenting with new fabric techniques and incorporating them into a design. Women have always told me how great they feel wearing something that I made. My clients always recognize and appreciate the attention to detail and the finest quality of fabrics, construction, and fit. That is my signature in everything I make.

RUDI
GERNREICH

Bold, original, and controversial, Gernreich was America's first fashion futurist, a social commentator who worked in the medium of clothes. Best known for his body-baring creations such as the no-bra bra and topless bathing suit, he also designed colorful knits and minidresses with clear plastic insertions. His love of modern dance and eternal youthfulness were themes that animated his designs.

JUSTIN
GIUNTA

The best is yet to come . . .

GARY
GRAHAM

Gary Graham's designs reference American culture and history with the perspective of a historian, the eye of an artist, and the soul of a punk. His passion for authenticity has been at the core of his collections since he launched his label.

Gary has an abiding interest in people and their stories, which is really what his clothes are all about. His work is genuine both in the sense that his references—whether they be the gypsies chronicled in the *New Yorker* stories of Joseph Mitchell or Dare Wright, the author of the beloved children's book *The Lonely Doll*—are culled from real experiences had by real people and in the cuts and techniques he employs. His Victorian-style jackets, strong tailoring, almost medieval-looking quilting, and textured, garment-dyed fabrics are design signatures that have a tangible sense of time and place. The signature look he has created—layered both literally and symbolically—is rich but never costume-y. Even right out of the store, his clothes look like they have not just a set of inspirations, but a history.

Joe Boxer began with a simple premise: I needed new underwear. Having moved from Canada in the early eighties, I was involved in design early on, printing T-shirts out of my apartment to make ends meet. To satisfy my need for new underwear, I started to silkscreen boxer shorts, sewing them at night and selling them at boutiques in the morning. One design in particular caught the attention of the Secret Service, a print of $100 bills that they said was too close for comfort. They confiscated them and burnt them. Seriously.

Really from that point on, everything we did was slightly (or completely) alternative in its thinking. We married customers in Times Square; we sent underwear into space, dressed in drag with Richard Branson, closed New York Fashion Week in Reykjavik (with Fern Mallis in a blond wig); we even did the World's Fastest Fashion Show in a parking lot of Kmart in Detroit by sending a human cannonball over the gathered crowds. Some people say we did social networking before it was even thought of. We used any means possible to get our story out.

But it wasn't all just about the marketing. We make great product, and people love it. The saying we coined, "The Brand Is the Amusement Park, The Product Is the Souvenir," was how we did and still do operate. People not only want to have an emotional relationship with a brand, but a great product as well, and at Joe Boxer, we still believe that every day.

HENRY
GRETHEL

Beautiful colors have always been paramount to my collections ... my strong suit. Color is the first decision he or she makes when shopping for clothing. When my collections were first introduced in Japan, I was described in the fashion press as "the color magician" ... magically making colors work together in a new and different way.

Recognizing the need for a slimmer cut in men's dress shirts, I introduced John Henry, "the fitted shirt," and built the brand successfully for both men's and women's tailored shirts. At the same time I changed the men's dress shirt industry from selling exact sleeve size to average sleeve length with an adjustable two button cuff. This became the new standard for the industry.

Selected by the U.S. Olympic committee as the first American designer to design the men's and women's opening ceremonies uniforms for the Albertville & Barcelona games was an honor I will always remember.

The committee wanted to break with the past to achieve a "world class look" for our athletes ... A daunting task, a huge job. Fortunately the results received accolades for the U.S. team from the international Olympic committee.... Designing for your country is as personal as it gets.

ULRICH

GRIMM

Shape and material are the foundation of my designs. Largely influenced by architecture, I am inspired by structures, colors, textures, and natural building materials. These references manifest in my accessories, interpreted in the heel of a shoe, hardware on a handbag, or accents on an eyewear frame.

My designs are clean and classic, but with a modern approach. I like to mix natural, traditional materials with more raw, industrial ones; finding balance among the tension in these combinations. The most interesting constructions descend from this modern play on form and function.

GEORGE

GUBLO

My goal for gunmetal, as the founder and creative director: to make sexy, feminine & beautifully crafted italian made shoes—using the best materials—that women could actually wear. My best compliment came from Halle Berry, who said "not only are they beautiful, but I feel like I could walk across Montana in them."

BILL
HAIRE

Bill Haire specialized in sequined and elaborately beaded evening dresses before he took up making sportswear for Fredericks a few seasons back. He obviously had no trouble making the transition.... He as obviously grasped the sportswear concept, and his styles have a special verve.

—Bernadine Morris, *New York Times*, October 8, 1975

JEFF
HALMOS
&
SAM
SHIPLEY

It should be noted that neither of us think of ourselves as "fashion" designers nor do we consider Shipley & Halmos a "fashion" label. When we sit down to design a collection, we never discuss how we're going to radically change what we offer our customer each season. Instead, our goal is to offer a consistency in quality, fit, and aesthetic while constantly thinking of unique, fun, and creative ways to build the brand itself.

In the process of branding, marketing can be as important as the product itself. We never approach a project the same way twice, whether that is a video installation, shooting and publishing a portraiture book, collaborating with artists, or conceptualizing partnerships with retailers. We feel our ability to think outside the box and never rely on a formula is what separates Shipley & Halmos from others.

HALSTON

The seventies belonged to Halston. Though he began
his career as a milliner, his shift to ready-to-wear clothing
made him a superstar. He was America's first minimalist
designer. By combining clean lines and classic fabric,
Halston designed clothing that was seasonless,
made for travel, and looked elegant night or day.
It is no surprise that many members of the burgeoning
"jet set" became his most celebrated clients.

TIM
HAMILTON

Tim Hamilton is one of the few American designers that is part of the conservation on menswear on an international stage. He has been a champion in mixing formal and casual, European tailoring with American sportswear, quality fabrics and unconventional finishing. His elegance has always a lived-in quality, a modern feeling, a downtown attitude in an uptown package.

—Stefano Tonchi, editor in chief, *W*

DOUGLAS
HANNANT

While my contemporaries are chasing the trendy scene, I have often been referred to as the Prince of Park Avenue, the undisputed heir apparent to dress the social set.

With his Midwestern roots, Douglas Hannant is not the first international fashion phenomenon to hale from the heartland; there were Bill Blass and Halston before him. And like them, Hannant has become known as the go-to designer for the Upper East Siders, attending charity lunches and black-tie galas, where they often see the designer himself. So given that kind of clientele, it is somewhat surprising to hear the designer talk about how his roots have influenced his designs. He has refined his luxury brand and blossomed into the celebrated designer of "Modern Classics." He prides himself on his Park Avenue socialites as his loyal client base but points out that similar types live in every city in America.

—Excerpt from *Avenue*, January 2010 article written by Jill Fairchild

CATHY
HARDWICK

For as long as I can remember, my favorite things to do have been to make clothes, sew, and knit. So when I was designing, I was naturally drawn to doing lots of knitwear as well as making things with beautiful fabrics.

KAREN
HARMAN

I cannot imagine a world in which the clothes of women become relentlessly conformist or once again, become contrived, stiff, and doll-like. I have always seen a woman in motion, and I see her still.

JOHNSON
HARTIG

"Johnson Hartig re-envisioned American ready-to-wear through the creation of Libertine, striking the perfect balance between directional aesthetics and functionality. Every one-of-a-kind piece that he creates is remade and, consequently, reinvented through his unique and fantastical vision. The art of transforming a found garment, whether it be a 1950s cream cashmere sweater or a dusty pink satin slip, into something new and never seen before is the heart and soul of what Libertine does best."
—Kate Mulleavy

"I'm still pretty surprised that when walking down any street to come across two or three of what must be by now twentieth genera-tion Libertine knockoffs.... A couple thoughts cross my mind, the first being 'Wow! What a big impact our little company has had!' quickly followed by 'If I had a nickel for every one of these....'"
—Johnson Hartig

JOAN
HELPERN

I create, I created, fashion essentials for those who care, those who dare to make positive differences for those in their towns, cities, countries across the globe. Thus, since 1968 I have designed for women (in ever-increasing and visible numbers) who run through airports! And, since 1980, for the men who run along beside them.

The person must always be stronger and more visible than what she wears. She must look wonderful. She will not if the shoes, the gloves, the dress, the shoulders are each screaming out to be noticed. Our customer is rarely taken in by the "emperor's new clothes." Unless she is in the fashion field, she does not consider fashion and the acquisition of product an all-consuming passion. She feels no great need to jump on a new fashion bandwagon every few months for fear she'll miss the parade. She is the parade.

LAZARO & JACK
HERNANDEZ   McCOLLOUGH

In 2004 the first annual CFDA/*Vogue* Fashion Fund was established to find
the next generation of American designers. As an inaugural recipient, Proenza
Schouler went on to play important role in reinvigorating American fashion.
Through funding and mentorship as well as exposure on a global scale, the award
allowed Proenza Schouler to transition from emerging designers to leading
talents in the industry. Proenza Schouler's continued growth and recognition
in the years that followed validated not only the success of the CFDA/*Vogue*
Fashion Fund, but also the idea of rethinking New York as an essential resource
for up and coming talent in the international fashion community.

CAROLINA
HERRERA

"The most boring subject is to talk about myself," says Carolina Herrera with the grace that is perhaps her greatest contribution to the worlds of fashion and style. "What I have been doing all these years is trying to make women feel more beautiful. I am not reinventing anything. It is only about beauty."

Beautiful, yes. But also mysterious, extravagant, magical.

Still, there is restraint in her indulgences. As in the crisp white shirts that have become her signature, Herrera makes clear that the simplest choices can often be the most elegant. Her clothes reach beyond the clichés of elegance. They are dramatic without suggesting costume and extravagant in ways that enhance a woman without hiding her: There are the portrait-framing sleeves, the deluxe fabrics, the richness of detail. Each sets the Herrera woman apart.

Legendary *Vogue* editor Diana Vreeland encouraged the Venezuelan-born Herrera to become a fashion designer, and she showed her debut collection in 1981. Today her runway collection remains a favorite of the best-dressed women all over the world.

CH Carolina Herrera, a lifestyle collection for women and men, builds on that strength. Her fragrances are among the top sellers in the business.

Timelessness is essential to Herrera, and she lays no claim to so-called innovations that are distractions to her mission. Known for remarkable technique and attention to detail, Herrera's designs celebrate sophisticated, real women who manage the challenges and excitement of family, career, and a vibrant social life.

"Style is not only what you wear, but how you live in the world around you," she says. "To have a fashionable life that goes beyond clothes, that is the essence of style. It can be done gracefully. I believe that an effortless attitude is the reward for discipline and focus. That is why I love a beautifully made white shirt."

For all the glamour of her clothes, Herrera's impact on fashion goes beyond the way women dress. Throughout her career, Herrera has demonstrated that to be a lady never goes out of style. "I'd like to be remembered for making women more beautiful."

TOMMY
HILFIGER

"Those who believe there are only so many ways to do preppy clearly haven't met Tommy Hilfiger, whose newest interpretation might just be his best one yet," said *WWD*, of the Tommy Hilfiger Fall 2011 collection.

When I launched Tommy Hilfiger in 1985, "preppy" was the standard way of dressing for a very niche set. Fashion-wise, it wasn't exactly young or exciting. But in those classic silhouettes, I found inspiration for a new way of dressing—one that all Americans could have fun with. By infusing a youthful spirit into classic chinos, oxfords, knits, and polos, I brought preppy to the masses. I made classics relaxed and embraced individuality and irreverence. When celebrating our twenty-fifth anniversary all around the globe in 2010, I was struck by how that preppy-with-a-twist idea we pioneered in America has flourished (and been reinterpreted) all over the world. Whereas "prep" used to mean Palm Beach and Nantucket, it's now found everywhere from San Juan to Jaipur, Buenos Aires to Tokyo. Our spirit of adaptability has never felt more relevant—and our preppy style has never looked more modern.

CAROLE
HOCHMAN

I am happy to be known as the queen of pajamas. I am thrilled to be responsible for making women everywhere feel pretty, comfy, cozy, and even sexy in their pj's. I made cotton jersey the most popular and biggest-selling fabric for sleepwear and lounging.

I started my career designing gorgeous, romantic, and very expensive lingerie for Christian Dior. The challenge for me was thinking no one really lived like that anymore. Women were changing and wanted to come home from work and get into something easy and comfortable. Everyone loved sleeping in their boyfriends' T-shirts.

The idea of a simple tee and drawstring pant, cut in the best-quality cotton knit, at a price that was affordable, was the beginning of a huge business. Now this category is everywhere, and I am still making them, in fabulous prints and colors that are always fresh and fun.

CHUCK
HOWARD

One of the adventurous young designers who put a distinctly non-Parisian accent on American clothing in the 1950s and '60s.

—Wolfgang Saxon, *New York Times*, October 5, 2002

CHRISTINA & SWAIM

HUTSON HUTSON

Swaim and Christina Hutson of Obedient Sons & Daughters made their most compelling IMPACT on American fashion by focusing on both their MEN'S and WOMEN'S collections of modern, tailored, and classic silhouettes. The brand became best known and gained both domestic and international attention for their clean and focused tailored, yet almost unisex, collections. The duo also made an IMPACT on both press relations and retail due to the brand's key craftsmanship and production of all of the collection pieces made in the United States.

SANG A

IM-PROPP

Since SANG A's launch in 2006, designer, Sang A Im-Propp has defined the niche that she calls "fun, innovative, and rebellious luxury," giving a new energy to American luxury handbags and accessories. Sang A executes her precise designs by always seeking out and developing her concepts with the best artisans and craftsmen in the United States. Sang A has energetically positioned herself both as a beneficiary and supporter of the art of American luxury.

ALEJANDRO

INGELMO

Alejandro Ingelmo has been at the forefront of the shoe industry since his collection debut for Fall 2006. As a fourth generation shoemaker, his understanding of this art form is vividly apparent in every design. Ingelmo's ability to intricately design and produce a shoe that enhances the wearer's physical form and presence is his biggest impact on American fashion.

MARC
JACOBS

The thought behind grunge, Marc Jacobs told *WWD* in 1992 at the time of his seminal collection for Perry Ellis, was to make everything wrong, which in turn "made most of it look very right."

Time has proven New York's then-enfant brilliant prescient. Grunge was new, audacious, shocking. It rocked Jacobs's world personally—he was fired—as it rocked all of fashion to its very core, shattering ironclad notions of just what made a designer collection *designer*.

Jacobs has moved on from garage-band knit caps and silks masquerading as lumberjack flannels. At times, it seems, far away, into an arena of ever more luxe and intricately crafted fashion. En route, he has celebrated the engagingly dark Violet Incredible and the adolescent, streetwalking Jodie Foster; he has taken us over the rainbow and on a mesmerizing surrealist reverie. One fall (2010) swung "conservative" with lush, ample classics; the next, sexual and severe. It's all unmistakably Marc Jacobs.

Throughout, an essential and overarching tenet remains from the grunge days: No matter how rich the clothes, no matter how painstaking their hand-worked constructions, perfection is never the goal. Rather, the goal of fashion for Jacobs himself, and the women and men who revel in his aesthetic, is self-expression uninhibited by external mandates of propriety.

Jacobs assessed the ultimate impact of grunge twenty years after its arrival, deeming it "the most liberating thing. It was," he said, "about a dismissal of everything that one was told was beautiful, correct, glamorous, sexy. I think that moment hasn't passed." Surely it lives on, season after season in ever-compelling, bold new ways in Marc Jacobs's remarkable work.

—Bridget Foley

HENRY
JACOBSON

Before launching men's lifestyle collection Henry Jacobson in 2002, I was responsible for transforming the way domestic men's neckwear producers approached product design. My company, Mulberry Neckwear, dominated the main floor men's designer neckwear business from the 1990s until 2008, when I sold the company to Phillips-Van Heusen.

When I founded Mulberry Neckwear in 1988, I created the first "pure" American neckwear design house. Mulberry controlled all aspects of the creative process, including the provision of original print designs, color variations, and screen separations to printing mills and original yarn dye and looming specifications for color, warp, and weft construction to weaving mills. Mulberry's innovation put enormous pressure on a creatively challenged industry to improve their design practices in order to compete and survive.

ERIC
JAVITS

Eric Javits opened his women's hat business after graduating from art school where he had studied painting and sculpture. By the late eighties he had become known as the hat designer of choice for the international set, royalty, and prominent society ladies as well as those celebrated in the worlds of music, television, and film.

During that early phase of millinery design, Eric heard clients voice concerns about premature aging due to sun damage. Many were being treated by dermatologists and getting cosmetic surgery to look younger. They were being told by the experts to wear sunhats in conjunction with sunscreen for added protection. Eric recognized the need for a packable straw sunhat that would provide ultimate protection.

Today Eric is regarded as one of the fashion accessory industry's foremost innovators. His trademark is elegance with gentility married to function. As an artist in his own right, Eric Javits has impacted women's wardrobes by creating designs that charm, endure, and are fun to wear.

LISA
JENKS

My interest in various ancient cultures, especially those of Egypt, Mexico, Africa, and particularly Polynesia, has served (and continues to serve) as the basis for my design inspiration. I have always valued the way that those societies used their art as a way to explain the universe and their way of life. I feel that my unique style and aesthetic are a direct result of my travels and my love for the exotic. My original collections, which focused mainly on sterling silver, led to work with gold and precious stones. I've continued to explore new viewpoints in order to expand my creative range and develop pieces that will both excite and inspire.

I like to fuse those seminal cultural influences with early and mid-twentieth-century design concepts, and in doing so, I've been able to establish my niche. As one of the vanguards of designer jewelry, my biggest impact on fashion has been pioneering this unique style: a modern and primitive mode with a new finish.

I hope that my impact on American fashion is a lasting one. My decision to pursue a career as a jewelry designer has never once been something I've second-guessed. I love creating and I love the process of developing new pieces and concepts; I simply cannot picture myself doing anything else.

JOHN P.
JOHN

As early as 1957, he was already on the defensive, arguing, "A hat cannot actually give one golden curls if the hair is mouse-colored and stringy; it cannot lift a face, pay overdue bills, subtract ten years from one's age, or transform a plain soul into a reigning princess. But it can lend practically any woman a temporary out-of-herself feeling. For the right hat creates a desired mood, and that isn't fiction or fancy, but fact, fact, fact."

BETSEY
JOHNSON

HALTER DRESS

← 0280

1965.
PARAPHERNALIA. 1st COLLECTION
XOX BETSEY.

I think, I brought, I bring ...
"FUN!"
A Party
A Pretty
Poofy
Petticoated
Punky
Princess
Party!
I think, I brought, I bring ...
"FANTASY!"
Fearless
Funky
Far-out
Affordable
Fashion
I think, I brought, I bring ...
"ROCK-N-ROLL!"
Racy
Raw
Raggity
Rough
Tough
Stuff
I think, I brought, I bring ...
Clothes to "brighten your day ...
& live life your way!"

ALEXANDER
JULIAN

Alexander Julian's impact is best summed up as the originator of the genre of menswear, which the press dubbed "Modern Traditional." "Traditional" in terms of natural, classic, raw materials, but "modern" in terms of innovative color, pattern, and silhouette. Dubbed "America's Master Colorist in Menswear" by the *New York Times*, he's given credit for introducing color to menswear, even though his earliest accolades were for introducing then-revolutionary new cuts, shapes, and details.

GEMMA
KAHNG

My biggest contribution to American fashion is the use of humor and sensual surprise to express glamour.

NORMA
KAMALI

Norma Kamali has come up with so many designs that she can only be described as a great American pioneer in fashion. While her aesthetic has always been grounded in sophistication, it's also based on the unorthodox juxtapositions of technique and material. She has transformed recycled army surplus parachute silk and down sleeping bags into cocoons of femininity. She reinvigorated the whole idea of glamour, updating Adrian's peplum suit and shoulder pads for her clients and fans, and in the process ignited the rage for vintage. She was the first to recreate the glamorous swimsuit, which has remained so influential in the marketplace. The way Coco Chanel took men's underwear jersey and made it a staple for women, Kamali made industrial grade gym sweatshirt fabrics into a groundbreaking collection in 1980 that practically launched the leisurewear revolution. And there is no image more memorable than Raquel Welch in a great Kamali siren dress or Paloma Picasso in a Kamali suit. Many of her shapes of the past three decades remain so contemporary, and at the same time, so timeless, that she still sells them in her shop. And you see her sleeping bag coats, which were a uniform in the seventies, on the streets every winter.

She's always been an independent, in both fashion and in retailing. Her first shop on East Fifty-third Street featured lizard and leather, then she moved it to Madison Avenue in 1974, and started attracting society girls. Four years later, she brought cutting-edge style to shopping with the launch of OMO. And she was one of the first designers to sell fashion on the Internet. In her way of thinking and in her work, always there is a streak of something imaginative and quite remarkable. She doesn't look to anyone, and she imitates no one but herself. It's always about her style. To me, she is America's Elsa Schiaparelli.

—André Leon Talley

DONNA
KARAN

The alignment of Donna Karan and New York.
That we celebrated women.
That we never stopped finding solutions to problems.
That we accentuated the positive and deleted the negative.
That we took her day into evening with comfort and ease.
That we kept evolving forward.
That we never felt the job was done.

JEANETTE

KASTENBERG

Jeanette Kastenberg is the Queen of Sequins. She loves their energy, their light-reflecting sheen, and she's employed them with a wit and sophistication that make every one of her designs unique and sequins new again. Jeanette was barely out of FIT when she took the fashion world by storm by turning hundreds of yards of overstocked black sequins into witty Chanel suits that Saks Fifth Avenue featured in its windows.

Jeanette has gone on to design everything from workout clothes to evening dresses, and to all of them she brings the zest and positive spirit that describe her own outlook on life. She draws on modern art and pop culture to create clothes that are trendsetting, youthful, and fun whether in a T-shirt emblazoned with a sequined Campbell's Soup can or a dress collaged from sparkling candy wrappers. But Jeanette's clothes are as feminine as they are playful. A physically fit mother who's always on the go, she cuts every piece to enhance a woman's body.

Warner Bros. was so impressed by Jeanette's designs that it commissioned her to make a clothing line for its studio stores, which put its DC Comics and Looney Tunes characters on the contemporary fashion map. When she produced a series of signed and numbered hand-beaded jackets of dazzling visual complexity, the art world took notice. One of them, an exuberant adaptation of a Kandinsky painting, is in the permanent collection of New York's Museum of Arts and Design. Jeanette also designed a group of outfits for the New York Knicks City Dancers, and her influence in their costumes can be seen to this day.

Brad Pitt Makes It Right in New Orleans

ROD

KEENAN

I've been making hats since 1990, but the day Justin Timberlake's stylist walked into my studio my world changed as did the entire hat industry. As soon as he donned our hats on his album cover, in concert, and in print, my business exploded, and hats were everywhere! Soon I was elated to see hats on men from airplanes to bars and social functions, and they were not baseball caps. Celebrities have always appreciated a handmade hat (and have always been happy to pay for them as it is our policy not to do giveaways), but after Justin we had Brad Pitt and many others calling our studio. In fact we hung up on Brad Pitt because we thought it was a prank call. Didn't do that twice! And to come full circle, when the Bill Cunningham documentary played at Film Forum the buzz began again. I hope that in some small way I have helped teach men that headwear can be more than a baseball cap!

PAT
KERR

Exclusivity has always been the hallmark of couture designers and, like most things she touches, designer Pat Kerr takes exclusivity to a whole new dimension. Kerr's designs have been labeled "the Fabergés and Fortunys of today" for their quality as objets d'art. Kerr is one of the world's leading collectors of and authority on antique lace and textile. Her friends in the fashion and lifestyle worlds have been known to describe Pat Kerr as a hummingbird, but a more up-to-date description would be "one-woman Internet of Microsoft proportions."

This genealogist-in-fabric began as a girl tourist in the Orient, when Pat collected antique textiles and ceremonial robes at the markets instead of jade and ivory. She went on to become one of the notable collectors of antique textiles and costumes of today. As a bridal designer she is renowned, and her spectacular collections of grand-entrance ball gowns are making history not only for their beauty, but for their totally pliable and noncrushable construction. Their enormous panniers and tulle petticoats curl up inside a tote bag and emerge pristine, without a crease.

—Eleanor Lambert, fashion icon, founder of the International
Best-Dressed List, Coty Awards, and the CFDA

BARRY
KIESELSTEIN-CORD

My career spans forty years across a great spectrum of products, from pure art to pure design. I am fortunate to have seventy-five pieces of my work in the permanent collections of the world's top museums, from the Louvre to the Metropolitan. My significant impacts are:

Creating/introducing matte gold and black gold.

Being the first American to employ 18.5-karat green gold in regular production.

Being among the first to establish signature luxury iconic accessories in the form of belts, handbags, eyewear, and fine jewelry with international impact.

Changing the copyright laws forever:
My most significant case made case law and is now required teaching in law schools. I proved an article can be both functional and art at the same time. This has protected billions of dollars worth of artists' and designers' work and formed the foundation of some of the world's largest corporations.

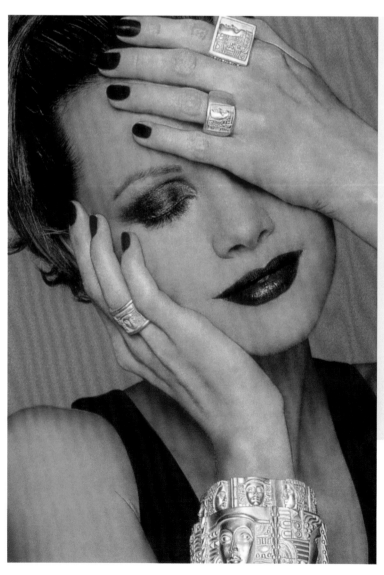

ADAM
KIMMEL

I have always said that I design menswear for my friends and contemporaries. For me that means designing clothing that is wearable, comfortable, and utilitarian and possesses the highest quality of tailoring and fabric. I aim for garments that are as luxurious as they are understated, and this is why my clothing tends to look rugged and feel soft. While I try to incorporate a certain classic timelessness into the brand, I don't design in a vacuum. There is a relevance to the here and now by way of the various inspirations I use for each new collection. In the last decade, I've looked to different American art movements, countercultures, and personal icons to inform the styles, cuts, and features of a collection, and in many ways, it's become my trademark to utilize film, photography, performances, and the Internet to express my vision. I can't pinpoint precisely what my impact has been yet on fashion, but I do know what I hope to stand for and what I hope the brand stands for.

CALVIN

KLEIN

"Calvin Klein created a fashion brand that made understated,
all-American glamour his own—at the same time
as building a vast billion dollar brand that includes
everything from pants to perfume and pillows."

—Joe Craven, *Vogue*, May 11, 2011

JOHN
KLOSS

The most revolutionary of Kloss's designs came about
as a reaction to the "ban the bra" movement in the seventies. He designed a bra for Lily of France in 1974 that
appeared not to exist, called the "glossie," which was made
from stretchy, sheer, glittery material. The design was
seamless, unconstructed, but underwired, so it provided
support for those women who needed it, yet wanted the
braless look. The glossie came in solid colors such as
amethyst, indigo, ruby, and mocha.

MICHAEL
KORS

"Michael really thrives on knowing his customer. It's the storytelling: She's in Palm Beach, she's in Aspen, she's going to Elio's for dinner. He speaks about his clients as his closest friends. You're never going to be a victim in Michael Kors, and that's a hard thing to pull off."

—Nina Garcia, *New York Magazine*

"He makes exceptionally beautiful clothes that are cross-generational and uniquely American . . . He is both smart enough and brave enough to design clothes that are about comfort, elegance and unselfconscious glamour."

—Anna Wintour

"Michael Kors is brilliant at conjuring a whole lifestyle in 64 runway looks."

—Nicole Phelps, *Style.com*

"He is quick to acknowledge his enduring fascination with the touchstones of upper-class American style: haute hippies, Fellini-era jet-setters, Park Avenue royalty."

—Ruth La Ferla, *New York Times*

"From the very beginning, I was convinced that you could be sexy and sporty at the same time. [Then] everything that was sporty was too sporty, too casual, and everything that was sexy was such a bombshell. I have always been intrigued by a sexy tomboy. That's my ethos. No matter what, that's going to be my ethos."

—Michael Kors, *WWD*

"I am the most indulgent and the most casual."

—Michael Kors, British *Vogue*

FIONA
KOTUR

It is every designer's dream that her work transcends the rise and fall of trends, essentially establishing itself as a hallmark of American fashion.

Kotur's minaudières have become the evening's ultimate accessory. Much of my inspiration is drawn from the incredible women who have made a resounding impact in the world of fashion and the arts, so it is only appropriate that my collections represent these muses. Silks, tweeds, chain mail, feathers, and other unique materials provide aesthetical freedom. The minaudière's silhouette is simple yet powerful as a statement, and it is just as important as the jewelry the Kotur woman is wearing.

I am always inspired by the possibilities of creating a beautiful accessory—and have always believed that the smaller the bag, the better the night.

MONICA RICH
KOSANN

I hope that my biggest impact on fashion has been to create a new category in fine jewelry, which embraces the idea of storytelling, memory, and family merged with enduring fashion and style. My one driving question when I design a piece of jewelry is, "Can a woman give this piece to her daughter in twenty years?" I like to think my collection offers my customers heirlooms for our generation. My goal is always to capture the essence of fashion while maintaining the timeless elegance of design. My jewelry tells a woman's story . . . or keeps her secrets.

REED KRAKOFF

REED
KRAKOFF

Reed Krakoff believes, of all the Coach collections he has created, the Hamptons Collection will prove over time to be his single most influential contribution to American fashion. Launched in Spring 2000 as part of a move to make luxury more accessible, Hamptons represented a turning point for the brand, at the time a sixty-year-old leather company. It was the first mixed-materials collection for Coach, combining fabrics with traditional leather trims, which later expanded to include the Coach signature jacquards, logo prints, and coated canvas.

At the time of its launch, Hamptons was described as classic and purposeful, but also undeniably fashionable. The collection's simple designs were and still are true to the brand's rich history and fundamental values of quality and craftsmanship. Reed's favorite piece from the original collection, the Book Tote, is a perfect example: Crafted with minimal hardware, the silhouette and hand-worked leather trim are quintessential Coach. The innovation—an exclusive double-faced cotton with a weatherproof rubberized layer in between—was the brand's future.

To this day, the Hamptons Collection remains seminal in defining Krakoff's approach to modern American design. He continues to juxtapose the principles of form and function with everything he invents.

MICHEL
KRAMER

During the American men's fashion revolution awakening:
I changed the wearing of men's neckwear from business uniform
to leisure, fun, relaxed wearing.

I did so by changing the shape of the necktie and scarf
and, more innovatively, by introducing the use of new fabrics—
cotton, linen, silk blend, quiana, and textured weaves such as
tussah, surrah, bourette, as well as batik print and knotty madras.

I also changed the personality of the tie by creating
conversation designs, border ideas, scenic motifs, sport themes,
love messages, allowing the gentleman wearer to choose and
express his own personality.

REGINA
KRAVITZ

The popularity of the jumpsuit in modern apparel is definitely the
major fashion contribution of my career. From 1978 to 1990, Regina
Kravitz was a top label in the emerging contemporary market. My
clothing was soft and sexy, predominantly in rayon crepe, tissue
faille, and a wide assortment of prints. My dresses were considered
"day to dinner," and hung with Nicole Miller, DVF, and other "dress"
labels of the time. The jumpsuit developed as a mistake. At the end
of each season, we would keep our sample room busy completing
half samples until the new season's ideas began. Prophetically, I put a
pleated, very low-cut, sleeveless top on top of a pair of loosely pleated
pants, all in tissue faille. A great item was born! It went into the
showroom and immediately started selling. At that time, I would see
them whenever I went out, including at Studio 54 and venues all over.
My customers said it made them look ten pounds thinner. I've always
been able to do this in designing clothing. More than fifty different
jumpsuit styles were developed in a five- to eight-year time frame, in
all sorts of fabrics for all seasons. No one quite had the same fit, and
the jumpsuit remains the iconic contribution of my career. It was the
mainstay of my business, and though it faded out for a long period of
time, it is once again timely and ready for my relaunch!

DEVI
KROELL

I made my debut in 2004, and at the same time made my first significant IMPACT contribution to American fashion. It was for my then line Devi Kroell (which I am no longer affiliated with today). The economy was in full boom; luxury and excess were all over the place especially with accessories, with tons of hardware, logos, and boxy, constructed shapes; sort of relics of the nineties that didn't get the memo that they were so last decade (and century). I yearned for something different, and delivered two revolutionary concepts in just one bag:

- an OVERSIZED hobo
- made entirely of PYTHON (believe it or not, exotics were not really on the radar, and many people did not know what python actually was and looked like). The python was treated so wildly with a metallic top coating, scales pushed up and their underside dyed in a contrasting color, that it looked out of this world and alien. This was the beginning of unusual and unexpected exotics.

NIKKI
KULE

Nikki Kule's biggest contribution to American fashion is that she sparked an outpouring of interest in designer clothes for children. When she started Kule in 2001, she was the first American designer whose central focus was children's wear. Just ten years later, the children's category is now recognized as a valuable way for designers around the world to grow and extend their brands.

CHRISTOPHER
KUNZ

&

NICHOLAS
KUNZ

NICHOLAS K's biggest impact on American fashion is successfully mixing two worlds that are normally contradictory to each other and creating a cohesive men's and women's collection. Having come from outdoor roots yet living most of their adult lives in New York City, the designers Nicholas and Christopher Kunz join these backgrounds into a collection that pioneered their boho luxe identity in the fashion world. They are continually inspired by the concept of busy lifestyles, travel, culture, and the fusing of remote destinations and modern environments. The design duo interweaves these concepts to create complementary men's and women's garments that are seemingly identical in fabrics, colors, details, and silhouettes, but naturally accentuate individual contours. NICHOLAS K's women's line has a signature tomboy aesthetic; however, it exudes an independent sensuality that is defined by precision tailoring. The design duo understands that as lives change, and things move faster, creating pieces that are versatile (can be worn several different ways), functional, comfortable, and transitional for different environments is an important factor in life.

BLAKE
KUWAHARA

Prior to the nineties eyewear, and sunglasses in particular, were designed and judged solely on their shape and color or, worse yet, considered just a medical device. In the creation of Blake Kuwahara's signature collection, KATA EYEWEAR, his groundbreaking concept was to take an integrated approach to creating eyewear that was at once artful and wearable.

Kuwahara is the founder and creative director of the interdisciplinary design firm Focus Group West.

STEVEN
LAGOS

I'm often asked what makes LAGOS different. There are many appropriate answers to that question.

Looking back—something I rarely do—I would say that LAGOS was a precursor in what is now called New Luxury, as LAGOS was one of the first brands to bridge the worlds of fine jewelry and accessibility. I never aspired to create an intimidating brand. Spawned from my belief that jewelry is one of the most personal, significant forms of art, I set out to create sophisticated, accessible pieces for the woman I know, pieces she could effortlessly wear every day.

My signature design—Caviar—is an example of that mind-set. The caviar-like beading of LAGOS signature collections brings texture to sterling silver and gold and transforms the precious metals into crafted jewelry that creates the feeling of a second skin.

It takes hundreds of tiny steps to complete the many facets of a single Caviar creation. I always start the creative process with a sketch. At the very end, the sterling silver is oxidized to create contrast. That last step is key to bringing out the sculptural, artistic qualities of the design.

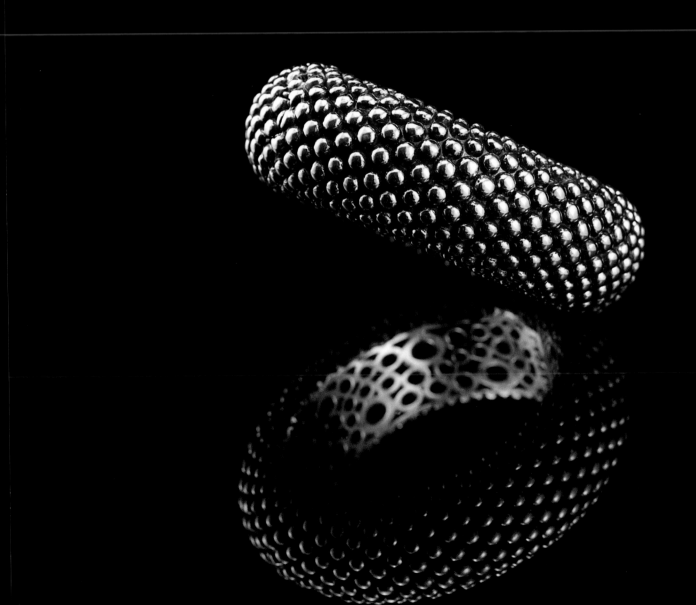

DEREK

LAM

I ask myself each time when I am designing:
How can I create clothing that has an emotional impact,
but done in the most straightforward and purest way?

ADRIENNE
LANDAU

I began my career by designing all kinds of little fur accessories and discovered nobody was doing anything like this at the time. I decided to present my accessories to all the high-end stores, and to my surprise they all bought my pieces!

One day I bought lots of sable tails and sewed them all around the bottom of a cashmere cape. It was an instant hit! This became my "signature" piece, and for some time I was known as "The Cape Lady." I then moved into my collage phase in which I mixed many skins, furs, and prints (my favorite, the timeless leopard print). Stylists and editors still come to my archive to pull these pieces for their clients and photo shoots—they *never* get old.

One of my most iconic pieces is my famous embroidered velvet, fur-trimmed kimono. Women of all ages have worn this piece, including huge names like Sharon Stone and Barbara Streisand, and they have even been featured in top fashion magazines like *Vogue Paris*. I am also proud to have expanded the Adrienne Landau brand to outerwear, handbags, gloves, men's accessories, and even a faux fur HSN line.

KENNETH JAY
LANE

Acclaimed by *Time* magazine as "the undisputed King of Costume Jewelry" and called "one of the three great costume jewelers of the twentieth century" by *Women's Wear Daily*, Kenneth Jay Lane transformed a previously undistinguished field into the height of fashion. "I believe that every woman has the right to be glamorous and have always believed that a woman can be just as glamorous in costume jewelry as million-dollar bangles and beads," Lane has said. "Style has little to do with money and expensive possessions; attitude and flair make all the difference."

It runs through everything he does, from his minimalism to his conspicuous absence from the American Fashion Awards. This is the way in which Lang really is trying to change the rules—to make fashion less about creating a spectacle for the press and more about the problem most people face when they think of fashion, which is simply what to put on in the morning.

LIZ
LANGE

I am flattered that so many recognize me for single-handedly pioneering the "new look" in maternity fashion and changing the way that women dress when they are pregnant. Before I began Liz Lange Maternity in 1997, maternity clothing was an ignored category. I designed maternity clothing strictly out of stretch fabrications and thus was able to design fitted and fashionable maternity clothing. This was groundbreaking at the time (though today it has come to be expected). I reached out to celebrities and dressed them when they were pregnant before regular designers had any interest in doing so. I became the first maternity designer to become a member of the CFDA and held the first-ever maternity fashion show at Bryant Park during New York Fashion Week in 2001. I was the first designer (non-athlete) personality to partner with Nike, creating Liz Lange for Swoosh (maternity athletic apparel). Liz Lange for Target is one of Target's longest standing designer partnerships—having been their exclusive in-store maternity apparel designer partner since 2002.

BYRON
LARS

Reinterpreting a men's button-down shirt into all manner of sexy, body-conscious womenswear would, I think, be what most people that know my work would say that my impact on American fashion has been. I am, however, a bit clueless on the subject, being too surrounded by the trees to really have a true sense of the forest.

At the end of the day, I try my utmost to make clothes that flatter the female form and get or keep a girl in touch with her feminine powers!

RALPH
LAUREN

"Ralph Lauren and American style have become
synonymous. And though he loves the history
and visual richness of our country, Ralph's work is never
really about being nostalgic. Rather it is a reinvigoration
of America's heritage, and America's ideas. He has
reminded us of America's roots, and he has celebrated
the roots, and made them once again relevant
and made them vital and even glamorous."

—Oprah Winfrey, The CFDA Legend's Award
Ceremony, New York City, 2007

JUDITH
LEIBER

Judith Leiber launched her namesake business in 1963, changing the way we think about luxury. The brand has earned its status as an American icon with a distinct heritage, timeless quality, and international appeal. In Washington, DC, the handbags have been carried to presidential inaugurations by the likes of Mamie Eisenhower, Jackie Kennedy, Nancy Reagan, Hillary Clinton, and many others. On red carpets all over the world, Judith Leiber bags and minaudières are staples seen on the arms of style-setters of all ages including Halle Berry, Jane Fonda, Eva Mendes, Gwyneth Paltrow, Rihanna, and more. In 1994, Judith Leiber accepted a Lifetime Achievement Award from the Council of Fashion Designers of America, wearing one of her miniaudières as a pendant to the awards ceremony!

LARRY
LEIGHT

"It was my mission to develop
progressive, flattering frames that fit well,
without sacrificing style."

—Larry Leight, Oliver Peoples founder and creative director

Larry Leight is credited with changing the direction of eyewear globally in the
late 1980s when he founded Oliver Peoples. He created and defined what is now
known as the intellectual category of eyewear, taking design cues from early
twenties and thirties American engineering and the styling of the late sixties.
The look he introduced was an extreme departure from the trends of the day,
which included loud colors and impractical geometric shapes.

NANETTE
LEPORE

The feminine fit, cheerful prints, and optimistic
spirit of my designs are my contribution to
American fashion. In 2001, my rainbow-striped
dress, shown on *Sex and the City*, captured that
breathtaking moment when the lights came
back on in New York after 9/11. I wanted to
celebrate all the vivacious New York women
who refused to be intimidated. My rose print
and work-wear–inspired designs for Spring 2011
are a continuation of that spirit—femininity and
tenacity endures. Likewise, my commitment to
saving New York City's Garment Center is for
aspiring designers all over America who, like me,
come to New York with nothing more than their
determination. I hope that I pass on my legacy
of femininity, optimism, and perseverance to my
daughter: I want her to always remember that
passion and joie de vivre are all that you need.

BETH
LEVINE

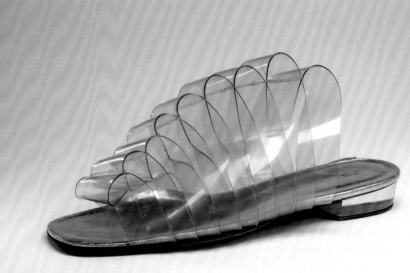

Beth Levine designed shoes for thirty years under the label Herbert Levine, named for her husband. She was known as America's First Lady of Shoe Design because of her prominence in twentieth-century fashion and because her designs were worn by the American First Ladies Lady Bird Johnson, Patricia Nixon, and Jacqueline Kennedy.

MONIQUE
LHUILLIER

Monique's designs are highly regarded as the essence of sophisticated luxury, femininity, allure, and glamour. Her love for fashion has been a lifelong passion, and her understanding of a woman's desire to look and feel beautiful is her signature trademark.

Monique grew up in the Philippines in a very close family. Her mother's sense of style and elegance were a big influence on Monique. At eleven, Monique would sketch designs, select fabrics, and customize her own dresses that were made by local couturiers in her hometown. Her parents noticed her potential and encouraged her to pursue her dream of becoming a designer. Monique moved to Los Angeles to attend the Fashion Institute of Design and Merchandising. While

studying at FIDM, she discovered her inclination toward bridal and evening gowns. It was at this time that she met her now husband, Tom Bugbee.

In 1996, Monique debuted her first bridal collection to the acclaim of retailers and magazine editors. One year later, Monique's vision to establish a couture house became a reality with Tom in place as the CEO. Their partnership has grown the business into one of the most successful international brands with a strong celebrity following. The business includes a ready-to-wear collection, a tabletop and giftware collection for Royal Doulton, a stationery and fine paper line, home fragrance, and a bed, bath, and home collection.

PHILLIP
LIM

Our vision of designer clothes at contemporary prices opened up and paved the way for the once dormant entry-level market. We have established ourselves as a respected business model, and we have shown that it is possible.

JOHAN
LINDEBERG

In 1996 I lived in NYC and had just left Diesel after six years. I decided to launch a new brand with a foundation in modern tailoring. I wanted to create a slim silhouette that felt more progressive and sharper than what most brands were offering.

After almost fifteen years the "Mick" blazer is still one of the bestsellers at J.Lindeberg together with the flat front straight-pant "Mark." I also took inspiration from this silhouette and created a new look in golf wear. My idea was to combine progressive tailoring and modern golf wear to create a new contemporary lifestyle brand.

After leaving J.Lindeberg in 2007, I recently launched my new project, BLK DNM, which has its core in progressive tailoring for both men and women in combination with jeans.

Every day I meet American men who tell me they have been wearing the suits I created throughout the years after being inspired to take a more modern approach with their wardrobes. The golf look I developed for J.Lindeberg by dressing professional players like Jesper Parnevik, Camilo Villegas, and Aaron Baddeley became a spearhead for contemporary golf wear that continues to inspire other brands in the field.

ADAM
LIPPES

I've always been a jeans and T-shirt guy, just in a dressed-up sort of way. As finding that polished and perfectly fit T-shirt was a challenge, I decided to create a collection of basics that could be at the core of a new American sportswear brand. Almost two years of development led to what Oprah has called "the T-shirt that can take you anywhere." A complete collection based on the same principles as the tee—ease, refinement, and simplicity—has led to ADAM.

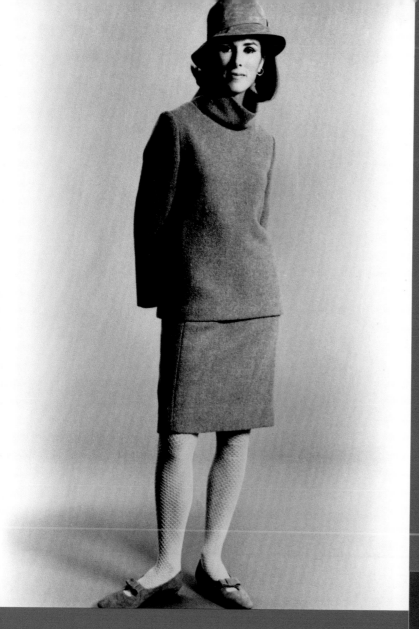

TINA
LUTZ

In a chapter of fashion history that will be known—among other things—for its collaborative, cross-pollinating approach to design, the "Guest Designer" series established by Tina Lutz serves as an important milestone for its prescient timing, unparalleled synergy, and enduring influence.

A fashion designer for more than thirty years, Lutz embarked on her most recognized venture in 2000, when she cofounded Lutz & Patmos, a women's ready-to-wear line that focused on luxury knitwear. She served as the brand's creative and branding director and made her impact on the industry with the creation and curation of the house's innovative collaborations known as the "Guest Designer" series.

As a result of this boundary-pushing approach to collaboration—a long-term component that gracefully dovetailed with Lutz & Patmos's own artful and enduring designs—the brand became known for its strong, contemporary vision.

DEANNA
LITTELL

She has made a success quickly by designing clothes that she herself wants to wear and has trouble finding. She fits them on herself, often models them in the showroom and gives them a heavy workout "hanging from a strap in the subways, getting in and out of taxis, walking quickly with big strides." This way, "sooner or later, I find out the kinks," she said.

—Bernadine Morris, *New York Times*, November 25, 1963

BOB
MACKIE

"Bob Mackie has given the fashion world sex appeal, drama, over-the-top wit, and drop-dead style. He's the master of curvaceous, show-stopping evening numbers that exude a heavy dose of glamour. And Mackie's skillful hand with exquisite beading, elaborate pleating, and seductive sheers is extraordinary. Cher often makes her much-publicized entrances in a Bob Mackie, but this designer can turn any woman into a ravishing siren."

—Etta Froio, contributing senior executive editor,
Women's Wear Daily

"'He understands exaggerations,' said Ann-Margret. Yet although Mackie's sensibility is 100% pop culture (not unlike Andy Warhol), each of his garments is crafted with the attention to detail characteristic of the haute couture. Rhinestones meet the gold standard. Mackie's work is unmistakably his own."

—Valerie Steele, director and chief curator,
Museum at the Fashion Institute of Technology

"The fantasy fashions that Mackie designed for Cher have entered fashion history. Even today it is astonishing to think of Cher wearing a see-through beaded Mackie gown on the cover of *Time* (March 17, 1975). But Mackie's contributions to fashion go far beyond the fantastic fashions that he created for Cher. Equally important are the hilariously brilliant costumes that he created for *The Carol Burnett Show*. For eleven years, Mackie designed the costumes and wigs for Burnett's popular variety show. Not only did he invent unforgettable outfits for Burnett's various alter egos, he also dressed the show's guest stars, often creating elaborate parodies of famous movies such as *Sunset Boulevard, Mildred Pierce*, and, of course, *Gone with the Wind*."

—Christie's catalog

CATHERINE
MALANDRINO

Catherine Malandrino captures the spirit of simplicity and sophistication of a woman who explores the romance of Paris and the rhythm of New York. This common link between my beloved two cities links my signature logo of urban yellow, which is edgy and is associated with the light of the city. The romance of Paris marries the freedom of America in every Catherine Malandrino piece.

    With designs that exude femininity, I enable women to embrace and emphasize their unique bodies. I imagine a woman that wears my clothes to speak a universal language of love and desire. The clothes murmur, suggest, and inspire, rather than impose. I pride myself on allowing women to express their most intimate and personal version of themselves. Ultimately, I aim to capture the spirit and sophistication of a woman. The search for individuality and feminine chic is at the heart of my work.

ISAAC
MANEVITZ

"What I am making is fashion jewelry, *not* costume jewelry. Costume jewelry is an imitation of real gold or silver, an effort to make one thing look like something else. My work on the other hand is made to stand alone," Isaac Manevitz said in an interview in 1980 when his brand Ben-Amun began gaining popularity.

It was the start of the decade that proclaimed "bigger is better." For the first time, women began to explore using jewelry to make their own statement about fashion and style. Manevitz was one of the first in the industry who preferred to work in unexpected man-made materials such as glass, Lucite, pewter, and brass rather than karat gold and precious stones. As a pioneer of this statement-making jewelry movement, Manevitz's message for Ben-Amun—clean lines, bold sculptural shapes, innovative designs, fresh materials, and unique combinations—has kept him on trend season after season. A sculptor by trade, he sees every piece in every collection as a work of art to be perfected, and quality is a top priority.

COLETTE
MALOUF

As a quintessential part of the acclaimed tradition of innovation in American accessories, Colette Malouf has singularly resurrected haute style to hair, creating a strong global brand known for its artistic elegance. Inheriting the DNA of classic couture from her family's luxury dress house established in the 1920s, Colette continues to infuse her collections with childhood impressions of the enchanting allure last remembered in the times of Audrey Hepburn.

MARY JANE
MARCASIANO

"In her desire to create beautiful and wearable knitwear, Marcasiano follows in the footsteps of women designers such as Coco Chanel, Sonia Rykiel, and Jacqueline Jacobsen (Dorothée Bis)—typical of European women designers who have influenced her work. Her personal innovations in the advancement of knit dressing in America, through the use of unusual yarns, stitches, and simplification of the shape of sweaters, are an inspiration to a new generation of young independent designers working on their own."

—Roberta Hochberger Gruber

ROBERT
MARC

Robert Marc is recognized as a visionary in the world of eyewear. He is credited with bringing eyewear to the forefront of fashion and elevating eyewear to its current position as a couture accessory. Robert launched his own signature collection of luxury eyewear in 1999—for which *Vogue* magazine announced, "Robert makes his Marc." Through his eponymous collection he revived the art of the handcrafted frame and developed a special hinge inspired by historical eyewear construction that has since become his trademark motif. He is celebrated for his inspired use of acetate, layering complementary and contrasting colors, patterns and textures to bring out their full visual potential, and maintaining the idea that excellence, innovation, and artistry have their own beauty. Nodding to the past while charging into the future, Robert Marc Eyewear is for modern men and women for whom luxury is defined by quality, craftsmanship, and subtlety.

DEBORAH
MARQUIT

In 1984, by taking on fabrics and colors traditionally used for clothes, designer Deborah Marquit invented the idea of fluorescent-colored bras and underwear to be worn as clothing and, by hand-dyeing nylon lace in fluorescent (neon) colors of pink, lime, orange, and yellow and by cutting and sewing her first collection, thus introduced the concept of "undergarments to be revealed as casual attire" and the first fluorescent bra. The fluorescent bra is her signature statement in the fashion market. The structure of the work is modeled after traditional foundations (such as mainstays like Playtex) whose purpose is to shape and enhance the body, to transform, and to "perform," constructing a blend of the architecture of bra design, fashion fabrics, and colors, therefore creating a trend.

LANA
MARKS

As CEO, owner, and designer of the LANA MARKS brand, Lana J. Marks brings architectural proportion and fashion-forward design to her exotic leather accessory collections.

LANA MARKS has fashioned an enchanting series of luxurious hand-sculpted belt buckles inspired by the Zodiac. Twelve constellations, each signifying a birth date, are elegantly depicted in the MARKS Zodiac series. Modeled after the astrological signs, each matte and shiny buckle is crafted of sterling silver hand-dipped in 24-karat gold. The versatile Zodiac buckles can be paired with a selection of colorful interchangeable belts.

JESSICA
McCLINTOCK

As a designer who has owned a fashion apparel company for forty-two years, I have a lot to express. I love my work! I love conceptual approaches to each of my design collections. For example, my love of lace is most always used as a romantic touch to a garment. Most of my inspiration comes from the romance I find in theater, art, and live experiences. I am mostly remembered for dressing girls for their proms, weddings, bat mitzvahs, quinceañeras, and other celebrations. My true goals are always to find creative ways to transcend time and maintain a high-end brand. I do believe my lasting impact on American fashion has been creating "reality designs." To me that means value in the designs.

VERA
MAXWELL

Maxwell became known as a designer in the 1930s when American fashion was struggling to be born and most designers toiled anonymously. She achieved fame with such designs as a weekend wardrobe of a collarless jacket with four patch pockets that she made in tweed and in gray flannel to be mixed and matched with a short pleated flannel tennis skirt, a longer tweed skirt with pressed-down pleats and a pair of flannel cuffed trousers—all designs so classic they could still be worn today.

—Anne-Marie Schiro, *New York Times*, January 20, 1995

KIMBERLY
McDONALD

The Kimberly McDonald brand has had the unique distinction of actually opening up an entire new genre of fine jewelry. Before this collection, unusual organic stones were found in fashion jewelry and in limited occurrence in fine jewelry, but typically just set in gold or with minimal "fine" materials. For my collection it was important to me to follow my roots as a curator of high jewelry collections, and though my choice of stones is unorthodox, the accompanying stones (diamonds and other precious stones) and the process of making each and every piece by hand keeps with the methods used in creating fine jewelry.

MARK
McNAIRY

To sum up my impact on American fashion, I should start with my footwear, Mark McNairy New Amsterdam. In the words of *GQ*, that's what made me "the most talked-about cobbler in, what, a century?" My obsession with footwear has deep roots. It all started with collecting shoes in junior high. I had a hundred pairs of basketball sneakers lined up around my room. My understanding and appreciation for footwear can be traced back to that time in my life. My stuff harkens back to a time of traditional cobblers and cordwainers. The shoes are a partnership between me and Sanders, a factory in Northampton, England. Since the collection's launch, in 2008, I've been integral in reintroducing classic Anglo silhouettes, styles, and details into high-end men's footwear—things like bucks, saddle shoes, and red brick soles. For New Amsterdam it's all about taking things back to their roots and doing the history justice, while still staying true to my own DNA. The heritage trend is more than a trend—it's men going back to wearing classics. I like to think I am doing my part.

DAVID
MEISTER

Starting out at Danskin, I quickly learned what fit and stretch in clothing could do for a woman—not only for her body, but for her comfort and confidence as well. I keep these ideas in mind with every garment I create; whether it be a custom red carpet look, a piece in my Signature collection, or a gown in my bridal line. Every woman—of every shape, height, or size—can put on a David Meister dress and feel beautiful due to the cut and drape of my designs and the stretch in the fabrics that I select. Matte jersey and stretch are two of my signature fabrics. Stretch is essential to modern dressing. It makes clothing more comfortable, fit better, move with the body, and it travels well. From a size 2 to a 24, I have discovered ways to make all women feel beautiful and comfortable by focusing heavily on the fit of my dresses. A woman can make a $500 dress look better than a $5,000 dress by selecting the appropriate fit for her body. I believe that my impact and contribution to American fashion is modern, sexy clothing that flatters all women.

ANDREAS
MELBOSTAD

"Phi masters proportions and straddles the line between function and femininity. Melbostad is taking utilitarian classics and, rather than (as is often the case with designers) simply rendering them in luxurious versions, is exploring the properties that make the garments essential in the first place: It is an intellectual approach to an emotional mystery, one that produces amazingly hip clothes that are fun to wear."

—Sally Singer, "A Fine Balance," *Vogue*, October 2007

GILLES
MENDEL

In an increasingly dense world where we start to think we've seen it all, where there's perhaps an overabundance of things and an overload on sensory perceptions, it becomes a rare and cherished moment when something can distinguish itself from the rest. Such could be said of the work and reinvention of craft dreamt and developed into being by Gilles Mendel, a fifth generation Franco-American furrier, for J. Mendel. Clear as crystal I can recollect his debut collections! The antennae went up and the inner voice repeated "There's something going on here! Pay attention!" What was going on was the reenvisioning of a material that had become ubiquitous with dusty, staid associations and, even greater, the revitalization of an increasingly waning industry.

In his hands, Gilles treated fur with the lightness and ease of fabric, devising innovative techniques along the way. He famously sheared mink into plush wide rail "corduroy" and lightened its weight with strips of tulle and chiffon! In spite of the codes of the trade, and to his furrier father's dismay, he daringly cut off the coveted long-hairs and re-pieced the pelts into glorious deco chevrons among countless other patterns. He over-dyed it into his favorite muted ballet pinks and dusty mauves rather than traditional and natural neutrals. The linings were as surprising and detailed as the exteriors, using pleated paisley silks and ruby patent seam trims. He made fur "fashionable" and year-round by treating it as "fashion," rather than putting it on the once in a lifetime, our mother's mother's, precious, winter fur pedestal. We owe Gilles for repositioning the place fur now holds in the modern-day closet, and the renaissance it enjoys today. Of course Gilles didn't begin and end with fur. He has gone on to further transform J. Mendel from a luxury furrier into a full-fledged fashion house. His day and eveningwear are likewise dreams of femininity, intricately crafted and draped with an eye and hand influenced by France but essentially embodying his American experience and freedom to create.

—Linda Fargo, April 4, 2011

CARLOS
MIELE

"I believe nothing is compartmentalized or segregated, as for me, life's frontiers are all imaginary. I'm most interested in creating a dialogue based on the tensions that exist between the contemporary and the traditional, the modern and the archaic, handcrafts and luxury. Working with communities in need in deprived areas, I found the traditional handicraft technique of my country hidden inside people's houses, instead of being shown to the world. I thought it would be interesting to bring these lost or forgotten skills, with all their richness, to the catwalk." Through the designer's initiative, he enables these artisans to earn a living while staying at home and caring for children that would have otherwise been left alone—through this he is empowering them in a unique and important way, and ensuring the care of the next generation while contributing to their family's income. "It's important for me to return what society gave to me," says Miele. Brazil is, after all, a modern country. But Miele's appeal is ultimately more timeless. His clothes celebrate beauty, joy, love of life. And that too is Brazil. Fashion and social activism are a modern mix, so it fits that Carlos Miele should be, in his own way, a leader.

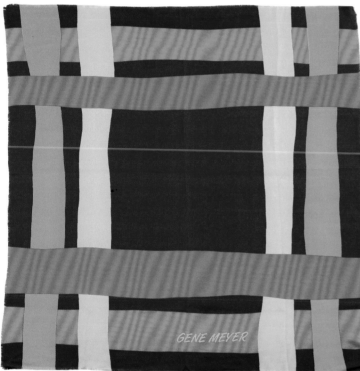

GENE
MEYER

"For two decades, Gene Meyer has been that rarest of fashion creatures, the designer's designer, influencing taste from the sanctuary of his studio. Apprenticed to Geoffrey Beene for eleven years, he learned to "pioneer the future," and then, under his own pale-blue label, he splattered menswear and home furnishings with kaleidoscopic rainbow-warping colors and arty, eye-teasing patterns. Along the way, he won two CFDA awards and earned a cult following—his ties, scarves, and couture (from his lavish, short-lived made-to-order collection) have become fetish objects among vintage-clothing connoisseurs."

—Amy Fine Collins, *Vanity Fair*, December 2003

GLEN
MILLER

Glen Miller for Ann Turk represents an original American luxury brand, made to order in America and exported worldwide. Miller's ornate hardware adorns his accessories like fine jewelry and is immediately recognized for its extraordinary quality, handcrafted beauty, and signature style.

Drawing upon his fine arts background for inspiration, he combined old-world craftsmanship with modern design technologies and materials for product innovation. Miller has created collections reflecting a fresh and genuine all-American spirit.

STEFAN
MILJANIC

Through my work in fashion, I wanted to address the Gilded Age, which gave birth to a uniquely American music, art, fashion, and lifestyle. Through the Gilded Age brand, I have projected and brought to modern fashion a part of the American heritage style that was not epitomized so much by the preppy style and Boston Brahmin attitude, but by a more masculine, gritty, subtly rougher, old New York style. I also wanted to change the archetype that the word *casual* is synonymous with *cheap*. We have shown that casual design can be luxurious, well made, and of greater value as well. There is nothing mediocre about a handmade cashmere cardigan (with all its imperfections) knitted solely by a pair of skilled hands and needles or a beautiful natural indigo garment dried on the ancient roof of a Kyoto house. There is a tremendous amount of effort, skill, and time needed to produce such an artisanal product.

Mass production? It is not!

NICOLE
MILLER

My unique perspective comes from a background in both fine art from RISD and haute couture from Ecole de la Chambre Syndicale de la Couture Parisienne. Aesthetics and engineering are equally important to me. My look is modern, feminine, body-conscious, and camouflaging. My clothing is always draped and often has elements of surprise.

   I realize fashion is a business and clothes must sell, but you have to be known for something to succeed. My breakthroughs were a little black dress and engineered pleating which became iconic. I have evolved both of these concepts, and they have become my signature today.

MALIA
MILLS

In 1993, we started Malia Mills with a simple idea . . . to engineer tops by bra size, to cut bottoms to show off a variety of shapes, to empower women to stand and stride to the water. Today, we have a designer swimwear collection created for the vixen within. We also have a fresh collection of ready-to-wear and delicious accessories curated in Malia Mills boutiques across America. We're passionate about celebrating women and articulating an inclusive and inspiring voice on the subject of women and beauty. Love thy differences!™

RICHARD

MISHAAN

Formal order is the best way to describe the sensibility of the type of clothes I have designed. To find the simplest line and to see the architectural potential in the garment are why I set out to design clothes at all. I have seen the fabric come to life when the form allows it to be the central focus. I am not suggesting that less is more, but that there should be a focus directing the eye to where more is even better. I hope that I have achieved that in my garments.

REBECCA

MINKOFF

In 2005, after spending four years working on a small apparel collection, I burst onto the handbag scene with the design of the "Morning After Bag." The bag became an overnight sensation, and I began solely concentrating on developing additional styles. My idea was to design a bag that was roomy enough to keep everything you need for the day (or an overnight stay). The "Morning After Bag" has become a must-have for modern trend-setting women and celebrities such as Rachel Bilson, Agyness Deyn, and Sarah Jessica Parker. This one popular style has become the foundation of my business and helped to develop Rebecca Minkoff into a full lifestyle brand.

BIBHU
MOHAPATRA

During my twelve years in fashion, I believe that I have designed clothes that are truly American in spirit. My clothes pay homage to modern American women who appreciate fine clothing with a modern outlook on old-world couture techniques. Over the years I have developed specific techniques and methods that use traditional materials such as fur, silk, and leather to produce untraditional collections that are both beautiful and incredibly modern.

With all of my work produced locally in New York, I believe that I have contributed to keeping the tradition of couture techniques alive while continually supporting and utilizing all that New York's garment industry has to offer.

PAUL
MORELLI

From a bright, Beaux Arts building circa 1901 in the heart of
Philadelphia, stunning, well-crafted jewelry has emerged for the past
thirty years. Here, Paul Morelli creates the kind of jewelry you know
will be handed down generation to generation, the antiques of the
future for the taste-makers of today with the know-how to collect.
Paul Morelli has created a culture of creativity, technical innovation,
and above all an eye for fine and detailed workmanship that is infectious. The people that surround Paul are what he calls his "monsters"
and are all as unforgiving and obsessive as their master in their
quest for quality, perfection, and poise in miniature. Thirty years of
making all these choices have positioned him to be a true heritage
luxury brand that will surely last another thirty years to come.

—Caroline Issa, *Tank* magazine

ROBERT LEE
MORRIS

Robert Lee Morris—the name itself seems like a branding ploy, but it was in his blood to make that name shine and become synonymous with sensuous, organic forms in gleaming metals that redefined the standard of fashion and costume jewelry. After only two years in New York, RLM made a name for his brand with his first cover of *Vogue* in 1976, with a bold gold bubble collar. Early in his career, a mythical image already popped into fashionistas' heads at the sound of his name; the knuckle ring, the Alpha cuff, the Beta cuff . . . soft undulating discs. When he opened his jewelry gallery ARTWEAR in 1977, fashion designers discovered a treasure of new accessories to play with, and Robert

began a long career of collaboration with Mr. Beene, Calvin Klein, Kansai Yamamoto, Karl Lagerfeld, Michael Kors, and most notably with Donna Karan. He is credited by the industry with being the man who fathered the new jewelry category called "designer jewelry" and "bridge," which has developed to be the leading category in the market today. To go with his 1981 Coty for his groundbreaking multimetal colored jewelry collection for Calvin Klein and his other two CFDA awards for his previous work, in 2007 Robert took home the Geoffrey Beene Lifetime Achievement Award.

MIRANDA & KARI
MORRISON   SIGERSON

Sigerson Morrison was started in New York City in 1991 by Kari Sigerson and
Miranda Morrison. The designers, who met while studying at the Fashion
Institute of Technology, were united by a simple design philosophy: "Style,
rather than fashion, is key." Always thinking ahead, they created quite a ruckus
with the invention of a dainty kitten heeled flip-flop. Thousands of pairs were
sold within hours! The classic rubber flip-flop was sexied up in new textures,
bold colors, and a perfectly proportioned low stiletto, which took the iconic
sandal from a beloved, informal basic to a chic instant classic. Soon after came
their cutting-edge take on the gladiator sandal, unabashedly sampled in cool
metallic hues and unexpected patterns—like ikat! An it-girl summer staple that
still sizzles today.

KATE
MULLEAVY

&

LAURA
MULLEAVY

"The Rodarte way of thinking is wonderfully unconstricted by eras or trends. The Mulleavy sisters are gifted and indefatigable cultural hunter-gatherers; their exquisite clothing, fearlessly imagined and precisely constructed, attests to their voracious curiosity and constant discernment."

—Susan Morgan, *New York Times Magazine*, September 5, 2008

MATT
MURPHY

Matt Murphy's sculptural, architectonic, and functional collection of handbags and leather goods, launched in 1995, was an integral part of the significant shift in accessory conceptualization at that time. Murphy's innovative process working with handmade 3-D paper models (evocative of building models from his architectural training) inspired his bags' distinctive fusion of clean forms, high-quality leathers, and artisan-crafted sterling silver and white bronze hardware. Using a special bonded-layer construction Murphy developed, produced on shoemaking equipment, the bags heralded the designer's signature non-trendy, timeless aesthetic.

From its inception to the present, the collection's concept and implementation have placed function and shape first, with a key goal that pieces from different years and collections can be interspersed and remixed, ultimately creating an accessories "toolbox" for the user over time. Murphy's logo, abstractly representing timelessness, reinforces this idea.

LEO
NARDUCCI

Impact? Well, let's see. When I first came to Seventh Avenue and wanted to do young affordably priced clothes, my options were not great. I loved to work in jersey, but couldn't stay in an affordable price range using expensive fabric. Then I remembered that my parents made very inexpensive missy dresses in Arnel jersey prints. My salespeople frowned . . . "old lady!" So I worked with Celanese, teamed up with a young print stylist, and did a contemporary black-and-white print, put it into some fresh young shapes, and Voilà!

Forward to the seventies. . . . What could I follow that up with? My partner introduced me to a company that was doing sequins by the yard with a new process that secured the sequins so that they wouldn't unravel. First I did it with BanLon, then Arnel double knit, prints and solids . . . magic! Affordable sequined evening dresses and sportswear that could be hand-washed. Soon everybody was doing it. Today synthetics are part of our industry in every price range.

I have been fortunate to spend the last fifty years in a career that I truly love. My goal has always been to be the best designer I could be. People ask me if I will retire, and my answer is always, "Retire? And do what?"

GELA & PAMELA
NASH-TAYLOR   SKAIST-LEVY

In richly saturated color, our velour tracksuit captured the fashion imagination of a nation and opened the floodgates for an era of relaxed luxury. The Juicy tracksuit quickly became a signifier of the in-crowd; tastemakers ranging from Madonna to *Vogue* editor-at-large André Leon Talley embraced the vivaciously fun and youthful clothing made in the "Glamorous U.S.A." Anchored firmly in fashion and popular culture, the athletic ensemble emerged as an entirely new category of dress. It became a wardrobe workhorse whose elements could as easily appear at cocktail hour as at the gym. Before us, women chose to look casual or sexy—after Juicy, women could be masters of both worlds. Our insouciantly posh ensemble became the go-to uniform for women everywhere and brought L.A. style to the world. As Sally Singer remarked, "The only thing that united the nation was an obsessive interest in Juicy velours."

We wanted to bring the idea of couture to everyone—for "nice girls who like stuff." So, we took the word "couture," previously a parlance of strictly high-fashion circles, and branded it into everyday vernacular. An entire culture has developed around the notion—the simple, yet influential notion of transforming athletic wear into fashion.

JOSIE
NATORI

Josie Natori has an intimate understanding of what makes a woman feel good—and has built her renown as a designer literally from the inside out. Starting in lingerie in 1977, she approached what was a staid category with a ready-to-wear sensibility. Her East-meets-West aesthetic, embroidery, prints, and color were exhilarating, and her monthly deliveries of new merchandise, unheard of. She parlayed that business into the World of Natori—a lifestyle empire that today includes multiple brand extensions in sleepwear, lingerie, and couture: Josie by Natori sleepwear and lingerie; Josie Natori ready-to-wear; a home accents collection; bedding; towels; sunglasses; fragrance; and swimwear.

VERA
NEUMAN

Known for her bold use of color and brilliant designs, VERA's artwork is still immediately identifiable today. She believed that fine art should not be relegated to the walls, but enjoyed in everyday life—specifically translated to women's fashion. Taking a global view, her travels from other cultures inspired the artwork she used for her collections. Known worldwide simply as VERA, she engineered her art onto blouses and dresses which were not only innovative and inspiring in the 1960's and 70's but still timeless today. She was at the forefront of using trademarks for her name and copyrighting her artwork to protect it. At the height of her business, her fashions were in over 20,000 stores worldwide. Because VERA signed the art that inspired each design, she is also credited with creating the first designer signature scarf. She later added the now recognizable ladybug to her signature for good luck! VERA's timeless art and philosophy were carried throughout each of her collections and continue to inspire designers around the world today.

—Susan Seid, President, The Vera Company

Vera paints the Vale of Kashmir

CHARLOTTE
NEUVILLE

Spring 1989, I was immersed in menswear inspiration: menswear fabrics (chunky Italian plaids, houndstooths, and foulard-patterned knits), eccentric, earthy colors, and above all, menswear silhouettes. I had been coming to work with my husband's sports coat on.... I just wasn't satisfied with archetypal women's proportions at the time and liked the feel of his, its roominess and ease. I yearned for a jacket that was oversize, slipping off a woman's shoulder, with a softer, more "feminine" construction.

Simply speaking, I called the new silhouette, "The Boyfriend Jacket." It took weeks of fittings to refine the new look. The Boyfriend Jacket ultimately spawned more than just the jacket—the Charlotte Neuville Fall 1989 collection featured luxe quilted car coats over menswear pants, big chunky mohair sweaters over tiny pleated schoolgirl skirts, and roomy silk faille smoking jackets for evening. Who would have known that the descriptive term "boyfriend" would survive more than twenty years later to mean anything oversize and roomy!

DAVID & MARCUS

NEVILLE   WAINWRIGHT

"The two Brits have succeeded in achieving what great
American fashion is about: an intelligent reflection on real
life and how we want to look as we're living it."

—Mark Holgate, *Vogue*, January 2011

Since its conception, rag & bone has been about the quality and craftsmanship of
its designs. Having started rag & bone without any formal fashion training, David
and I were able to come into the industry with a different perspective than many
of our peers. We wanted to create clothes without branding that had a sense of
luxury, timelessness, and accessibility. Instead of focusing first and foremost on
fashion, we were able to concentrate on the quality of the clothes, where they were
made, and how they were made. We chose to have most of our manufacturing
done in U.S. factories that still sew clothes in the manner they did fifty years ago.
Consequently, our brand isn't traditionally designer, but rather designer quality
that reflects our English heritage and utilitarian, made-in-America ethos. We feel
proud to be among a new generation of designers who are spearheading a regen-
eration of American fashion and a new kind of American fashion business.

IRENE
NEUWIRTH

I design a collection of fine jewelry that is modern and timeless, with an element of edge and surprise. The tone is bold, slightly unexpected, optimistic, and intelligent. I favor strong colors and shapes, and tend to use stones in unexpected combinations. I never shy away from color, and this has become a signature of my designs. I love bright lapis blue, carnelian, chrysoprase, emeralds, turquoise, opals, and diamonds. I don't feel there had been a youthful, clean, not overly designed collection where precious stones like emeralds and diamonds are whimsically placed before me. Ultimately, I like my collection to feel like the fine version of a costume jewelry line.

I have always loved layering, and my collections reflect that. The jewelry is meant to be built upon season to season. My chains have become signature layering pieces, as have my flat gold earrings and bangles. I like to keep fine jewelry young and playful, and believe it should be worn and enjoyed every day.

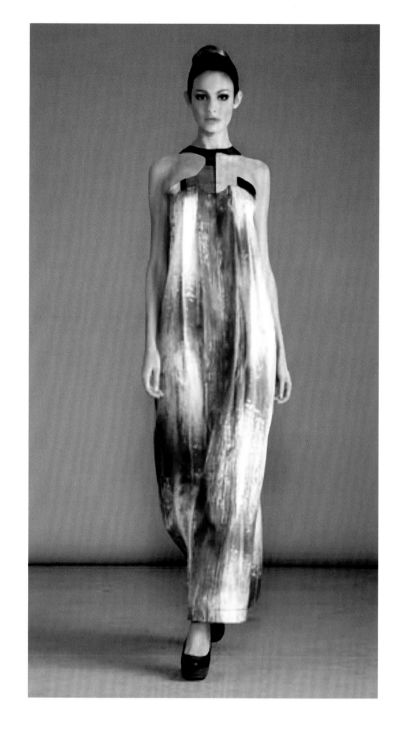

ROZAE
NICHOLS

Throughout twenty-five years of making clothing, I have always striven to create innovative techniques of finishing, construction, texture, textiles, craft, and print. If there have been any trends stemming from my collections, I hope that my works have inspired others to be thoughtful and sensitive to the inner workings of handmade garments for the modern woman. Artisanal, thoughtful construction details and authenticity are the key points of my approach in design.

ROLAND
NIVELAIS

Twenty years ago, I had designed two strikingly dramatic, black velvet, full-length dresses with strapless necklines distinguished by very graphic scrolls (creating a kind of positive/negative effect). After my fashion show, the immediate reaction to those two dresses was unbelievable! Besides being bought by Bergdorf's and Saks immediately and being featured in their windows, there was a deluge of requests from stylists to use the dresses for some of the most coveted photographers.

The highlight of those requests was for the ad for the famous Elizabeth Arden "Red Door," which turned out to be featured in every fashion magazine including *Vogue*, *Harper's*, *Elle*, *Town & Country*, *W*, etc., and most of the time on the highly desirable back cover! This ad went on to be highly circulated for four years! That year, the CFDA extended the invitation to me to become one of their members, and I gladly accepted.

VANESSA
NOEL

One of the most iconic contributions I have made to the American fashion industry is my stretch alligator over the knee boots. Worn by Kim Cattrall in the *Sex and the City* movie, highlighted on the couture runways of Paris and the ready-to-wear runways in New York, the boots have become one of the most coveted necessities for international and American socialites. Embracing my love for the natural beauty of alligator, I worked closely with the tanneries in Europe to develop this new technology. The process of creating the actual stretch alligator skins took me more than four years to accomplish. Vanessa Noel stretch alligator boots are today's luxury fashion armor.

CHARLES
NOLAN

Charles Nolan was a master at tweaking the traditional with an element of surprise: classic coats made new in whimsical popcorn Melton; timeless shapes in amped-up colors used in unexpected odd pairings; toggles and stripes added to a classic balmacaan to reference a fireman's coat; daytime iconic Icelandic sweaters or sweatshirts repurposed by beading for evening.

Charles prided himself in creating clothing that worked on an eighteen-year-old as well as an eighty-year-old. His spring 2006 show included his eleven-year-old niece, his seventy-year-old mother, and the eighty-six-year-old mother of his partner, Andrew Tobias.

With the start of his own label, Charles began to create shows that were warm and inclusive, in contrast to the typical elitist presentation. Charles put nieces, nephews, moms, aunts, and friends on his runway. He sprinkled real people into the mix of models to show the versatility of the clothing.

Charles repeatedly stated that his goal in life was to dress the first woman president. When the famous kiss between Tipper and Al Gore happened at the 2000 Democratic National Convention, Tipper was wearing Charles Nolan. Charles once successfully dressed Arianna Huffington as Queen Elizabeth on the fly for a Renaissance weekend skit using a hotel tablecloth and a roll of tin foil. Elaine Stritch at the Carlyle and on Thirty Rock in Charles Nolan. Charles loved having his shop on Gansevoort Street, mainly because it put him face-to-face with these women.

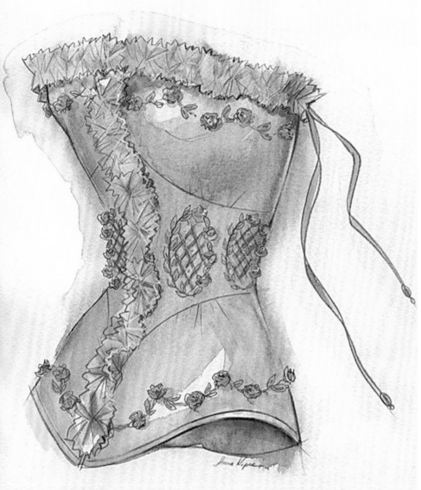

JUAN CARLOS
OBANDO

Telling a story is about being sincere, and expressing those ideas you want to be remembered for and followed by. Fashion should always be current and express a point of view. It should seduce and evoke, inspire and comfort. Its body should portray modernity, but its heart should be rooted in traditional craftsmanship, portraying values that make it both original and timeless.

I want my lasting impact in fashion to become my desire to preserve the values of handcraftsmanship in today's fast-paced world by endorsing innovation led by focus on good design.

MAGGIE
NORRIS

Within the world of couture, there is a deep respect for the process of making clothing. Each piece doesn't just leave your hands as a garment, but as a work of art because of the craftsman element. The garment becomes more of a gift to the world, highlighting its unique and special quality. In a world so technologically advanced, the work of couture artists becomes more important, as their work has the ability to transcend time and modern technology to hold its own as an independent art form.

As an American designer working in the world of couture, Maggie Norris has not only upheld the traditions of the couture process in her atelier, she makes it a priority in her work to celebrate the craftsmanship of other artisans around the world, sharing their talents with us through her collaboration with each one. Maggie Norris Couture continues to sculpt the female figure through the architectural aspects of corsetry, bespoke shirts, tailored shirts, and opulent evening gowns.

ASHLEY & MARY-KATE
OLSEN   OLSEN

We believe THE ROW's largest impact on the American fashion industry is our
commitment to support the U.S. garment industry and continuing to build jobs
domestically while pushing the standards of excellence in ready-to-wear. THE
ROW has become a luxury label that focuses on making clothing of the highest
quality and fit. Our clothing is carefully designed with the discerning customer in
mind, and this has translated into strong sales that help contribute to the stability
and growth of the American garment industry. Our dedication to domestic
production and job creation is one that is vital to the ethos of THE ROW and one
that we will continue to support.

SIGRID
OLSEN

An artist by trade, Sigrid Olsen founded her eponymous brand featuring her colorful hand-printed textile designs in 1984 and immediately found a receptive audience with specialty retailers across America. Her artistic point of view and creative approach to fashion set her apart from other designers in the industry and created a niche market that loyally followed her evolution for almost twenty-five years until the line was shuttered in 2008. Over the years she developed an iconic sportswear brand with distinctive prints, artisanal sweaters, and unique detailing which made her style unmistakable. She established a solid customer base with baby boomers by offering fashionable clothing that was made to fit real women without being matronly or dowdy. Soon her label was a staple in most American women's closets.

RICK

OWENS

'Dust' is what I call the warm soft grey colour of gently slipping into unconsciousness....

The clothes I make are my autobiography. They are the calm elegance I want to get to and the damage I've done on the way. They are an expression of tenderness and raging ego. They are an adolescent idealization and its inevitable defeat

MOLLIE

PARNIS

I've always had a theory that good designing doesn't mean dresses you have to throw away every year. Things shouldn't go out-of-date overnight.

MARCIA

PATMOS

Marcia Patmos has left her mark on American fashion by examining and redefining what luxury means in our lives today. She created one of the first lifestyle brands, her ten-year collaborative line Lutz & Patmos, by following her conscience and designing for lifetimes rather than trends, working with artisan communities and creating partnerships with charities, frequently with guest designers, a concept L&P pioneered. These principles continue to guide her new brand M.PATMOS.

Patmos was an early adopter of eco-friendly and sustainable design; in fact, from an early age, Marcia's grandmother taught her to sew, knit, crochet, and repurpose just about anything, instilling an appreciation of the power of a personal touch. The sourcing of materials, whether it is the use of state-of-the-art, no-waste technology or collaboration with communities of artisans working in ancient traditions of hand work, contributes to the overall sustainability and low environmental impact of her work. But ultimately, it all comes back to the clothing, and features such as reversible color combinations, two in one or multifunctionality, and the versatility and quality to be worn season to season and year after year make the strongest statements for her commitment to fashion in harmony with her worldview.

JOHN
PATRICK

I envision a world in the near future where people
won't ask 'Is it organic?' but say 'Of course, it's organic!'

I have spent the past decade working on my passion
for transparency and sustainability. In that time I have
discovered more and more about myself and my work that
takes me to a new and unexpected place. It is a gift
to be able to work in the creative world, and I do not take
it lightly. I hope that I am remembered as being one
of many pioneers who believed that the entire world
could live in sustainable harmony.

MONIQUE
PÉAN

When I began my line in 2006, there were very few choices for consumers interested in sophisticated yet eco-friendly fine jewelry. I aimed to create a collection that would blur the lines between art, sustainability, and luxury. One of the first decisions I made was to work exclusively with recycled gold and platinum and conflict and devastation-free stones. I then combined these items with rare repurposed eco-friendly materials such as fossilized woolly mammoth and fossilized walrus ivory ranging between 10,000 and 150,000 years old. I like to think that each piece that I create is a combination of art, history, nature, and fashion.

I believe that my impact on American fashion is the creation of a covetable fine jewelry collection that has a positive impact on society and the environment. My collections have a philanthropic focus, and a portion of the proceeds from each jewelry sale provides clean drinking water to impoverished communities in collaboration with charity: water and Partners In Health. In an effort to support native arts around the world, I start each collection by identifying a group of artisans in a particular region to work with. In many instances, I collaborate with artisans to adapt and incorporate traditional art forms.

ROBIN
PICCONE

"The art to cutting a perfect silhouette:
It's not always about what
the suit covers but how it frames
what remains bare."

—Robin Piccone

Robin Piccone revolutionized the swimwear industry with her innovative use of neoprene for BODY GLOVE swimwear in 1986. Inspired by the wetsuits worn by surfers, her sleek body-conscious suits marked a turning point in swimwear design. Piccone's interpretation of the surfer style created a fashion standard that has been widely imitated throughout the fashion industry. The Costume Institute of the Metropolitan Museum of Art's permanent collection includes two of her neoprene swimsuits. For her achievements in changing the swimwear landscape, Piccone was honored with the California Designer of the Year award.

Noticing the lack of fashion in contemporary swimwear, Piccone launched her signature label in 1992. Characterized by modern styling and innovative details for a wearable and flattering cut, ROBIN PICCONE accentuates a body's unique lines and curves without relying entirely on briefness to create a cutting edge look. ROBIN PICCONE has been featured in magazines and newspapers such as *Vogue*, *Cosmopolitan*, *Lucky*, *Sports Illustrated*, *Seventeen*, *Self*, *More*, *GQ* and *Women's Fitness* and is available at department stores and specialty chains throughout the United States.

MARY
PING

In honor of the fifty years of the CFDA, my humble contribution to American fashion is based on a very classic design philosophy and a resulting body of work that is committed to that same meaningful practice. The label is best described as "a logical dissection of fashion," an investigation into the basic elements of what we wear.

Slow and Steady Wins the Race is a conceptual clothing and accessory line by Mary Ping founded on the design philosophy that things can be timely and timeless, unique and universal, ageless and cross-cultural. The work is seasonless and proves that good design can be universally intellectual and emotionally responsive. The entire body of work is a living archive, a reference library.

JILL
PLATNER

I feel that my biggest contribution to the fashion community has been transforming and elevating the idea of silver jewelry. This is especially true of my gallery pieces, which are limited editions created and fabricated as pieces of art, rather than production works. The real testament to my work, though, is that I am still designing and creating in the same spirit of challenging boundaries twenty years later. Although my jewelry and technique have certainly evolved from my early days, the original ethos is still the guiding force behind my work.

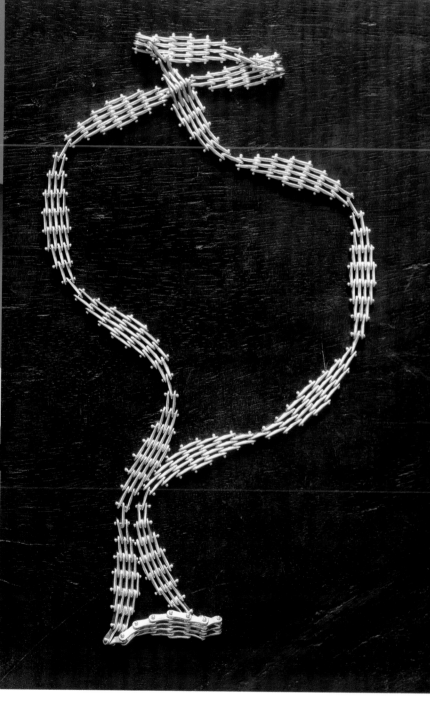

LINDA
PLATT

&

TOM
PLATT

LIFE IS COMPLICATED,
CLOTHES SHOULD BE SIMPLE!

CARMELO
POMODORO

Throughout his all too brief career, Pomodoro continued to develop this series of women in white, and these were arguably his most successful artistic and commercial fashions. From the eggshell cotton crochet cover-up from his resort 1990 collection, both a tribute to the 1960s and an avant-garde prefiguration of the 1993 crochet craze, to virginal white cotton organza overshirts and cotton silk lace tank dresses also appearing that year, Pomodoro brought forth inspirational designs that made women feel and project their most beautiful selves. Whether or not his attraction to monochromatic compositions came from his skills as a black-and-white photographer (he did much of the photography for his company's advertising campaigns himself), it is clear this propensity distinguished him among other artists of his generation such as Charlotte Neuville, Zang Toi, Jennifer George, and Rebecca Moses.

If white was his best noncolor, knitted fabric was his best medium for making art through dresses. A master technician, he understood not only pattern making and construction but also his materials. In knitting, with its ability to hold a shape, to drape, to cling, and to stretch, Pomodoro gave his designs a comfort quotient not possible from any other technique. What made his knits extraordinary was the mixture of mostly natural fibers with a minuscule amount of the newest microfibers developed for him in Japan.

ZAC

POSEN

Creating modern glamour for a diversity of women and
presenting this on the runway as fashiontainment—while
always looking at both the history of fashion as
an art form and how to evolve its future.

ANNA MAXIMILIAN
POTOK

Potok was known for her use of sumptuous furs,
especially sable, chinchilla, mink, broadtail, and ermine.
She developed a technique for working sable so the
skins looked fatter and more opulent than those
used by other furriers. She also liked combinations
of furs, like broadtail with mink or sable.

—Bernadine Morris, *New York Times*, April 23, 1987

LILLY
PULITZER

In 1950-ish Palm Beach, Lilly Pulitzer created American resort fashion. Living the life-style was the key . . . and seeing a way to infuse bright, happy prints and color into an affluent-at-ease wardrobe is something Lilly pioneered. Hard to imagine life before a bright pink floral-printed shift dress! It has become a part of American history, and Lilly Pulitzer will be known forever as step one toward happy, resort, chic.

—Lilly Pulitzer Fashion Director, Janie Schoenborn

JAMES
PURCELL

My greatest impact came from something very small: just a swatch of fabric, really. An afterthought. But it showed me the influence a trend could have. I created an overskirt to go over one of my dresses. Some gathered fabric with a satin waistband tied in a bow. I showed it to a buyer. She bought. Then it sold . . . and sold, and sold, and sold. Soon I was creating them in many colors and fabrics. New stores came to my showroom to buy the collection because they wanted the latest thing, too. The fashion press loved it. And then I saw it interpreted by others. First one, then another . . . soon I kept a folder of clips documenting its spread. From high to low, it appeared in French couture and catalogs. I was thrilled. But the crowning moment was when I was sitting on a beach, and a woman walked by. She had put one over her bathing suit for a *promenade sur la plage*. Even I would never have thought of putting silk gazar near saltwater. But she had, and all heads turned. And that is the impact of fashion.

TRACY
REESE

My love of design came early, and with my mother's help, I was sewing my own clothes at ten. My passion soon brought me to New York to attend Parsons School of Design. Three years after graduating, I launched my first line with a loan from my father. Eighteen months later, financing ran out, and I was forced to close the business. I took this as an opportunity to increase my experience, and by the mid-nineties, I was ready to try again. I was focused, knew what I wanted, and had a game plan.

With three successful womenswear brands and multiple category extensions, I've found my place in the industry, by staying true to my aesthetic, putting my customers' needs first, providing great fit and a consistent point of view that transcends trends. My story is one of perseverance, determination, and breaking barriers in the American fashion industry. I am proud to be one of the first African-American designers to show during NYFW, presenting consistently for more than twenty-six seasons. I'm among the very few female African-American designers to be featured in *Vogue* and other top publications. Seeing an incredible style influencer like First Lady Michelle Obama wear my designs reminds me just how far I've come. Doing what I love for a living and reaching women across the world through my designs is an incredible blessing. Overcoming adversity is an opportunity to grow stronger. I hope future generations will see that, no matter your color, status, or any potential setbacks, true success is possible!

BILLY
REID

William "Billy" Reid grew up in Amite, Louisiana, where his mother operated a women's clothing boutique. The shop would later influence his interest in design. Billy got his start in designer fashion in 1998 with William Reid. The brand went on hiatus in 2001 and relaunched under the name Billy Reid in 2004 with a new business model: to build a designer brand around his authentic lifestyle and establish retail shops that reflect his upbringing, his personality, his aesthetic. In Fall 2008, Billy added a women's capsule collection to complement his men's and accessories collections.

Billy's modern approach to traditional Americana mixed with Southern dandyism has come to define the brand. *GQ* and the CFDA awarded Billy the Best New Designer in America Award in February 2010. His win resulted in a capsule collection with Levi's for Fall 2010. In November 2010, Billy won the CFDA/*Vogue* Fashion Fund Award, becoming the first-ever designer to win both awards in the same year. As a part of his win, Reid designed a men's capsule collection for J. Crew for Summer 2011. Billy has collaborated in his own collection with other like-minded brands such as Stetson on hats and winter accessories and K-Swiss on a canvas lace-up sneaker.

Today, Billy works out of his flagship shop and studio in Florence, Alabama. The store is furnished with Reid family heirlooms and other reclaimed materials.

MARY ANN
RESTIVO

The decade of the sixties was a most liberating time for fashion designers. Luckily I came on the scene during this era and became known as an ingénue who could deliver exciting, saleable clothes. By the time the eighties came around, I knew that I wanted to design clothes for the executive woman emerging on the scene, filling the void between very expensive couture houses and what was then known as "better" sportswear.

Mary Ann Restivo became the go-to label to aspire to and wear if you were a woman in business. During this period, women such as Gloria Steinem, Candice Bergen, and Matilda Cuomo, the then first lady of New York, were clients.

During the CFDA's most formative years of the mid-eighties to the mid-2000s, I was privileged to sit on the board and be part of the force that guided the organization to the level of prestige that it enjoys today. I cannot imagine any other career that could be more rewarding to me, except perhaps singing like Jo Stafford.

ROBIN
RENZI

With its sophisticated, modern, and carefree style, Me&Ro has become a favorite brand over the last twenty years for many longtime devotees. Me&Ro's art is inspired by the human need both to adorn and to communicate through jewelry. Equally important is the power jewelry has to express the human values of strength, love, and faith. Me&Ro emphasizes the wearability of its designs, even when working with materials that verge on excessive. Known for its stackable rings, hammered bangles, personal amulets, and hoops of all sizes, Me&Ro pursues an aesthetic of simple beauty.

JUDITH
RIPKA

The concept of "wearable" fine jewelry was relatively new when I started designing, as women had thought of jewelry as an accessory only to be worn on special occasions. I would teach my customers how to have fun with their jewelry, and I became known for my versatile designs, as well as creating classic jewelry with a modern twist. I developed a distinctive look incorporating signature design elements and a proprietary formula for the color of my gold, which I named Celadon because of its slightly greenish tint. This shade of gold flattered all skin tones, making the skin appear to glow, which, with my signature matte finish, gave the jewelry a look of understated elegance. In 1986, I designed my "Pearl Necklace System"—a strand of pearls with a detachable loop and toggle closure. This one piece, based on fluidity and a system of interchangeable components, laid the foundation for my collection. The inherent flexibility encouraged women to embrace their own creativity and wear my designs in countless ways. Today, more than twenty years later, women tell me that this concept was a stepping-stone for them to have fun with their jewelry, as the design can be worn as a long or short necklace or doubled, with a detachable clip-on, or even as a bracelet, from blue jeans to black tie and everything in between.

BILL
ROBINSON

Bill Robinson was a rare breed of designer—articulate, modest, and enormously intuitive. He was one of the few American menswear designers to achieve a worldwide reputation in the 1980s. His clothes had their roots in classic American styles but also reflected a tradition of European design. They were an amalgam of fashion basics and sophisticated, elegant sportswear.

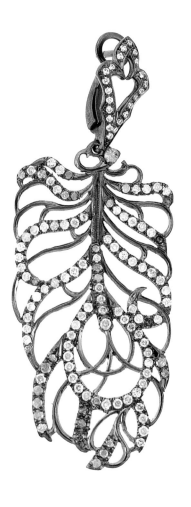

DAVID
RODRIGUEZ

Since launching in 1997, there have been many career milestones, but the constant in my path has been the commitment to maintaining a made-in-New-York ethos. I have always kept not only my sampling process but also my production in the Garment District. The satisfaction I feel is from knowing that through my creative process I am providing the livelihood for my team and the countless workers that are employed by the sewing contractors, fabric finishers, and furriers that are such an essential part of the American fashion industry.

LOREE
RODKIN

When I launched my jewelry line in 1988 there was nothing unconventional on the market. No one was doing heraldic or edgy or distressed applications. Rock and roll jewelry was yet to be a phrase in our vocabulary. Diamond skulls, articulated diamond armored bondage rings. Grey diamonds, rough-cut diamonds. Black-rhodiumed and dull-finished jewelry weren't a part of our vernacular. When I started, jewelry was still conventional and grown up.

I think my impact was to make diamond jewelry a fashion forward accessory. Besides designing jewelry for Elizabeth Taylor, Cher, Madonna, and most of rock and roll's and film's glitterati. I've put fashion forward jewelry in the White House, having designed the pieces for Mrs. Obama from the election through the inauguration. I'm the only jeweler to hang on permanent display in "The First Ladies at the Smithsonian" exhibtion. That's a little impact, I hope.

NARCISO
RODRIGUEZ

For Narciso Rodriguez, design is an ever-evolving process that is first and foremost about the body. Simultaneously refined, elegant, and accessible, his creations celebrate the body, conveying a sensuality without an overt sexuality—a sensuality that is above all about the way a woman moves.

Focused on fashion that is approachable, Narciso Rodriguez's work is meant to provide a frame to enhance, not overwhelm, an individual or her personality. It is no coincidence that Rodriguez has designed dresses for two fashion icons, marking highly momentous occasions in American history. As the designer of Carolyn Bessette Kennedy's wedding dress and Michelle Obama's election night victory dress, Rodriguez captured each moment in a transformative manner with a singular vision.

Narciso Rodriguez creates timeless pieces that fit and function well—that look good and feel good. Acclaimed for both pure and elegant eveningwear as well as sophisticated sportswear, Narciso Rodriguez's clothing enhances a woman's body with clean lines, precise tailoring, and luxurious materials. Rodriguez seeks to balance an underlying architectural structure with a seamless fluidity that is soft and sensual. His signature elements include fine craftsmanship, discreet well-considered structure, and a discerning sense of color and detail.

ROBERT
RODRIGUEZ

I am always inspired by the beauty of nature
and the history of architecture around me.
The one thing that fascinates me about
designing is my ability to control and
manipulate different fabrics in order
to create surface interest and dimension.
I think this would be the biggest impact
I have on American fashion.

PAMELLA
ROLAND

Pamella Roland's impact on American fashion has come one
woman at a time—we design and produce each piece with the
goal of having each woman who wears it look and feel amazing.
We pride ourselves on our craftsmanship and fit. Our beaded
dresses are finished by hand. Our gowns are draped with close
attention to every detail. Our line is known for quality, and that
quality must be present in every step of the process—from selection of luxurious fabrics to the finished garment.

The Pamella Roland line is best known for elegant gowns
and fun and flirty cocktail dresses. One other distinguishing
characteristic of Pamella Roland is our diverse customer base.
We can dress a fifty-year-old mother as well as her twenty-year-
old daughter—our dresses flatter women of every age, shape, and
size. Our goal is to make each of our customers feel as special in
one of our dresses as an A-list actress on the red carpet.

LELA
ROSE

Color and femininity have always been the foundation of LELA ROSE. They are the overriding themes for every collection. By offering form-flattering dresses in vibrant colors with innovative details to classic silhouettes, Lela creates an alternative to the little black dress. She speaks to the modern American woman—one who finds the need to look put together with the ease of one zip. Lela's bold color palette reflects her belief that wearing color gives women a sunnier outlook on the day.

CHRISTIAN
ROTH

When did sunglasses become more than sunglasses? In 1984, when Christian Roth and Eric Domege launched Christian Roth and Optical Affairs Eyewear and forever transformed a functional basic into a covetable fashion accessory. Seen on the runways of top designers and shot for the most prestigious international fashion magazines, Christian Roth Eyewear impacted the industry by making eyewear a desirable piece of fashion and paving the path for many brands to follow. The line's innovative use of silhouette, technique, and color positioned it on the forefront of both trends and technology. Roth became a pioneer in the use of titanium and handmade acetate, and in doing so created a luxury optical market. He was the first eyewear designer to be inducted into the Council of Fashion Designers of America. As proof of Roth's timelessness and resiliency, the label still stands out more than twenty-five years later. Today, the Christian Roth name is synonymous with impeccable, subtle design, pursued by the savviest of collectors.

RACHEL
ROY

"I give women the means to express themselves and be who they are and who they aspire to be, and I think there is real beauty in this. Everything I design is made to enhance the woman who is wearing it whether she's running a company, the country, or her family."

—Rachel Roy

"Clothing from the designer Rachel Roy recalls a time when women had impeccable manners, hourglass figures and the good sense to flaunt them with clothes on."

—Jennifer Tung, *New York Times*

CYNTHIA
ROWLEY

"Cynthia Rowley is a serious person with a serious business.... This is reflected in the clothes she creates, which are crisp and classic and designed to make women look appealing—but not by making them look like hookers or space aliens or men."

—Bill Blass for *Esquire*, "Women We Love"

From a pop-up book set inspired by Kara Walker's cut-outs to a drop-cloth reveal or a serenade by Scarlett Johanssen, Cynthia Rowley's runways always pair compelling performance with beautiful clothing. Rowley has built her company up into a globally recognized brand most well-known for sophisticated silhouettes, lavish textiles, and attention to fine detail work. The Cynthia Rowley collection is about breaking boundaries and taking fashion in new directions, whether in the creation of designer Band-Aids and wetsuits, a capsule for the Gagosian Gallery, a collaborative exhibit for MoMA's PS1, or the founding of the groundbreaking art-retail site Exhibition A. The brand lives where art and fashion fuse, where ingenuity and innovation reign, and where the possibilities are limitless.

RALPH
RUCCI

"I am always honored and humbled by the accomplishments and innovations that my staff and I are permitted to introduce; but, you see, it is not the inclusion with other designers that leaves me speechless but, rather, the voice that God has given me to use within this métier."

—Ralph Rucci

"Rucci reminds me of a mad monk in the Inquisition," says journalist Tim Blanks. "He has that kind of fierceness and fanaticism that's unique in fashion. He's like the Dark Prince of Seventh Avenue. He has shown a devotion to the artistry of what he does that is above and beyond the call of duty. It's fanaticism. What he does is not just craft, it's art. And that's a formidable proposition for fashion people. They say 'Where's the humor and sex appeal?' History will be kind to him."

—From *The Art of Weightlessness*
by Valerie Steele, Patricia Mears, and Clare Sauro

GLORIA
SACHS

Gloria Sachs was trained as a fine artist, painter, and sculptor. She brings those aesthetic considerations to the designing of clothes. "I approach the designing of clothes as I would approach any form of art—no differently than if I were creating a painting or piece of sculpture. Designing clothes is not unlike sculpture, because I create form; not unlike painting, because I dye the yarn as I would mix paints on a palette. The process is no different."

Sachs designs not only her clothing, but also her textiles, which are printed for her in Italy. All her cashmeres are knitted in Scotland. In the last fifteen years, Sachs has been involved in designing horsehair textiles woven for her in China. These are used by top architects in hotels worldwide. She is also working on a major museum show about China with Wu Hung, the artist Xu Bing, and the architect Pei Zhu.

KELLY
RYAN

The beauty of design is the ability
to share the view of one's imagination.

JAMIE
SADOCK

BROKEN BARRIERS
My philosophy has always been
"CORROSION OF CONFORMITY."

THE ART OF MY PASSION and THE SPIRIT OF MY ART are integrated into
my designs in a way that has enabled the "Jamie Junkies," as they call themselves,
to recognize that I cater to the fact that your youth and your spirit don't age, just
the outward body does. You don't lose those feelings and emotions or sense of
vitality because you're a little bit older today than yesterday. Your body can age,
but not your soul or your youthfulness.

231

FERNANDO
SANCHEZ

He introduced dressmaker techniques
to slips and caftans so that they
transcended their functional boundaries.
Things like finished seams and linings
made innerwear acceptable as outerwear
and foreshadowed the mainstream
acceptance, two decades later,
of women wearing lingerie like
garments in their daily wardrobes.

—Eric Wilson, *New York Times*, July 3, 2006

SELIMA
SALAUN

When Selima Optique launched in the mid-nineties, decades of
conspicuous branding were barely behind us, and the fashion
world clearly suffered from "visible logo overdose." While
many competitors have since followed her lead, founder Selima
Salaun's decision to stay clear of any visible branding was
revolutionary in the world of luxury eyewear. Fashion has seen
waves of logo-mania come and go, but the Selima Optique logo
has always been and will always be discreetly printed inside
the frame.

Working with multiple colors within a single frame—by
fusing two or more (sometimes vintage) laminates together—
changed the look of eyewear. Selima Optique was at the
forefront of this technique and started creating multicolored
frames when most designers were hesitant to venture beyond
a dark, safe palette. Today it seems impossible to imagine the
fashion world without high-end colorful eyewear.

BEHNAZ
SARAFPOUR

My approach to designing women's fashion has always been focused on a fundamental idea of merging functionality with beauty. It is with this idea in mind that I have developed my collection of designer sportswear. One of the most important elements in my work has been how textiles can be used in creating both shapes and surface interest in the pieces I have designed.

I have always believed that each piece should contain a classical element that either consciously or subconsciously resonates with women without being directly or obviously rooted in the past, a familiarity that allows the wearer to connect with the piece and adopt it into her daily life. In an increasingly global field where everything can be found everywhere, I attempt to bring authentic and unique influences from other cultures as well as other forms of art into my work, while inventing new approaches in construction that give a more weightless and mobile quality to each piece.

JANIS
SAVITT

A design by Janis Savitt represents a unique style and taste, something you won't find anywhere else. As a woman, my customer has always been a reflection of my own taste and love of jewelry. My impact is a new interpretation of wearable diamond and costume jewelry alike that embodies the modern woman. The former, the wearable diamond piece, is fine yet poignant; this is a functional everyday diamond whose brilliance is nothing short of timeless and chic—something that never will see the inside of a vault. I have been known to design diamond pieces that are so subtle, they draw your eyes, attention, and focus. This diamond becomes an everyday statement

DON
SAYRES

Don Sayres began his career designing suits and revolutionized that category of dressing. At that time, a suit was usually two pieces that matched and were never worn separately. Sportswear separates were just being introduced, and the vast choices of combinations were overwhelming for many women not used to having to be that creative. Don Sayres for Wellmore was Sayres's next endeavor. He brought his easy sense of elegance to a collection of knitwear comprising dresses and suits—day into evening. The pieces offered a maximum splash of style with a minimum need for care. They were the traveling woman's dream.

ARNOLD
SCAASI

Arnold Scaasi is known for his impeccably tailored suits and glamorous eveningwear and cocktail dresses trimmed with feathers, fur, sequins, or fine embroidery. In 1968, he caught the eye of a worldwide audience when Barbra Streisand wore his sheer overblouse and pants ensemble to collect her Academy Award for *Funny Girl*. Scaasi has dressed first ladies Mamie Eisenhower, Barbara Bush, Hillary Clinton, and Laura Bush, in addition to such notable personalities as Joan Crawford, Elizabeth Taylor, Princess Yasmin Aga Khan, Lauren Bacall, Brooke Astor, Diahann Carroll, Catherine Deneuve, Arlene Francis, and Mary Tyler Moore.

JORDAN
SCHLANGER

Matrixmetal™ is one of many technological innovations developed by Jordan Schlanger in his quest to expand the possibilities of design beyond the limitations of traditional craft.

Fibers of metal are drawn to the thinness of hairs and woven into a flexible web. Various textile techniques such as braiding and knitting are applied to the metal fibers creating soft, open constructions which are formed by hand. This allows metal, an otherwise intransigent, solid material, to be formed in space like ceramics or blown glass but with the openwork reminiscent of corals, sea fans, lace, and basketry.

Matrixmetal™ was a hit from its inception, appearing in the most prestigious press and retail venues worldwide, and collected by celebrities who loved the bold but delicate, organic look.

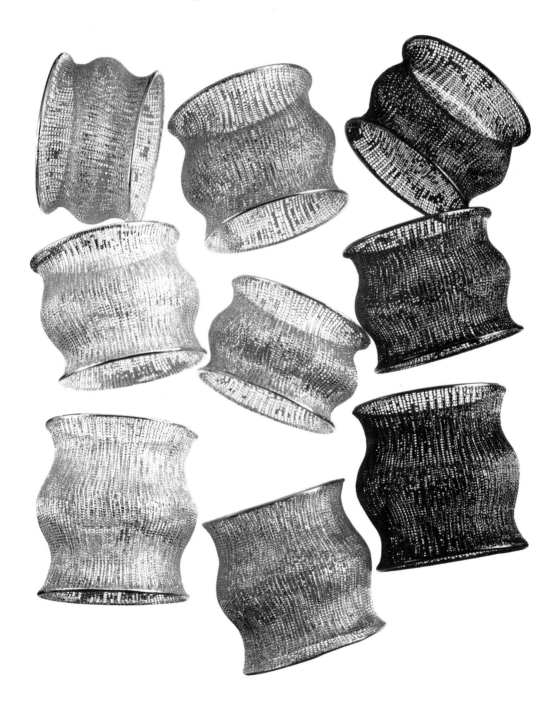

LORRAINE
SCHWARTZ

Lorraine Schwartz has reinvented the concept of jewelry. She has fashioned the most memorable trends, revolutionizing the way women wear jewels. One of the most iconic moments in jewelry history was the incredible 115-karat emerald drop earrings custom made by Schwartz for Angelina Jolie for the 2009 Academy Awards. The simplicity of the design coupled with the opulent green hue is unforgettable.

Lorraine has created the chicest trends showcased on the red carpet. From the multi-circle diamond earrings in which Beyoncé won her first solo artist award to the titanium hand piece B tells us to put a ring on with, these works have made women worldwide see jewelry in a new and powerful light.

A look at the red carpet is just a glimpse into what Schwartz embodies. Her pieces, though dramatic, are meant to be worn and adorned. They look great with everything from jeans to black-tie gowns. "Lorraine always does what you are thinking about or what you are dreaming about," Mary J. Blige says of her longtime friend. "She's not limited with her artistic ability."

"Ronaldus Shamask's one big thing came in 1981, the spiral jacket, created from one piece of fabric, curved by a seam like a lemon peel."

—Amy M. Spindler, *New York Times*, August 12, 1997

RICKY
SERBIN

I was incredibly fortunate to be designing jewelry in New York in the early 1980s, just as a vibrant generation of American designers was coming into their own. My first job was as silversmith assistant to Robert Lee Morris. A short time later Carolina Herrera asked me to design runway jewelry for her early collections. She graciously introduced me to *Vogue*, *Bazaar*, and her friend Oscar. She helped launch my business, and soon I was creating for the American designers whose work I so admired: Oscar de la Renta, Geoffrey Beene, Adolfo, Marc Jacobs, Bill Blass, Michael Vollbracht, and Bob Mackie. The clothes demanded dramatic jewelry, and glamorous excess was my forte. I fashioned elaborate crystal necklaces, dangly multicolor earrings, and especially whimsical pins that were meant to stand out on the boldly colored, strong silhouettes of the day. When Michael Jackson was photographed wearing my cross and crown brooches on his yellow sweater, it made an immediate impact on popular fashion. It was a heady, exciting time, and for me, a literally gilded age. My contribution was to help define the accessories that were so much a part of the total designer look of the day.

GEORGE
SHARP

Creative director George Sharp
is influencing American fashion
by transforming St. John into a modern
lifestyle collection that is best defined
as "effortless chic."

MARCIA
SHERRILL

My belts, which are in the collection of the Metropolitan
Museum of Art's Costume Institute, changed buckles and exotic
skins and how they were perceived by affluent customers. They
are appealing to men and women.

When I owned the label KLEINBERG SHERRILL and
now Sherrill Ltd., we radically changed the *look* of exotic skin
belts, not staying with the over-the-top disco belts of the day but
offering, then and now, elegant alternatives to western buckles
and plain traditional buckles. They radicalized the industry.

My Scarlet Alligator Bag with an 18-karat gold breast
cancer ribbon with genuine faceted rubies was the most expensive new bag ever auctioned at Sotheby's, and the bag fetched
$20,000. It was created and sold for charity in support of my
book, *Portraits of Hope: 52 Stories of Breast Cancer Survival*,
published by The Monacelli Press. All produced in America,
these luxury accessories are handcrafted.

FABRICE
SIMON

Born in a mountain town in Haiti, Fabrice migrated to New York to begin a career in a textile firm. While at this firm his style and elegance and impressive artistic ability were first recognized. After being promoted to the company's art department, Fabrice was encouraged to attend the Fashion Institute of Technology. It was there that formal art training took form in textile design and fashion illustration, a seemingly natural extension of his early exposure to couture.

Ambition and courage enabled Fabrice to start his own design company at age twenty-five. Original, one-of-a-kind, hand-painted crepe-de-chine tunics were an immediate success, followed by revolutionary beaded designs with a dark sparkle, which added a newly hip and sexy look. Worldwide recognition came in 1980 as he was named Essence magazine's Black Designer of the Year, and by 1981, the Coty Award was his.

In a half-page obituary, written by Anne-Marie Schiro in the New York Times, Schiro "celebrated this extraordinary man, his life and his career." His career exemplified the black American experience success story—he truly lived the "American Dream."

MICHAEL
SIMON

Michael Simon created the conversational novelty concept, not only popularizing it, but totally dominating the category. Michael started the category almost by accident with a group of artists he had hired from the best art schools in the country to shake up fashion. They designed a couple of "conversational" sweaters for fun, and suddenly everyone wanted more. New designs quickly followed. The sweaters were unique and the workmanship was extraordinary; to the consumer the designs said something more personal, identifying themselves to others. It started a conversation for people who may otherwise have been quiet, introducing the saying "conversation pieces," and brought joy to people celebrating life during the holidays.

So how did a 24-year-old kid from the Bronx start a fashion business and go on to build an internationally known brand and be the market leader of conversational novelty fashion? The answer is simple: with no formal industry training or preconceived ideas of what fashion should be, Michael Simon went where the others feared to thread.

ADELE
SIMPSON

The longevity of Adele Simpson's fashion business might be attributed to her acute awareness of the needs of her clientele: busy women who were frequently in the public eye, traveled quite a bit, and who required practical, well-made clothes to please not only their husbands and their observers, but themselves. Avant-garde or bizarre fashions would not do for these women. Simpson consistently offered conservative, yet pretty and feminine versions of current trends. The garments were made of ordinary fabrics such as cotton—Simpson was the first American designer to treat cotton seriously as a fashion fabric—or sumptuous fabrics inspired by the textiles she saw and collected on her frequent world travels.

PAUL
SINCLAIRE

The work that Paul Sinclaire did for *L'Uomo Vogue* preceded the new silhouette created by Hedi Slimane for Dior and the work of Thom Browne in the U.S. At a time when the Armani slouch was a predominant look on both sides of the Atlantic, Paul's work was clearly going in a different direction. His approach to styling created a parallel world in which the masculine was rendered in a deeply poetic way. This was years ahead of the work that any other major stylist was doing in menswear.

—Alex Gonzalez

MICHAEL
SMALDONE

If I could be so lucky as to leave a mark on American fashion, I would hope it would be with two words: Tradition Transformed. These words have both a beautiful irony and an intrinsic connectivity. From my earliest days in the business until now, my inspiration has come from taking something traditional and transforming it into something modern and relevant.

While at Banana Republic, this meant reimagining the rules for men, rethinking what a suit could be and, subsequently, ushering in a more fashionable man. To me, the era of casual Fridays was not about comfort, but about redefining casual in an elegant way.

As chief creative officer at Talbots, I work with my team to transform the very definition of traditional. We see tradition transformed in the face of Linda Evangelista, the repertoire of Julianne Moore, and of course, the actions and innate style of our first lady. Michelle Obama has redefined the notion of style for generations young and old. When I see her in Talbots, I am thrilled to know a brand so rich in history, is now a part of history. And yes, excited to know I played a small part.

It is often believed that for a designer to be accomplished, one must create desire for an item or a collection. My most rewarding moments, however, come when I am able to recognize a need that people don't even know they have, and then fill that need so effortlessly it becomes inherent to who they are.

AMY
SMILOVIC

When asked a question like "What will you be remembered for," my first reaction is to say that I hope I haven't discovered it yet. Tibi is my passion, I love what I do, I embrace personal style and I'm proud to have accomplished something like a global brand and family-owned company from scratch. I'm honored to be at the helm of Tibi, and to be able to share that excitement with my family and employees. The impact, I think, is yet to be determined. Every day I walk into work excited to discover our next cult-favorite piece or must-have style. I always look forward to proclaiming (and truly believing) "this collection is our absolute best ever" with each new season. When I'm able to name my biggest contribution to the fashion industry, that's when I'll be able to retire!

MICHELLE
SMITH

Blazing a bold new fashion trail out of the minimalist nineties, Milly designer Michelle Smith's collection debut in September 2000 created a sensation with her vibrant use of color and print. Her youthful, luxurious take on feminine dressing, delivered with wit and glamour, epitomizes uptown sophistication meeting downtown cool.

Milly has developed into an iconic brand known for exquisite prints and colors, luxurious fabrics, and attention to detail—a timeless aesthetic now recognized throughout the globe with a devoted following. Celebrities such as Gwyneth Paltrow, Victoria Beckham, Beyoncé, Thandie Newton, and Taylor Swift are counted among Milly's loyal fans.

WILLI
SMITH

Willi Smith was inspired, he said, not by Paris but by Sunday church in Harlem. His WilliWear line, founded in 1976, was characterized by loose silhouettes in brightly colored fabrics. Exuberant and witty, his clothes were sophisticated, yet inexpensive. Signature garments, such as violet linen blazers and loose cotton separates, appealed to both men and women. His "street couture" had a significant impact on fashion in the 1980s.

MARIA
SNYDER

Maria Snyder is a pioneer in the eco-fashion movement as a fashion trend. In 1999, Felissimo stores exhibited Maria's eco-creations as art. Their press release states: "Felissimo is proud to exhibit Maria's multi-dimensional work because it reflects the same kind of inspirational sources and environmental concerns. Maria is one of the first designers to introduce an exclusive collection made from fiber from post consumer plastic bottles. The theme for recycling further underlines Maria's love for nature and respect for the earth."

MIMI
SO

Traditionally, fine jewelry has always been perceived as classic and conservative; less about design and more about the gemstones. My biggest impact on American fashion has been to infuse design and style in fine jewelry to dress the contemporary woman.

PETER

SOM

"Som is emerging as the freshest mixmaster
on the block—my eyes could not keep up with the
multitude of fantastic clothes."

—FabSugar

"As a full-fledged member of a new generation
of designers, Peter is leading the tradition of Great American
Sportswear firmly into the 21st century."

—*Infomat.com*

"Since its spring 2001 debut, the label has been
celebrated by industry leaders, winning Som numerous
accolades, including consecutive nominations for the CFDA's
prestigious Swarovski Perry Ellis award and a finalist spot for
the *Vogue*/CFDA fashion fund."

—*NYmag.com*

MICHAEL
SPIRITO

The spirit of America is tangibly evident in the jewelry of Michael Spirito. The rebelliousness, the individualism, and the immaculate craftsmanship combine to create a unique experience for the wearer.

I discovered my business partner Michael's extraordinary talent a decade ago, at a party at his loft in Brooklyn. We had met socially, and I was intrigued to talk more to this tall, striking, tattooed man. I was working as a trend forecaster; Michael was laboring for a staid, traditional jewelry maker. When he showed the small crowd the exquisite wearable art he was creating at a small table in his living room, we were all astounded. His jewelry was cutting edge with flavors of rock 'n' roll and punk, but created with a soft hand and an eye for gemstone color and placement. I had seen nothing like it before.

Now, in our eleventh year of business together, we have weathered the storms of fashion. Michael was edgy when that was a dirty word to retailers. We fought to have this type of work taken seriously, and the new generation of designers have benefitted from our battles. With each new collection, a deeper element of his talent and ingenuity is revealed.

—Sloan Mandell, brand director, Michael Spirito NYC

SIMON

SPURR

"The suit is as much a part of the brand,
as the brand is becoming a part of the suit."

—Simon Spurr

"His knowledge of the industry and comprehension
of the nature of this business are evident through
the success of the expansion of his collection. . . .
Simon has proven his creativity, ingenuity and forward
thinking methods in his approach to design."

—Jim Moore, creative director, *GQ*, 2010

My aim has always been to readdress the way that a modern man approaches the suit. I have brought my own inherent style and the Savile Row aesthetic to the next generation of American men, resulting in a brand that redefines the boundaries of sartorialism. Understanding the fine balance between tradition without being traditional, the SIMON SPURR brand has become a leader at the forefront of American menswear that has been embraced by the likes of Bradley Cooper, Zac Efron, and Kellan Lutz.

LAURIE
STARK

&

RICHARD
STARK

Our greatest impact on American fashion will be what we've still kept close to the vest. While Chrome Hearts has, for more than twenty years, put out many of the most iconic and identifiable signature design motifs, our impact lies in the curiosity we've evoked in our customers, who are always fascinated by what we will explore next.

Aesthetically, we'll always be known for outfitting some of the most legendary style visionaries of our time—Cher, Karl Lagerfeld, Iggy Pop, only to name a few—in their most acclaimed looks. With pride, we will continue to produce all Chrome Hearts in the United States of America.

GEORGE
STAVROPOULOS

Throughout his career, George Peter Stavropoulos maintained a relatively low but highly respected profile in the fashion world. He was one of a small number of designers in America who exclusively produced ready-to-wear clothes of the quality and caliber of Parisian haute couture. Stavropoulos presented two ready-to-wear collections, produced in his own atelier each year for thirty years, and never ventured into lower-priced lines, licensed products, or perfumes, as did many of his contemporaries. Nor did he venture into the further reaches of avant-garde design. While many of his designs were innovative and strikingly beautiful, they were never shocking or arresting, and his innovations were subtle to the degree that they were apparent only to the wearer or noticed either upon close inspection or when the wearer moved about.

CYNTHIA
STEFFE

Fashion is nothing if not about change and evolution. When I first launched my own collection, I recognized that American women were ready for a change. With women occupying prominent positions throughout society and countless others aspiring to do the same, clothing became more of a personal statement.

Youthful, detail-oriented clothing with a feminine edge has become the signature of my collections. I was an early proponent of the contemporary area that has now come to dominate most channels of the American market as well as women's closets.

SHELLY
STEFFEE

"Throughout her career, Shelly Steffee has always had a singularly unique approach to design, making her a true original in the American fashion community."

—Lauren David Peden, fashion journalist

Shelly Steffee launched her eponymous collection in 1999 with the goal of creating accessible luxury that evokes an emotional response and empowers women to feel like the best possible version of themselves. In doing so, she predated the affordable luxury movement by nearly a decade. Equally impactful: The SHELLY STEFFEE collection has always been manufactured in New York City's Garment District. But Steffee's most lasting impact on American fashion can be felt through her cutting-edge design techniques. While renowned for her razor sharp tailoring and flattering cuts, Steffee is also a master craftsperson.

SUE
STEMP

Sue Stemp burst on to the New York fashion scene with the cover of *WWD* in August 1995. The dress was a silk chiffon cocktail dress hand-printed with geometric shapes and lightning bolts and a pivotal piece in her debut collection for Spring 2009. Stemp's impact on American contemporary fashion has been in bringing an unashamed girlishness and young, flirty confidence back. Her vibrant clothes are not for wallflowers and reflect her own personal aesthetic: feminine, free-spirited, and effortlessly sexy with a hint of DIY rock-n-roll attitude. With an emphasis on getting dressed up and going out, they draw on Stemp's passion for color and textiles, in particular prints (pieces are often hand silkscreened). Stemp was one of the first young designers to successfully appeal to both the New York uptown and downtown (of which she was a permanent fixture) fashion sets. She was also at the forefront of designer collaborations, often working with artist friends on textile designs.

SCOTT
STERNBERG

Band [of Outsiders] is about
bringing a sense of humor and levity
to all of this fashion stuff.

ROBERT
STOCK

Since its inception in 2001, Robert Graham by Robert Stock has revitalized and reinvented the art of a man's shirt. Not only does Robert Graham deliver the most unique patterns, designed and drawn in-house, but every collection embraces intricate embroidery and luxury fabrics, thus creating a truly recognizable entrée of woven shirts.

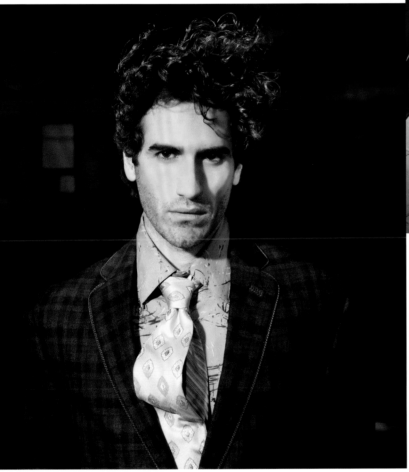

STEVEN
STOLMAN

I'll never forget the moment I walked into a home furnishings fabric showroom in New York's D&D Building and in those toiles de Jouy, chinoiseries, florals, and damasks, I saw—as if struck by lightning—simple little dresses, trousers, and skirts. From the very first slip dress that I sent down the runway cut from F. Schumacher's "Florentine Griffin" ultimately to ball gowns made from Brunschwig and Scalamandré florals and brocades, I managed to carve out a niche. Who would want to wear clothes made from the drapes? Thankfully, an awful lot of great gals to whom I owe my career—along with my dear friend and mentor, the late Pauline Trigère, who by example taught me the meaning of "chic." A day doesn't go by that I don't think of her.

Now, I have the pleasure of applying that kernel of an idea to the Jack Rogers label—one that's known more for an iconic sandal than for apparel. To me, it's a match made in heaven—a highly decorative shoe serving as the foundation for equally decorative clothes.

JILL
STUART

Redefining and interpreting what
it means to be feminine each season.
Recognizing shifts in trends and
the need to move forward, while still
maintaining the belief that every
woman wants to look beautiful.

JAY
STRONGWATER

A serendipitous desire to create jewelry one summer while
between semesters of art college has inspired my passion for
creating collages of metal, enamel, and crystals. At first my focus
was on manipulating these materials into fantastical bejeweled
necklaces, earrings, and brooches. A fortuitous opportunity
to show Oscar de la Renta my work led to an amazing decade
of creating one-of-a-kind jewelry to adorn his most beautiful
clothes. Working with Oscar was a master class of learning
about the world of fashion.

In 1995 I turned a page by taking my jeweler's craftsmanship and creating an all-metal picture frame. Every detail was
meticulously finished in oxidized metal, hand-enameling, and
set with hundreds of Swarovski crystals. This first frame quickly
grew to a collection fondly known as "Jewels for the Home." I am
very proud to say that we have created a world of luxury product
that had never existed before. Each design is a reflection of the
artisanal craftsmanship I so passionately believe in.

KAREN
SUEN-COOPER

SUEN | COOPER luxury leather goods, founded by Karen Suen-Cooper in 1991, was on the forefront of ushering in an era of luxury exotic skin handbags in American fashion when tastes were fueled by the exclusive and the exquisite SUEN | COOPER handbag shapes drawn from an architectural discipline countered by sensual interior details such as French plonge lambskin lining in sumptuous signature red, which in China is the color of life and prosperity. Combining modern ideas of form and function, her exotic skin handbags were uniquely dimensioned to house laptops and briefs, mobile phones and eyewear, among the myriad of modern accoutrements.

ANNA
SUI

A Timeless Vision

"She is an artist who is era-less. . . .
Her fashions, fragrances, and boutiques
live in their own time. They look,
smell, and feel powerful and beautiful,
with no era imprisoning them."

—Jack White

KOI
SUWANNAGATE

With the label founded in 2000, Koi Suwannagate has changed
the way you think about wearing a cashmere sweater. Each of
her designs is a completely unique, one-of-a-kind handmade
garment, and each reflects her own personal vision. Her signature style is to sculpt and shape each piece to enhance and
beautify the natural contours of the female body, draped in
a way that allows fluid movement and ultimate comfort.

ALBERTUS
SWANEPOEL

The idea of an accessory making an impact on American fashion can be hard to do. Ready-to-wear always seems to take front stage to what Albertus likes to call "the dot on the *i* of fashion": the hat.

But Albertus managed to create a buzz about this quiet luxury early on in his career by partnering with the right fashion houses on the New York scene. We first saw this collaboration with Proenza Schouler and their Fall 2007 collection. The presentation was an army of cloches on almost every single model that came down the runway. Suddenly, the "vintage" look of a flapper style was now new, fresh, chic, and modern.

It is this sort of impact that Albertus Swanepoel has managed to maintain on the American fashion scene. Whether it was the plumed fedora at Carolina Herrera or the *Blade Runner* helmets at Narciso Rodriguez, Swanepoel has created a modern buzz around the age-old craft of millinery.

VIOLA
SYLBERT

Viola Sylbert's forte is a subtle elegance, while the sportier furs by Anne Klein are big and dashing. One of the best black minks in town is Sylbert's: its hem is midcalf, the shoulders are natural, and its scale would not overwhelm a small-boned woman. She uses smoke-colored mink skins on the diagonal for another coat, and in a rare foray into bigness, has designed a belted bathrobe with raglan sleeves in golden sable.

—Angela Taylor, June 16, 1984

ELIE
TAHARI

When I launched my company in 1972, it was a time of women's liberation, and women were starting to climb the corporate ladder. I started making suits because a lot of New York women needed to get dressed to go to work. Women were wearing a lot of printed dresses, so the suit was something new and fresh looking and no one else was really making them for women then. My store on Madison became the place to go, and that's how I built my business in the seventies. I started putting my name on the label, and the business really took off from there. Women became clients for life because of the suits' incredible fit: They felt confident and comfortable in the suits; they could be themselves and know that they looked great. Our company has grown exponentially over the years, and we are now a lifestyle brand encompassing men's, women's, handbags, shoes, jewelry, and outerwear lines sold in more than six hundred stores in more than forty countries—but I still get so many people coming up to me and thanking me for creating the perfect suit!

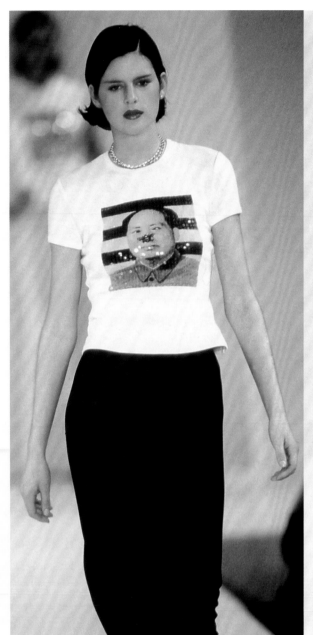

VIVIENNE
TAM

Vivienne Tam more than anything represents the globalization of fashion. Before the 1990s, fashion was very much a European and American sportswear-dominated world. When I started my collection, I naturally gravitated to design that reflected growing up in the former British colony of Hong Kong, which evolved into my signature East-meets-West style. Today, we see influences in fashion from the far corners of the earth, and I'd like to think that I helped break some of those barriers.

Because there was no place in Hong Kong for my designs, I came to America. Chinese people were only looking to the West, for western designs. It was America that gave me the opportunity, accepting my designs and my creativities, and the freedom to be who I am. America enabled me to bridge to the western world: I am an ambassador of Chinese culture to America. As the first Chinese-born designer to establish a successful label here, I helped pave the way for a generation of Asian designers.

In my work, I've always played with the language of eastern dress and culture. I combine elements like the cheongsam, the Mao suit, Pop Art, bold patterns, and traditional techniques while consistently embracing modern technology. This contrast adds up to a world-wise design sensibility that embraces and empowers femininity without condescending to it. I design for a modern woman, appreciative of the myriad influences and cultures around her.

Fashion critic Richard Martin once said that I possess an "idealistic globalism that transcends politics and offers a more enchanted, peaceful world." I hope to continue to live up to that.

REBECCA
TAYLOR

Since her childhood growing up on the beaches of New Zealand, watching her amother hand-stitch artisanal beaded ballet costumes for her, Rebecca Taylor has been drawn to all things that glitter, sparkle, and shine. She launched her signature collection in 1996, introducing the contemporary market to embellishment and a special attention to detail formerly accessible only through the designer or couturier collections. Unconventional hand-tooled beadwork, encrusted jewel placements, delicate fabric manipulations, and intricate embroidery and seam work have earned the label a reputation for exquisite craftsmanship and a loyal following globally.

Every day for the past fifteen years, Rebecca has been in the design studio, personally selecting materials that make each piece in the collection unique. From red carpet gowns to T-shirts, Rebecca Taylor clothing has a signature feminine aesthetic that separates the brand from others in the better contemporary arena. In addition to outfitting clients in attire for formal occasions, Rebecca Taylor intertwines beauty with lifestyle, making "special" accessible in everyday pieces with elements like her signature rhinestone buttons.

While trend and inspiration may vary from season to season, whether it be dresses covered in laser-cut chiffon rose petals, pieces with jewel-kissed tulle overlays, flowing micro-pleated gowns, corseting or rows of elaborate pin-tucking, Rebecca Taylor remains true to form: truly feminine and always magical.

YEOHLEE

TENG

My work has had an impact on fashion in the following areas:

FASHION + ARCHITECTURE—My work has been widely acknowledged as evocative of architectural principles and modernist in the selection of materials, development of details, and minimalist attitude. The shapes and forms that I innovated in that context have had an indelible influence on fashion. My theories have helped define ongoing conversations on the subject and influenced how fashion as a design discipline is being viewed today.

URBAN NOMAD—I dress the urban nomad, a term I coined in 1996 while observing the people passing on the street in front of my window and looking at the denizens traveling through the twenty-first century environs of Renzo Piano's Kansai International Airport in Osaka Bay. The term describes a system of clothing I designed for the built environment, allowing the wearer the greatest efficiency and freedom in global travel whether traversing from New York to Kuala Lumpur or Red Hook to Midtown. This concept that I pioneered has been widely adopted, and its impact has grown as energy and economy in dress have become more and more important.

BILL
TICE

Tice was known for designing dresses and pajamas that could be worn inside or outside the home. He was part of a small group of designers who put at-home wear into the wardrobes of shoppers by pricing the garments in the moderate range.

—J. Michael Elliott, *New York Times*, March 29, 1995

SOPHIE
THEALLET

It is very difficult and feels pretentious for me to state the impact of my work on American fashion, especially because I am at the early stages of a, hopefully, long journey. That said, one thing I know that I bring to the New American Fashion landscape, is the Parisian tradition of construction and couture techniques that I was taught. I am particularly proud to make my garments with these techniques in New York City. I would like to be remembered as a Modern Couturiere with a Bohemian sensibility who loves freedom, effortless chic, and sophistication—a multicultural, subtly sexy, and substantially democratic fashion brand with soul.

MONIKA
TILLEY

My greatest impact on American fashion was that I took the athleticism of actual clothes used for skiing, tennis, and other sports and translated that sleek, functional style into clothing that could be worn every day, by every woman. Truly *sportswear*.

Within the CFDA, I headed the admissions committee from its inception by Perry Ellis for twenty years. As a way of saying thank you for all the help I received when I began, I started the merit-based scholarship seventeen years ago, which paved the way toward democratizing the fashion hierarchy, opening doors to the next deserving design generations.

ZANG
TOI

"Toi has a flair for the dramatic
and the exotic: he's inspired
by Malaysian orchids, wildly colored
batiks, and intricate gold jewelry.
Rich, vibrant colors—[chartreuse],
fuchsia, and vermillion—are mixed
up in lavish ways. Opulent fabrics
such as gold lace, deep-colored silk
shantung, and organza are signatures.
The shapes are clean-lined, so
clothes never look overly ethnic."

—Laurie Schechter, *Vogue*, March 1990

In the early nineties, I was one of the young fashion
designers in America who were not afraid to explore
the possibilities of pairing bright hues together, such
as shocking pink and orange, bright red and shocking
pink, chartreuse and purple, etc. In the era when
American fashion was still dominated by Armani's
neutral-toned sportswear, I decided to do something
completely different. It was a bold and risky step,
but that was also how I caught the attention of Anna
Wintour in 1989.

ISABEL
TOLEDO

The packing skirt from my spring 1988 collection encapsulated an evolution of ideas that began in 1984 with a beach bag I sold at Fiourrucci. This design was a triple impact blessing.

Because I come from the school of the self-taught, the design was to be the first of many experimentations with circles and geometric patterns to come to fruition. It sold out at Bergdorf Goodman.

The brave and astute journalist who blessed the design with her validation was Wendy Goodman, who featured it in her best-of-the-spring-collections article for New York Magazine in 1988. The sculpture- and art-filled photograph by Michael O'Brien was the perfect summing-up of art and fashion. The model was Naomi Campbell, who was just at the start of her meteoric and prolific career. The stars were aligned. I was to add my contributions to the American sportswear tradition.

This breakthrough led the way and provided a platform for me to evolve my work.

On January 20, 2009, I got the opportunity to Impact history when First Lady Elect Michelle Obama chose to wear a lemongrass coat and dress designed by me to the presidential inauguration of her husband, Barack Obama.

RAFE
TOTENGCO

My design philosophy is rooted in my personal experience. Filipino people are open and inclusive, a melting pot of European, American, and Asian cultures, and this mix reflects in my impact on American fashion. Rafe stands for classic silhouettes with Asian handcrafted influences, beautiful materials, and an uncompromising attention to functionality while remaining accessible for every woman. I know I've succeeded when on the same day I can see an immaculately dressed career woman in midtown Manhattan with a five-year-old Rafe bag that she just can't stop wearing, and then see a chic bohemian girl at a café in the West Village toting the same design. The best compliment I was ever paid was when I was told "this is my happy bag"—I'd like that to be my epitaph.

PAULINE
TRIGÈRE

Trigère become known especially for her impeccable and imaginative tailoring of women's suits and coats. She made use of all weights of wool, from sheer crêpes for eveningwear to thick tweeds for daytime coats. She was recognized early in her career as an innovator for such fashions as evening dresses made of wool or cotton, reversible coats and capes in all shapes and sizes. Another characteristic Trigère feature is the luxurious touch of fur trim at necklines, cuffs, and hems. Before the 1960s, her palette was fairly subdued and she rarely used printed fabrics; during the 1960s and 1970s she began to use more prints and softer fabrics, always retaining a tailored touch. Her application of prints is bold and deliberate, the pattern is often used to complement the structure of the piece. Notwithstanding her extensive use of wool and tailoring techniques, Trigère's clothing has always been unmistakably feminine.

TRINA
TURK

A genuine California local, Trina Turk is informed as much by her upbringing as she is by a collector's appreciation for the modernist artistry and craftsmanship born in the Golden State. She has championed the effortless élan and sunny optimism of the native mind-set through world-wise women's ready-to-wear and accessories, a menswear line called Mr. Turk, and residential decor and textiles since launching the brand with her photographer husband, Jonathan Skow, in 1995. Turk draws from their lives split between two mid-century marvels they restored in Los Angeles's creative enclave of Silver Lake and in Palm Springs, as well as travels up and down the coastline. From an urban architectural detail to a flowering desert succulent, Turk absorbs the graphic patterns and dynamic colors into a joyfully chic, flourishing lifestyle brand. Like her clothes, her shop interiors merge vintage and new in a seamless timelessness. Turk's own archive of vintage modernist jewelry triggered the innovation to replace the prosaic metal rings long a bikini staple with hardware flavored by her favorite period pieces—a move that not only caught on with devotees, but the entire swimwear industry, which dove in after her lead. It's one facet of a carefree glamour the Trina Turk brand defined early on that continues to inspire followers and fans alike.

MISH
TWORKOWSKI

The first time I met Mish Tworkowski, nearly twenty years ago, I am pretty sure it was love at first sight. Unfailingly polite and impeccably tailored, he wore festive bow ties and an enormous grin that was an immediate tip-off to his infectious good humor and endless genuine charm. The good news was that the same combination of glamour and wit was reflected in his designs. Almost as wonderful as the jewelry itself is the shop where it's showcased. One day I walked in to find a famous pop star singing a bar or two of his greatest hit, a delightfully over-the-top gesture I'm sure Mish loved. He is, after all, the designer of the monkey cuff links inspired by the same Palm Beach swizzle sticks I collected as a child. I bought a pair for my father, who loves Mish almost as much as I do. How could you not? He's still the same wonderful human being I first laid eyes on. Except that now he also happens to be a world-class jeweler.

—Julia Reed

PATRICIA
UNDERWOOD

I believe that I have contributed to keeping alive the classic American form of millinery, with its simplicity of line and style. Believing strongly that hats have their own relevant function, I design with that function—be it fashion, weather, or beauty—in mind. Believing that the hat uniquely enhances the wearer and complements the clothes, I have been fortunate to collaborate over the years with many other CFDA members in creating distinctive looks for their collections. Many leading editors and photographers have used my hats editorially and in advertising—appreciating, as I do, the graphic elements that hats can bring to images. Last, but definitely not least, there are many "leading ladies" and dedicated hat aficionados who have worn my hats over the years and who provide the ultimate stamp of approval for my work.

KAY
UNGER

Dressing the modern American working woman: Kay didn't just dress her, she grew up with her . . . she *was* her. What Chanel had "theorized" would be the needs of the modern woman (the first wave of feminism), Kay actually lived (the second wave of feminism). As Kay graduated from Parsons School of Design and started work, she created a line that other "career girls" like her could embrace as they entered the job market. Influenced by the classic femininity of Jackie Kennedy in the White House and Audrey Hepburn on the screen, as well as street level expressions of nonconformity, Kay created a compromise to the contradictions of the time, an alternative to the LBD—colorful suits and dinner dresses that were flattering, comfortable, feminine, versatile; with function as inspiration for form, enhancing the positive (showcasing feminine curves and waist) and hiding flaws (strategic draping and zipper placement—to build confidence). Easy solutions to changing lifestyles to go from day to night, from work to drinks seamlessly; balancing the line between feminine and flirtatious embellishments, while maintaining the "career woman's" confident sense of power and newly acquired independence.

KAY UNGER N.Y.

CARMEN
MARC
VALVO

I believe my contribution to American fashion was the creation of a new level of designer eveningwear. When I first started, there were couture gowns, and there was the bridge market. I wanted to give my customers the couture-quality gown but at an accessible price. Since then, many of my contemporaries have followed in my footsteps to the benefit of glamorous women across America, giving them a choice they never had before.

KOOS

VAN DEN AKKER

Koos Van Den Akker's biggest impact on American fashion is COLLAGE.

"Van Den Akker, as everyone will describe, is a collagist as much
as a designer of apparel. But the obvious, though generally
unstated, fact is that his pictorial effects are conceived and applied
to an inherently three-dimensional form. Any single view of Van
Den Akker's work is necessarily only a partial one. His designs
complete themselves in motion, for it is only in a full 360-degree
view that his applied compositions can fully be comprehended."

—Harold Koda, curator of the Costume Institute at the
Metropolitan Museum of Art, New York City, May 2002

JOHN
VARVATOS

The world of John Varvatos is a continuously evolving counterbalance of modern and vintage charged with an authentic infusion of rock-n-roll swagger. It's a parallel existence where the contemporary man can gather the finer artisan craftsmanship and bespoke tailoring of his father's repertoire and yet be effortlessly cool in a modern environment. It's the feel of luxury without being ostentatious or pretentious, allowing style to express a man's signature instead of it being dictated by fashion.

JOAN
VASS

"If you like something, why shouldn't you
be able to go back to a store to replace it?"

—Joan Vass, quoted in *The Washington Post*, 1979

Joan Vass, a popular knitwear designer in the eighties and
nineties whose elegantly understated sweaters stood in contrast
to her reputation as a bohemian and a provocateur, believed that
the only purpose for a label in a piece of clothing is to show the
wearer which way to put it on.

Coming from a background in both the publishing and art
worlds, Ms. Vass began a cottage industry in the early seventies
when she brought her personal interest in hand knits and crochet
to women who needed an outlet for their marketable skills.
Vass immediately made an impression with her style, as well
as with her outspokenness. She was an American woman with
strong ideas and concerns, which were reflected in her designs,
and frequently expressed. When everyone was wearing Pucci's
psychedelic prints, she wore black. In her collections, she favored
classic shapes, and repeated them frequently.

Her beautifully crafted, easy-to-wear designs in simple
and unstructured shapes were predominantly made of natural
fibers, usually in subtle colors.

ADRIENNE

VITTADINI

Knitwear is where I have made my strongest impact. It is the most creative fashion expression. I love it because it is modern, moves with you, travels well, and is sensual and close to the body. Balancing my love of European elegance with American practicality, I innately understood the needs of women seeking clothing that reflected their current lifestyles. I used knitwear to cater to all those needs, encompassing total lifestyle dressing, from day wear to sportswear to eveningwear.

MICHAEL
VOLLBRACHT

During the late seventies and through the eighties, Michael Vollbracht was best known as a fashion designer—a very, very good one, I might add. But he was, and still is, an illustrator as well. During the last three decades, he's sketched almost every style icon. I've always though that his drawings show both authority and spontaneity, a rare combination that was surely nurtured by his dual profession. Vollbracht is perhaps most famous for the shopping bag he designed for Bloomingdale's: it didn't have the store's name on it. Bloomingdale's thought his illustration—of one eye and a mouth—so memorable that it didn't seem to mind.

EGON
VON FURSTENBERG

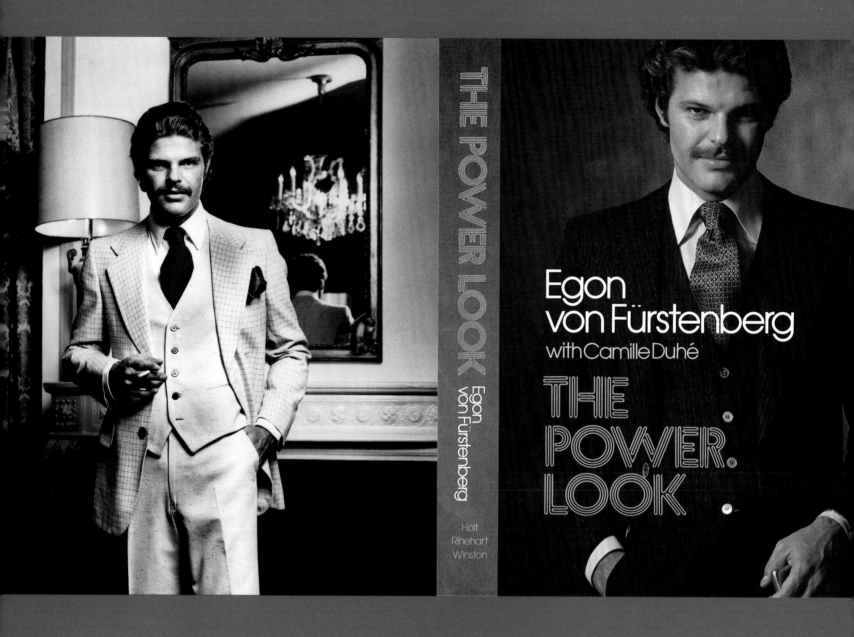

Eduard Egon von und zu Furstenberg (1946–2004) was an Austro-Italian aristocrat, a prince, in fact, by birth.

He was exposed from an early age to the multifaceted aspects of "elegance," thanks to his wealthy and international background. Shortly after moving to New York in the late sixties, he traded an early banking career for one in fashion.

While embracing the American culture and the excitement of life in New York in the seventies and eighties, von Furstenberg found his place in the fashion scene by translating his own experience into the role of "mentor." He focused his attention mainly on the young career man and began designing comfortable and classic garments that could help men feel at ease and elegant, without sacrificing the much fêted "personal style." By the late seventies, his line of menswear in Europe and the United States included suits, shirts, and sweaters as well as several licensed products such as eyewear, jewelry, and cologne.

His book *The Power Look*, published in 1978, is a true bible of fashion advice and grooming. Egon von Furstenberg was easygoing, and his sunny disposition and good looks never failed to make an impact on people. His own keen sense of style is shared in this "how-to" manual, where the designer takes the reader on a journey of self-help through a maze of patterns, colors, styles, and looks.

—F. Dantes, Diane von Furstenberg Studio

PATRICA
VON MUSULIN

I have designed and manufactured in the United States, a collection of accessories that is unique and identifiable worldwide. I have experimented with materials in a way that had not been done before. I have created a collection that has been continuously sold to the finest stores worldwide for more than thirty years and shown almost every season in runway shows with different clothing designers since the original creation.

ALEXANDER
WANG

It's easier for me to describe the biggest impact fashion has had on *me*. The one thing that never loses its excitement over time is seeing my clothes being worn in real life—on the street, in the subway, in different cities. I remember the first time I saw one of my pieces; my first reaction was to go up to the girl who was wearing it and ask her a million questions about where she got it. Of course, I refrained, but truly nothing is more rewarding than seeing normal people wearing the collection in their everyday lives.

VERA
WANG

Vera Wang has created a unique aspirational world that alludes to sensuality and youthful sophistication. Exquisite details, intricate draping, and a nonchalant sense of style characterize the Vera Wang aesthetic.

Vera Wang, a native New Yorker, understands women who embrace fashion. As a child, Vera accompanied her mother as she shopped Parisian and American couture. Vera studied at Chapin, Sarah Lawrence College, and the Sorbonne. By age 23, Vera was the youngest ever *Vogue* fashion editor and stylist, where she remained for sixteen years before moving to Ralph Lauren as a design director. In 1990, Vera Wang opened her first flagship store on Manhattan's famed Madison Avenue, introducing fashion to the bridal industry with revolutionary designs and refined detailing. Since then she has expanded her collections to include ready-to-wear, footwear, eyewear, fragrance, china and crystal, silver and gifts, bedding, mattresses, fine papers, luggage, hospitality, and her first book, *Vera Wang On Weddings*.

In 2005, the Council of Fashion Designers of America awarded Vera "Womenswear Designer of the Year." Vera further established herself as a style authority in 2007 by sharing her modern sensibility with millions of American women through her Simply Vera Vera Wang line available at Kohl's department stores nationwide. In Spring 2011, Vera launched her highly anticipated inaugural collection for David's Bridal, White by Vera Wang, which brings the acclaimed Vera Wang aesthetic to a new set of brides.

The year 2010 marked Vera Wang's twentieth anniversary as a brand, a celebration of two decades spent at the forefront of fashion.

CATHY
WATERMAN

As the CFDA celebrates fifty years, I'm happy to say it's been twenty years since I sold my first fine jewelry collection to Barneys. Little did I know that by weaving together a reverence for history with a passion for nature I would change how fine jewelry was perceived and be the first of a new generation of voices to offer a woman the opportunity to find her own voice through the jewelry she wears.

It's a quest for the sense of wonder that makes us human and that will whisper to the future about who we were in the early twenty-first century.

HEIDI
WEISEL

Is there anything more luxurious than cashmere? It might be combining it with other beautiful fabrics like satin, chiffon, lace, and leather; or turning a classic jewel-neck fitted sweater into a little dance dress by attaching it to a floaty chiffon skirt—simply held together by a satin ribbon. That is exactly what I did! I loved the idea of wearing a cashmere sweater and skirt to a party one night but wanted it to be one piece—comfortable and elegant and so very modern! I made one for myself and included it in my collection. I was so inspired by the women who loved wearing the cashmere and chiffon dresses that I expanded the concept to include cashmere-topped ball gowns, my famous cashmere and chiffon gowns, sexy siren gowns, wedding gowns, dresses, and little satin-trimmed cardigans. My signature look was launched! Eveningwear that is unfussy—with the ease and modern appeal of sportswear and decidedly American!

JOHN
WEITZ

If John Weitz wasn't the first American designer to make a big name for himself, he was certainly the most dashing—with his aristocratic good looks, impeccable manners, and a voice that could lift the ladies of the fashion press right out of their sling-backs.

—Cathy Horyn, *New York Times*, February 20, 2000

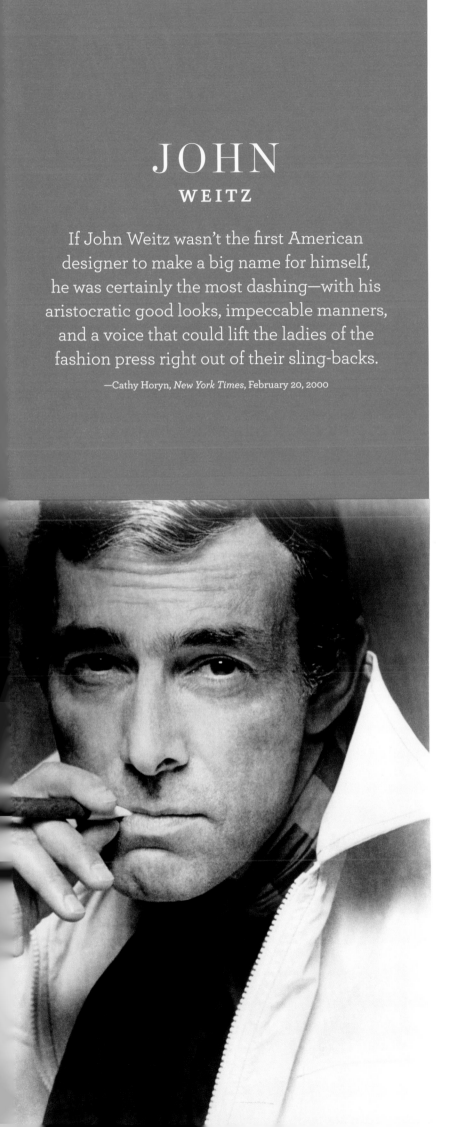

STUART
WEITZMAN

In 2002, after noticing for years that when it came to red carpet fashion, attention was mostly paid to the gowns and expensive jewels, I decided that beautiful footwear was due praise. So, I teamed up with The Platinum Guild and one of their jewelry designers, Kwiat, to create what was the first shoe of its kind—a four-and-a-half inch, open-toe silver sandal adorned with one million dollars worth of diamonds and platinum. We named the shoe the "Million Dollar Sandal," and it was worn by Laura Elena Harring on March 24, 2002, to the 74th Annual Academy Awards. This iconic evening shoe stands out among all others that I have created, and it was reported on in hundreds of media outlets worldwide. A "shoe-cam" was even created on one of the major cable news outlets for red carpet coverage following this milestone. Our brand name became recognized immediately all over the world, and as a result, I have long considered this to be "the tipping point" for our company and one important way that we have made an impact on American fashion. After all, the glamour of the red carpet is a theme that certainly resonates with American fashion lovers.

CARLA
WESTCOTT

While I was a student at Parsons School of Design, my senior critic, designer Jennifer George, took me to her studio and put matte jersey into my hands. "This is what you want," she said, and she was right. Thus began my love affair with matte jersey, the perfect fabric, wearable, refined, and quiet. I see no value in dominating a woman with a gown so visually noisy and opulent that her identity becomes of little interest. To complement the customer is harmonious design; she is and will always be more important than the garment.

Sometimes clothes just need to shut the hell up.

JOHN
WHITLEDGE

Trovata has impacted American fashion by showing that compelling designs are about telling stories, about tapping into the aspiration, creation, and fantasy involved in the daily fashioning of who you are and who you might be.

According to the *New York Times*, Trovata's clothes are "a perfect balance of casual California culture and crisp East Coast boarding school style. Each season, they [base] their collection on charming fictional stories involving adventurous travelers and [weave] messages into the linings, cuffs and collars." Trovata became known for tying these quirky seasonal narratives to unorthodox fashion week presentations, using capoeira dancers and yodelers to paint a picture not of garments hanging on a rack but of real and imagined places,

EDWARD
WILKERSON

Crisp, classic, easy, iconic, the white shirt was in style fifty years ago, it will be in style fifty years from now, and nobody does the white shirt better than Edward Wilkerson! His work for Lafayette 148 embraces every shape, size, and age. He believes in practical magic, and he designs accordingly, always recognizing the need for a few go-to staples that work as perfectly at the office as they do at a black =-tie gala . . . which brings us back to the white shirt. Truth be told, not all white shirts are created equally, but Wilkerson is a master of tailoring. The way he cuts, his choice of fabric, his attention to detail, his creativity, his wit, his simplicity, his bravado all come together to turn every one of his white shirts into a collector's item. It's no wonder that I regularly feature these pieces in the pages of *O Magazine*.

—Adam Glassman, creative director, *O, The Oprah Magazine*

GARY
WOLKOWITZ

As founder and chief creative officer of Hot Sox, Gary Wolkowitz's impact on American fashion is no less than the creation of the fashion hosiery category. In 1971, the world was wearing mostly solid-colored socks. Wolkowitz left his position as art director at CBS/Columbia Records that year based on response to the hand silkscreened socks that Hot Sox showed at the New York National Boutique Show.

As a designer, Wolkowitz drew on his fine arts background, applying a painterly eye for color and detail. The means to produce his visions did not yet exist, so he reengineered knitting machines, leading to the computer technology that we now take for granted in manufacturing. One result was the Hot Sox iconic toe sock, which sold millions of pairs the first year.

Hot Sox changed how hosiery does business by bringing a seasonal, sportswear mentality to the industry. Gary Wolkowitz's record of innovation across design, manufacturing, and business practices earned him a membership in the CFDA in 1992.

PINKY
WOLMAN

When I came from the Midwest to New York City, after graduating from Washington
University in St. Louis, it was a huge leap of faith. I immediately became immersed
in the fashion world of Seventh Avenue. Soon after, I began thinking about "what
else was out there" with my design partner, Dianne Beaudry, and we set off to explore
Europe and eventually Asia.

In the mid-seventies, we began to show and sell our collection, Pinky & Dianne,
from Milan to shops all over the world. I led the way in Asia in creating and importing
New York City style and around in the world in the global fashion scene well before
it was the norm. It was a wonderful experience and since 2003 I've been back in Japan
with my own label, Pinky Wolman New York, doing what I love, actively designing
and licensing.

JASON
WU

As a Taiwanese-American designer who has lived all over the world, I am incredibly proud to be part of the CFDA and to be a part of the New York fashion community. My aesthetic merges American sportswear with old-world glamour and modern sophistication, creating a supremely feminine sensibility.

The heart and soul of my collection lie in the craftsmanship and timeless quality my clients have come to expect from Jason Wu. The focus of my designs is always in their minute details, with the garments crafted as beautifully inside as out. I have stayed ahead of the curve by never following trends, and I've always designing by the motto "Quality over quantity." I always seek to push the boundaries of my work by integrating new materials and haute couture–inspired techniques into my collections.

One of the proudest moments in my career has been the opportunity to dress First Lady Michelle Obama for the Inaugural Gala. The dress will be preserved forever in the Smithsonian as a part of American history. Having had such a monumental moment has driven me to work harder every season to exceed expectations and to lend my support to the American fashion industry.

I am able to maintain the strictest quality standards by having 90 percent of the Jason Wu collection produced in New York. This also supports my belief in the New York Garment Center and its important role in the New York economy and to the New York fashion industry.

ARAKS
YERAMYAN

"My stance has always been that if your bra straps are going to show, you might as well wear a bra that is worthy of being shown off. What is more, you can use this as an opportunity to add a hit of color to whatever else you're wearing—in fact, I like to think of it more as a basic underpinning than an undergarment."

—Anne Christensen, "The Moment," *New York Times*, May 27, 2009

My brand is known for its clean and pointillist construction, modern finishing, and my obsessive attention to color. I create underpinnings that are refined, effortless, and something to wear every day. Something to be seen, but quietly seen—the idea of innerwear as outerwear, lingerie for women to wear and feel beautiful everyday.

I feel that I have created a different kind of appeal—underpinnings for a woman, confident, dressing for herself, and still sensual. It is now considered an accessory to be seen. You can find the influence everywhere, there is a whole category that blurs the distinction between innerwear and outerwear that didn't exist before.

GERARD
YOSCA

Gerard Yosca is one of fashion's rebels. Twenty-eight years ago, when costume jewelry was just beginning to break out of its well-mannered ladylike box, he discovered the archaic medium of colored enamel. Why couldn't jewelry be Day-Glo lime? Studded with spikes? Big and graphic? The impact of these early collections was instantaneous. His idiosyncratic designs encouraged women to express themselves, to say who they are and want to be. They still do. Collections inspired by architecture, outer space, and motorcycles followed.

The common theme? Always, "What's next?" The dainty flowers and bugs of Victorian scrapbooks led to hand-painted butterfly barrettes. A revolution for hair.

The value of Gerard's work is that there is a strong point of view. The design process always includes research and experimentation. A craftsman's hand is apparent; nothing too perfect or measured. These are the keys to his longevity. Collections change dramatically in material and theme; some collections are awash in color, some devoid. His knack for anticipating what his fans will want or need next keeps him relevant.

JEAN
YU

I believe my work will have a lasting impact on American fashion for its rigorous discipline in technique, aesthetics, and original design. This is achieved by the intimate knowledge and process of sculpting the fabric around the three-dimensional body. The originality comes from building the design from the ground up, inside out. This dynamic is notable, as the whole of the industry works from the outside in: assembling desired parts from other garments as the chief design methodology. While this is efficient and economical, it lacks the very ingredient that pulled me in in the first place: the art of fashion and its impact to create desire. My designs are distinguished by old-world dressmaking techniques and a purity of form that is modern yet sensual. Each piece is patterned, draped, and designed by me personally. This is not efficient/economical and its result is quite subtle; however, such nuances, in any medium, are deeply meaningful and inspire the work of others.

Those who design as an art form are a very small community around the world but specifically so in American fashion. My body of work has been chronicled among a rare breed of artist in American fashion, and the recognition inspires me to move forward with my art that I hope will move others.

DAVID
YURMAN

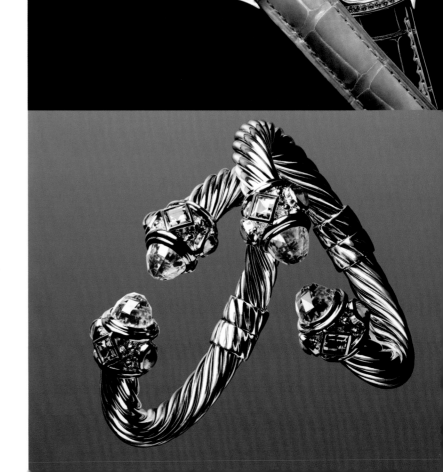

David Yurman's first love was fine art—specifically sculpture. His early years were spent learning from some of the great master sculptors of the twentieth century. It wasn't until he channeled that passion and technique into decorative arts that David Yurman, the jeweler, was born. The creation of the Cable Bracelet made David Yurman jewelry an instant contemporary and historical classic. The Cable collection, now trademarked, has become the cornerstone reference for almost all of the designs that have followed. Prior to this, jewelry was divided into categories and driven entirely by materials. In a uniquely American way, David Yurman rewrote the global rules of jewelry and made design a requirement in its classification; he is also the first jeweler to create an innovative, world-class lifestyle campaign.

Beyond his clear impact on jewelry design, David Yurman is also considered the grand master of fine jewelry as accessible luxury. His constant focus on great design, fine materials, and building a democratic distribution platform allowed women to buy fine jewelry for themselves. Historically, jewelry was most often purchased by men for women, and in many ways this change has allowed women to have their own unique and independent relationship with jewelry as a category.

KATRIN
ZIMMERMANN

"I think of a waterfall when I see the fine
silver strands cascading down a neckline.
In its artful simplicity, its design flexibility
invites interaction with playful asymmetry.
Though a perfectly contemporary design,
I regard it as uniquely timeless."

—Maxine Weintraub, Museum of Contemporary Art, Chicago

My most well-known piece of jewelry, the one with which I have
made the greatest impact on American fashion and on the
world of design, is the African Necklace. Inspired by the neck
rings worn by two completely unrelated tribes, the Ndebele of
South Africa and the Karen of Thailand, this series of cascading
sterling silver cables is secured at the back with a simple silver
tube. As a design, it accomplishes the impossible—forming a
necklace that does not fasten around the neck. As a piece of
adornment, it is democratic: no matter the size of the wearer's
neck, it fits. As jewelry, it is multifaceted—pulling the cables into
different formations makes the piece look completely new.
The origin of its inspiration in two different, unrelated conti-
nents and its expression of form in many different looks that
are versatile, easy, yet polished make it the quintessential
"American" jewelry—an expression of its multifaceted past and
of its multicultural present and future.

ITALO
ZUCCHELLI

I have strived to rewrite men's iconic American sportswear; constantly exploring new ways to make it modern and relevant. Through research and technology, I have experimented with innovative fabrics to create inspirational yet approachable clothes. Fabrics are really the "soul" of my designs. A classic silhouette is something completely different using new materials. I always like to combine these high-tech fabrics with more traditional ones, finding a unique balance in the contrast. It's like opposites attract; the juxtaposition of luxury and the industrial, precious materials and techno elements, the iconic and unfamiliar—two different worlds combined. The result is very modern.

Color also plays a key role in the dynamic. I like to use strong colors to make bold, graphic statements. Injecting these powerful colors and incorporating new materials into iconic silhouettes has become a signature of my design style.

"Capturing the tension—literally in high-tech fabrics and figuratively in design—is the essence of modern menswear. And Calvin Klein plays that perfectly. . . . By contrast, on the runway, there was nothing but the extraordinary: a regular padded nylon raincoat, but in vivid blue; a tweed suit, but sculpted in rubbery shapes; a tailored evening suit with flashes of gilding from luminous taping at the streams. But somehow the designer Italo Zucchelli manages to pull off this futurism for the present. . . . The original Calvin Klein aesthetic was to bring sensuality to the simple. The 21st-century approach is different, but it has a refreshing effect on sportswear."
—Suzy Menkes, *International Herald Tribune*, February 14, 2011

"In a generally strong collection, Zucchelli once again experimented with shape and construction. . . . Zucchelli continues to make his mark at Calvin Klein for his play with new fabrics and proportions."
—*Women's Wear Daily*, February 14, 2011

"The design leader of the modernist moment in men's fashion today is Italo Zucchelli, an Italian designing for Calvin Klein, where he evokes the energy, hard edges and technology-packed life of urban citizens for this American brand."
—Godfrey Deeny, *Fashion Wire Daily*, June 20, 2010

BEN
ZUCKERMAN

"He held a unique and special place in the history of our business," the designer Mollie Parnis said yesterday, adding; "He never really was replaced. There's nobody who does uniquely and exactly what he did. He had a marvelous flair for fabric and color and putting them all together. He took such pride in his clothes that nobody could sell them better than he could."

—Joan Cook, *New York Times*, April 11, 1979

Joseph Abboud
Amsale Aberra
Reem Acra
Alexa Adams
Frank Adams
Carey Adina
Adolfo
Miguel Adrover
Adri
Waris Ahluwalia
Akira
Steven Alan
Simon Alcantara
Karen Alexander
Victor Alfaro
Fred Allard
Linda Allard
Jeanne Allen
Carolina Amato
Ron Anderson
John Anthony
Miho Aoki
Nak Armstrong
James Arpad
Patricia Ashley
Joseph Assatly
Richard Assatly
Bill Atkinson
Brian Atwood
Bonnie August
Dominick Avellino
Lisa Axelson
Lubov Azria
Max Azria
Yigal Azrouel
Mark Badgley
Michael Ball
Kara Varian Baker
Jeffrey Banks
Leigh Bantivoglio
Christina Barboglio
Jan Barboglio
Jhane Barnes
John Bartlett
Victoria Bartlett
Gaby Basora
Dennis Basso
Michael Bastian
Matthew Batanian
Britta Bauer
Shane Baum
Bradley Bayou
Vicki Beamon
Geoffrey Beene
Alvin Bell
Jaques Bellini
Stacey Bendet
Richard Bengtsson
Russell Bennett

Diane Bennis
Dianne Benson
Chris Benz
Magda Berliner
Gaston Berthelot
Neil Bieff
Becky Bisoulis
Alexis Bittar
Alice Blain
Bill Blass
Sherrie Bloom
Franklin Bober
Kenneth Bonavitacola
Sully Bonnelly
Eddie Borgo
Monica Botkier
Jeannene Booher
Ole Bordon
Marc Bouwer
Bryan Bradley
Barry Bricken
Thomas Brigance
Eleanor Brenner
Steven Brody
Donald Brooks
Thom Browne
Brian Bubb
Dana Buchman
Andrew Buckler
Jason Bunin
Sophie Buhai
Tory Burch
Stephen Burrows
Anthony Camargo
David Cameron
Patti Capallo
Pamela Capone
Albert Capraro
Victor Caraballo
Paula Carbone
David Cardona
Betty Carol
Zack Carr
Kevin Carrigan
Pierre (Pierrot) Carrilero
Liliana Casabal
Allen Case
Oleg Cassini
Edmundo Castillo
Salvatore Cesarani
Richard Chai
Julie Chaiken
Amy Chan
Charles Chang-Lima
Natalie Chanin
Kip Chapelle
Georgina Chapman
Ron Chereskin
Wenlan Chia

Sandy Chilewich
Susie Cho
Malee Chompoo
David Chu
Eva Chun
Doo-Ri Chung
Liz Claiborne
Patricia Clyne
Carol Cohen
David Cohen
Meg Cohen
Peter Cohen
Anne Cole
Kenneth Cole
Liz Collins
Michael Colovos
Nicole Colovos
Sean Combs
Rachel Comey
Robert Comstock
Kathryn Conover
Bern Conrad
Martin Cooper
Jo Copeland
Anna Corinna Sellinger
Maria Cornejo
Andrew Corrigan
Esteban Cortazar
Francisco Costa
Victor Costa
Jeffrey Costello
Christian Cota
Erica Courtney
James Coviello
Steven Cox
Keren Craig
Philip Crangi
Maureen Cullinane
Angela Cummings
Eloise Curtis
Lilly Daché
Sandy Dalal
James Daugherty
Robert Danes
David Dartnell
Erica Davies
Vicki Davis
Oscar de la Renta
Donald Deal
Maxine de la Falaise
Peter de Wilde
Louis Dell'Olio
Pamela Dennis
Jane Derby
Lyn Devon
Kathryn Dianos
Stephen DiGeronimo
Piero Dimitri
David Dion

Dominic
Arthur Doucette
Henry Duarte
Keanan Duffty
Randolph Duke
Henry Dunay
Holly Dunlap
Stephen Dweck
Marc Ecko
Libby Edelman
Sam Edelman
Warren Edwards
Lola Ehrlich
Florence Eiseman
Mark Eisen
Perry Ellis
Melinda Eng
Karen Erickson
Olga Erteszek
Miss Ero
George Esquivel
Luis Estévez
David Evins
Gene Ewing
Fabrice
Steve Fabrikant
John Fairchild
Carlos Falchi
Joseph Famolare
Gaetano Fazio
Han Feng
Pina Ferlisi
Luis Fernandez
Erin Fetherston
Andrew Fezza
Alfred Fiandaca
Patricia Ficalora
Elizabeth Fillmore
Cheryl Finnegan
Eileen Fisher
Alan Flusser
Anne Fogarty
Dana Foley
Tom Ford
Roger Forsythe
Istvan Francer
Julie Francis
Isaac Franco
Robert Freda
R. Scott French
Carolee Friedlander
James Galanos
Nancy Ganz
Annemarie Gardin
Eric Gaskins
Wendy Gell
Nancy Geist
Robert Geller
Jennifer George

Geri Gerard
Jean Paul Germaine
Rudi Gernreich
Geoffrey Gertz
Mossimo Giannulli
Tess Giberson
Flora Gill
Justin Giunta
Gary Graham
Nicholas Graham
Marc Grant
Cindy Greene
Rogan Gregory
Henry Grethel
Ulrich Grimm
Joy Gryson
George Gublo
Prabal Gurung
Daphne Gutierrez
Jon Haggins
Scott Hahn
Bill Haire
Everett Hall
Kevan Hall
George Halley
Jeff Halmos
Halston
Tim Hamilton
Douglas Hannant
Cathy Hardwick
John Hardy
Karen Harman
Dean Harris
Johnson Hartig
Sylvia Heisel
Nancy Heller
Joan Helpern
Gordon Henderson
Stan Herman
Lazaro Hernandez
Arturo Herrera
Carolina Herrera
Tommy Hilfiger
Nick Hilton
Kazuyoshi Hino
Catherine Hipp
Carole Hochman
Mara Hoffman
Carole Horn
Donald Hopson
Chuck Howard
Janet Howard
Christina Hutson
Swaim Hutston
Sang A Im-Propp
Alejandro Ingelmo
Pat Iuto
Marc Jacobs
Henry Jacobson

Eric Javits, Jr.
Lisa Jenks
Mr. John
Betsey Johnson
Nancy Johnson
Wini Jones
Alexander Jordan
Andrea Jovine
Victor Jovis
Alexander Julian
Gemma Kahng
Bill Kaiserman
Kalinka
Norma Kamali
Larry Kane
Jen Kao
Donna Karan
Lance Karesh
Kasper
Jeanette Kastenberg
Michael Katz
Ken Kaufman
Jerry Kaye
Jenni Kayne
Kazuko
Shaun Kearney
Anthony Keegan
Rod Keenan
Randy Kemper
Pat Kerr
Naeem Khan
David Kidd
Barry Kieselstein-Cord
Bud Kilpatrick
Eugenia Kim
Adam Kimmel
Alexis Kirk
Kip Kirkendall
Gayle Kirkpatrick
Calvin Klein
John Kloss
Nancy Knox
Ronald Kolodzie
Michael Kors
Monica Rich Kosann
Reed Krakoff
Michel Kramer
Regina Kravitz
Devi Kroell
Nikki Kule
Flora Kung
Christopher Kunz
Nicholas Kunz
Blake Kuwahara
Steven Lagos
Derek Lam
Isabel Lam
Eleanor Lambert
Tony Lambert

Richard Lambertson
Adrienne Landau
Kenneth Jay Lane
Helmut Lang
Liz Lange
Byron Lars
Hubert Latimer
Ralph Lauren
Helen Lazar
Jack Lazar
Susan Lazar
Ron Leal
Eunice Lee
Helen Lee
Soo Yung Lee
Judith Leiber
Larry Leight
Nanette Lepore
Michael Leva
Beth Levine
Brett Lewis
Marilyn Lewis
Monique Lhuillier
Andrea Lieberman
Phillip Lim
Johan Lindeberg
Marcella Lindeberg
Antoinette Linn
Adam Lippes
Deanna Littell
Deborah Lloyd
Elizabeth Locke
Dana Lorenz
Jean Louis
Holly Lueders
Tina Lutz
Jenna Lyons
Kerry MacBride
Bob Mackie
Marion Maged
Jeff Mahshie
Catherine Malandrino
Maurice Malone
Colette Malouf
Isaac Manevitz
Melissa Joy Manning
Robert Marc
Mary Jane Marcasiano
Georges Marciano
Stanley Marcus
Fiona Kotur Marin
Lana Marks
Luba Marks
Deborah Marquit
Jose Martin
Frank Masandrea
Leon Max
Vera Maxwell
Lisa Mayock
Matthew Mazer
Marie McCarthy
Jessica McClintock
Jack McCollough
Kimberly McDonald
Mary McFadden
Marlo McGriff
Maxime McKendry

Mark McNairy
David Meister
Jonathan Meizler
Andrea Melbostad
Tony Melillo
Gilles Mendel
Cecilia Metheny
Gene Meyer
B. Michael
Carlos Miele
Stefan Miljanic
Derrick Miller
E. Jerrold Miller
Glen Miller
Nicole Miller
Malia Mills
Rebecca Minkoff
James Mischka
Richard Mishaan
Isaac Mizrahi
Leon A. Mnuchin
Bibhu Mohapatra
Mark Montano
Vincent Monte-Sano
John Moore
Paul Morelli
Robert Lee Morris
Miranda Morrison
Rebecca Moses
Kathy Moskal
Kate Mulleavy
Laura Mulleavy
Sandra Muller
Matt Murphy
Anthony Muto
Blake Mycoskie
Morton Myles
George Nardiello
Leo Narducci
Gela Nash-Taylor
Craig Natiello
Josie Natori
Vera Neumann
Charlotte Neuville
Irene Neuwirth
David Neville
Rozae Nichols
Lars Nilsson
Albert Nipon
Pearl Nipon
Roland Nivelais
Danny Noble
Vanessa Noel
Charles Nolan
Norman Norell
Maggie Norris
Nicole Noselli
Peter Noviello
Matt Nye
Juan Carlos Obando
Todd Oldham
Frank Olive
Ashley Olsen
Mary-Kate Olsen
Sigrid Olsen
Luca Orlandi
Marie-Anne Oudejans

Rick Owens
Yonson Pak
Thakoon Panichgul
Gregory Parkinson
Patricia Pastor
Mollie Parnis
Marcia Patmos
John Patrick
Edward Pavlick
Monique Péan
Sylvia Pedlar
Diane Pernet
Patty Perreira
Christina Perrin
James Perse
Thuy Pham
Sarah Phillips
Paloma Picasso-Lopez
Robin Piccone
Mary Ping
Maria Pinto
Jill Platner
Linda Platt
Tom Platt
Alexandre Plokhov
Laura Poretzky
Carmelo Pomodoro
Regina Porter
Zac Posen
Anna Maximilian Potok
Gene Pressman
Martin Price
Lilly Pulitzer
James Purcell
Jessie Randall
David Rees
Tracy Reese
William Reid
Robin Renzi
Mary Ann Restivo
Brian Reyes
Kenneth Richard
Bettina Riedel
Robert Riley
Sara Ripault
Judith Ripka
Bill Robinson
Patrick Robinson
Shannon Rodgers
Loree Rodkin
David Rodriguez
Eddie Rodriguez
Narciso Rodriguez
Robert Rodriguez
Carolyne Roehm
Jackie Rogers
Alice Roi
Pamella Roland
Dominic Rompollo
Charlotte Ronson
Lela Rose
Ivy Ross
Kara Ross
Martin Ross
Ippolita Rostagno
Christian Roth
Christian Francis Roth

Cynthia Rowley
Rachel Roy
Sonja Rubin
Ralph Rucci
Sabato Russo
Miriam Ruzow
Kelly Ryan
Gloria Sachs
Jamie Sadock
Selima Salaun
George Samen
Arthur Samuels, Jr.
Pat Sandler
Angel Sanchez
Fernando Sanchez
Giorgio Sant'Angelo
Lauren Sara
Behnaz Sarafpour
Fernando Sarmi
Janis Savitt
Don Sayres
Arnold Scaasi
Robert Schaefer
John Scher
Jordan Schlanger
Lorraine Schwartz
L'Wren Scott
Harriet Selwyn
Ricky Serbin
Christopher Serluco
Michael Seroy
Ronaldus Shamask
George Sharp
Susan Sheinman
Marcia Sherrill
Alexander Shields
Sam Shipley
Tess Sholom
Joan Sibley
Helene Sidel
Kari Sigerson
Daniel Silver
Howard Silver
Elinor Simmons
Michael Simon
Don Simonelli
George Simonton
Adele Simpson
Paul Sinclaire
Pamela Skaist-Levy
Stella Sloat
Michael Smaldone
Amy Smilovic
Eric Smith
Frank Smith
Michelle Smith
Willi Smith
Wynn Smith
Mark R. Snider
Maria Snyder
Mimi So
Peter Som
Eva Sonnino
Kate Spade
Gunnar Spaulding
Peter Speliopoulos
Michael Spirito

Simon Spurr
Laurie Stark
Richard Stark
George Stavropoulos
Carole Stein
Cynthia Steffe
Shelly Steffee
Sue Stemp
Marieluisa Stern
Scott Sternberg
Robert Stock
Dan Stoenescu
Steven Stolman
Jay Strongwater
Jill Stuart
Lynn Stuart
Karen Suen-Cooper
Anna Sui
Charles Suppon
Koi Suwannagate
Daiki Suzuki
Albertus Swanepoel
Gene Sylbert
Viola Sylbert
Robert Tagliapietra
Elie Tahari
Richard Tam
Vivienne Tam
Gustave Tassell
Rebecca Taylor
Rodney Telford
Yeohlee Teng
Marcus Teo
Sophie Theallet
Gordon Thompson III
Olivier Theyskens
Ben Thylan
Bill Tice
Frank Tignino
Monika Tilley
Zang Toi
Isabel Toledo
Julian Tomchin
Susie Tompkins
Rafe Totengco
Bill Travilla
Pauline Trigère
Gil Truedsson
John Truex
Trina Turk
Mish Tworkowski
Richard Tyler
Patricia Underwood
Kay Unger
Germán Valdivia
Tony Valentine
Carmen Marc Valvo
Koos van den Akker
Nicholas Varney
John Varvatos
Joan Vass
Adrienne Vittadini
Michael Vollbracht
Diane von Furstenberg
Egon von Furstenberg
Patricia von Musulin
Diane Vreeland

Ilie Wacs
Marcus Wainwright
Tom Walko
Norma Walters
Alexander Wang
Vera Wang
Gale Warren
Cathy Waterman
Chester Weinberg
Heidi Weisel
Jon Weiser
John Weitz
Stuart Weitzman
Trish Wescoat Pound
Carla Westcott
John Whitledge
Edward Wilkerson
Arthur Williams
Harriet Winter
Judith Wister
Nancy White
Brian Wolk
Jenny Bell Whyte
Gary Wolkowitz
Pinky Wolman
Andrew Woods
Sydney Wragge
Angela Wright
Lee Wright
Sharon Wright
Peter Wrigley
Jason Wu
Araks Yeramyan
Gerard Yosca
Jean Yu
David Yurman
Gabriella Zanzani
Katrin Zimmermann
Italo Zucchelli
Ben Zuckerman

INDEX

Designers are listed by last name, name brands listed by first name.
Page numbers in *italics* refer to images.

PHOTO CREDITS

Page 6 (top, middle right): Photographs by PatrickMcMullan.com

Page 6 (middle left): Photo by Andrew H. Walker/Getty Images for CFDA

Page 6 (bottom): Billy Farrell/BFAnyc.com

Page 9: Time & Life Pictures/Getty Images

Pages 12, 14, 16, 19, 28, 29, 32, 33, 34, 49, 64, 85, 100, 103, 108–109, 113, 117, 119 (top right), 125, 134 (top right), 141 (top right), 152, 153, 164, 165, 173, 177, 183 (top left), 209 (bottom left), 216, 232 (bottom right), 235, 244, 258, 262, 263, 266, 268, 275, 283, 289 © Fashion Institute of Technology | SUNY, FIT Library Dept. of Special Collections and FIT Archives

Page 17, 18: Courtesy of CFDA

Page 23: Photograph by PatrickMcMullan.com

Page 30, 185 (top right): Copyright © Steven Meisel/Art + Commerce

Page 35 (top): Copyright © George De Sota/Liaison

Page 35 (bottom left): Photo by Rose Hartman/WireImage

Page 36: Photo by Ron Galella/WireImage

Page 37: Courtesy of Stan Herman, illustration by Don Morrison

Page 38: Courtesy of Diane von Furstenberg

Page 39 (left): Machalaba/Women's Wear Daily/Condé Nast Archive. Copyright © Condé Nast

Page 39 (middle): Stone/Vogue/Condé Nast Archive. Copyright © Condé Nast

Page 39 (right): Heidi Levine/AFP/Getty Images

Page 42: Photo by Rose Hartman/Getty Images

Page 42: Courtesy of Lisa Wells/Reem Acra

Page 43: Photo by Alexander Tamargo/Getty Images

Page 43 (right): Coffin/Vogue/Condé Nast Archive. Copyright © Condé Nast

Page 44: Grace Kelsey

Page 45 (top left): Courtesy of Steven Alan

Page 45 (bottom left): Peggy Sirota/Trunk Archive

Page 45 (top right): Terry Richardson/Art Partner

Page 46 (bottom left): Copyright © John Huba/Art + Commerce

Page 46 (top right): Courtesy of

Jeanne Allen and Marc Grant

Page 47 (bottom left): Photo by Ron Contarsy

Page 47 (top right): Michael Waring

Page 48 (top left): Courtesy of John Anthony

Page 48 (bottom right): Courtesy of Nak Armstrong

Pages 49 (bottom right), 234 (bottom left): Tom Munro

Page 50: Courtesy of Max Azria and Lubov Azria

Page 51 (top left): Courtesy of Yigal Azrouël

Page 51 (bottom right): Photo by Frazer Harrison/Getty Images for Mercedes-Benz

Page 52 (top left): Courtesy of Jeffrey Banks

Page 52 (bottom right): Courtesy of Jhane Barnes

Page 53 (top left): Courtesy of John Bartlett

Page 53 (bottom right): Gwen Stefani by Mark Squires

Page 54 (bottom left): Courtesy of Dennis Basso

Page 54 (bottom right): Courtesy of Shane Baum

Page 55 (bottom left): Courtesy of Bradley Bayou

Page 55 (bottom right): Courtesy of Vicki Beamon and Karen Erikson

Page 56 (right): William Laxston/Geoffrey Beene

Page 56 (left): Photo by Jack Deutsch

Page 57: Andrew Eccles/Trunk Archive

Page 58 (bottom left): Courtesy of Alvin Bell

Page 58 (bottom right): Courtesy of Susan Bennis and Warren Edwards

Page 59: Courtesy of Dianne Benson

Page 60 (bottom left): Courtesy of Chris Benz

Page 60 (top right): Courtesy of Mada Berliner

Page 61: Courtesy of Alexis Bittar

Page 62 (top right): Courtesy of Monica Botkier

Page 62 (bottom left): Courtesy of Sully Bonelly

Page 63 (bottom right): Photo by Jim Smeal/WireImage

Page 63 (top right): Photo by Paul Lange

Page 65: Courtesy of Thom Browne

Page 66: Courtesy of Dana Buchman

Page 67 (top left): Tung T. Bui

Page 68 (right): Tierney Gueron/

Trunk Archive

Pages 68 (left) and 69: Jennifer Livingston

Page 70: Courtesy of Stephen Burrows

Page 71 (bottom left): Courtesy of Anthony Camargo

Page 71 (top right): Mert Alas and Marcus Piggot/Art Partner

Page 72 (top left): Courtesy of Marc Baptiste/Liliana Casabal

Page 72 (bottom right): Photo by Al Pucci/NY Daily News Archive via Getty Images

Page 73 (top left): Courtesy of Edmundo Castillo

Page 73 (top right): Courtesy of John Moe/Salvatore J. Cesarani

Page 74: Photographed by Marcelo Gomes for *The Last Magazine*

Page 75 (top right): Courtesy of Amy Chan

Page 75 (bottom left): Courtesy of Julie Chaiken

Page 76: Copyright © Robert Rausch 2010

Page 77: Courtesy of Georgina Chapman and Keren Craig

Page 78 (bottom left): Courtesy of Ron Chereskin Studios

Page 78 (top right): Courtesy of Wenlan Chia

Page 79: Courtesy of David Chu/Mikael Jansson

Page 80: Hearst Communications, Inc./Trunk Archive

Page 81 (bottom left): Photo by Luis Bañuelos Aréchiga

Page 81 (top left, sketch): Courtesy of Doo-ri Chung

Page 82: Sketches and photos courtesy of Art Ortenberg

Page 83: Courtesy of Art Ortenberg/Liz Claiborne Foundation

Page 84: Courtesy of Patricia Clyne

Page 86 (left): Photo by Annie Leibovitz. Courtesy of the artist

Page 86 (right): Courtesy of Kenneth Cole

Page 87: Courtesy of Kenneth Cole

Page 88: Courtesy of Liz Collins

Page 89: Dusan Reljin

Page 90 (top right): Courtesy of Rachel Comey

Pages 90 (bottom left), 128 (top right), 132, 189, 243 (bottom right), 250, 292: Courtesy Dan and Corina Lecca

Page 91: Courtesy of Kathryn Conover

Page 92 (top left): Courtesy of Martin Cooper

Page 92 (bottom right): Mark Borthwick

Page 93 (bottom left): Courtesy of Dana Foley and Anna Corinna

Page 93 (bottom right): Norman Jean Roy/Trunk Archive

Page 94: Copyright © Craig McDean/Art + Commerce

Page 95 (far left): Photo by Frazer Harrison/Getty Images

Page 95 (second to left): Photo by Peter Kramer/Getty Images

Page 95 (center): Photo by Steve Granitz/WireImage

Page 95 (second to right): Photo by Joe Raedle/Getty Images

Page 95 (far right): Photo by Jason Merritt/Getty Images

Page 96: Illustration Courtesy of Al Hirschberg

Page 97 (bottom left): Courtesy of Randy Brooke/Jeffrey Costello and Robert Tagliapietraa

Page 97 (top right): Courtesy of Erica Courtney

Page 98: Platon

Page 99: Raymond Meier/Trunk Archive

Page 101 (bottom left): Courtesy of Robert Danes

Page 101 (sketches and bottom right): Courtesy of Donald Deal

Page 101 (top right): Jason Riker

Page 102 (right): Courtesy of Lyn Devon

Page 102 (top left): Demarchelier/Vogue/Condé Nast Archive. Copyright © Condé Nast

Page 104 (right): Courtesy of Keanan Duffty

Page 105 (top left): AMFAR

Page 105 (bottom right): Courtesy of Stephen Dwek

Page 106: Courtesy of Mark Ecko

Page 107 (top left): Courtesy of Sam Edelman and Libby Edelman

Page 107 (bottom right): Courtesy of Mark Eisen

Page 108 (left): Courtesy of Melinda Eng

Page 109 (top right): Coffin/Vogue/Condé Nast Archive. Copyright © Condé Nast

Page 110 (bottom left): Courtesy of Steve Fabrikant

Page 110 (top right): Courtesy of Carlos Falchi

Page 111 (top right): Courtesy of Andrew Fezza, photo by Herb Ritts

Page 111 (bottom left): Marisa Crawford

Page 112 (top left): Courtesy of Cheryl Finnegan

Page 112 (right): Jennifer Antola/ Contour by Getty Images

Page 115, 205: Mario Testino/Art Partner

Page 116: Courtesy of R. Scott French

Page 118 (bottom left): Courtesy of Robert Gellar

Page 118 (top right): Courtesy of Jennifer George

Page 119 (bottom left): Courtesy of Geri Gerard

Page 120 (bottom left): Courtesy of Justin Giunta

Page 120 (top right): Courtesy of Gary Graham

Page 121 (top left): Courtesy of Nick Graham

Page 121 (top right): Reprinted with the permission of the USOC

Page 122 (bottom left): Anthony Cotsifas/Art Partner

Page 122 (top right): ClintSpaulding. com

Page 122, 122 (middle right, bottom right): Courtesy of George Gublo

Page 123: Courtesy of Shipley & Halmos

Page 126 (top left): Courtesy of Tim Hamilton

Page 126 (top right): Courtesy of Douglas Hannant

Page 127 (bottom left): Courtesy of Cathy Hardwick

Page 127 (right): Courtesy of Karen Harman

Page 128 (bottom left): Courtesy of Johnson Hartig

Page 129: Courtesy of Lazaro Hernandez and Jack McCollough

Page 131: Courtesy of Antoni Bernad

Page 134 (top left): Courtesy of Carole Hochman

Page 135: Courtesy of Swaim Hutson and Christina Hutson

Page 136: Courtesy of Sang A Im-Propp

Page 137: Courtesy of Alejandro Ingelmo

Page 139: WWD Archives

Page 140 (bottom left): Courtesy of Henry Jacobson

Page 140 (top right): Photo by Michael Thompson

Page 141 (bottom left): Courtesy of Lisa Jenks, photo by Chris Callis

Page 142: Courtesy of Betsey Johnson

Page 143 (left): Courtesy of Alexander Julian

Page 143 (top right): Arthur Elgort/ Vogue/Condé Nast Archive. Copyright © Condé Nast

Page 145: Mark Seliger

Page 147 (top left): Courtesy of Donna Karan

Page 147 (top right): Copyright © Patrick Demarchelier

Page 147, 147 (middle left, middle right): Photos by Peter Lindbergh

Page 147, 147 (bottom left, bottom right): Photos courtesy of Donna Karan/ Mikael Jansson

Page 148 (top right): Benson/ Architectural Digest/Condé Nast Archive. Copyright © Condé Nast

Page 149: Courtesy of Pat Kerr

Page 150: Courtesy of Barry Kieselstein-Cord

Page 151 (top left): Courtesy of Ari Marcopoulos/Adam Kimmel

Page 151 (bottom left): Image Courtesy of Jim Krantz/Adam Kimmel

Page 151 (top right): Courtesy of Meredith Danluck/Adam Kimmel

Page 155: Photos by Mario Testino

Page 156 (top left): Courtesy of Monica Rich Kosann

Page 156 (bottom right): Courtesy of Fiona Kotur, illustration by Sheila Camera Kotur

Page 157: Courtesy of Reed Krakoff

Page 158 (bottom left): Courtesy of Michel Kramer

Page 158 (top right): Courtesy of Regina Kravitz

Page 159 (bottom left): Jaime Chard

Page 159 (top right): Courtesy of Nikki Kule

Page 160 (bottom left): Courtesy of Christopher Kunz and Nicholas Kunz

Page 160 (top right): Courtesy of Blake Kuwahara

Page 161: Courtesy of Steven Lagos

Page 162: Copyright © Craig McDean/Art + Commerce

Page 163: David Sims/Art Partner

Page 166: Photo by Gail Albert Halaban

Page 167: Noah Chen Photography for Byron Lars Beauty Mark

Page 169 (top, middle far right, bottom middle): Bruce Weber/ Trunk Archive

Page 169 (middle center, bottom right): Francois Halard/Trunk Archive

Page 169 (middle right): Sheila Metzner

Page 169 (bottom left): Courtesy of Ralph Lauren, photo by Carter Berg

Page 170: Copyright © John Bigelow Taylor

Page 171: Courtesy of Larry Leight

Page 172: Ruven Afanador

Page 174 (left): Courtesy of Monique Lhuillier

Page 175 (right): Photo by Kevork Djansezian/Getty Images

Page 175: Courtesy of Phillip Lim

Page 176 (bottom left): Courtesy of Johan Lindeberg

Page 176 (top right): Courtesy of Adam Lippes

Page 177 (bottom right): Courtesy of Tina Lutz

Page 178: Courtesy of Bob Mackie

Page 179: Courtesy of Catherine Malandrino

Page 180 (top left): Diane Vasil Photography

Page 180 (bottom right): Courtesy of Isaac Manevitz

Page 181 (top left): Courtesy of Robert Marc

Page 181 (bottom right): Elisabeth Novick

Page 182 (top left): Courtesy of Lana Marks

Page 182 (bottom right): Photo by Frazer Harrison/Getty Images

Page 183 (bottom right): Courtesy of Jessica McClintock

Page 184 (bottom left): Courtesy of Kimberly McDonald

Page 184 (top right): Courtesy of Mark McNairy, photo by Justin Chung

Page 185 (bottom left): Courtesy of David Meister

Page 186: Courtesy of Gilles Mendel

Page 187 (top): Mark Roskams

Page 187 (bottom right): Michael Roberts

Page 188 (top left): Courtesy of Stefan Miljanic

Page 188 (bottom right): Courtesy of Glen Miller

Page 190: Courtesy of Malia Mills

Page 191 (left): Courtesy of Rebecca Minkoff

Page 191 (bottom right): Courtesy of Richard Mishaan

Page 192: Courtesy of Bibhu Mohapatra

Page 193: Courtesy of Paul Morelli

Page 194: Courtesy of Robert Lee Morris

Page 195: Courtesy of Fabien Baron

Page 196: Autumn de Wilde

Page 197 (top right): Courtesy of Leo Narducci

Page 197 (bottom left): Courtesy of Matt Murphy

Page 198: Tim Walker/Art Partner

Page 199: Martyn Thomas/Trunk Archive

Page 200 (bottom left): Courtesy of Vera Neuman

Page 200 (top right): Courtesy of Charlotte Neuville

Page 201 (middle): Photo by Terry Tsiolis

Page 201 (left, right): Courtesy of Marcus Wainwright and David Neville

Page 202 (bottom left): Courtesy of Irene Neuwirth

Page 202 (top right): Courtesy of Rozae Nichols

Page 203 (top right): Courtesy of Vanessa Noel

Page 203 (bottom left): J. R. Duran

Page 204: Courtesy of Charles Nolan

Page 205 (top left): Courtesy of Maggie Norris, Illustrated by Anna Kiper

Page 206: Courtesy of Mary-Kate Olsen and Ashley Olsen, photos by Beatrice Kim

Page 207: Laspata DeCaro

Page 208: Corrine Day/TrunkArchive. com

Page 209 (top right): Courtesy of Marcia Patmos, photo by Nico Iliev

Page 210: Courtesy of John Patrick

Page 211: Courtesy of Monique Péan, photo by Marco Pedde

Page 212: Michael Reinhardt

Page 213 (left): Courtesy of Mary Ping and Slow and Steady Wins The Race, photo by Isabel Asha Penzlien

Page 213 (right): Courtesy of Jill Platner, photo by Maria Robledo

Page 214: Photos by Barbara Nitke, graphic design by John Lynch, hair and makeup by Andrea Wilson

Page 215: New York Post/Splash News

Page 217: Courtesy of Lilly Pulitzer

Page 218: Courtesy of James Purcell, photo by Gideon Lewin

Page 219: Luis Acosta/AFP/Getty Images

Page 220: Courtesy of Billy Reid

Page 221 (top left): Courtesy of Robin Renzi

Page 221 (bottom right): Courtesy of Mary Ann Restivo

Page 222 (bottom right): Courtesy of Judith Ripka

Page 223 (top left): Courtesy of Loree Rodkin

Page 223 (bottom right): Courtesy of David Rodriguez

Page 224: Photo by Joe Raedle/Getty Images

Page 225: Denis Reggie

Page 226 (bottom left): Courtesy of Robert Rodriguez

Page 226 (top right): Courtesy of Pamella Roland

Page 227 (bottom left): Courtesy of Lela Rose

Page 227 (top right): Courtesy of Christian Roth

Page 228 (top left): Courtesy of Cynthia Rowley, photo by Don Ashby

Page 228 (bottom right): Courtesy of Rachel Roy

Page 229: Courtesy of Ralph Rucci

Page 230 (top left): Eric Micotto

ACKNOWLEDGMENTS

We have entered the Golden Age of American fashion with the Council of Fashion Designers of America celebrating its fiftieth anniversary. Over the last five decades, we have counted the greatest designers in the world among our ranks, and our current roster of talent is no exception.

It is these members, both past and present, that have truly made our anniversary book very special. When all is combined there are over six hundred designers who have been part of the CFDA. This book is an authentic representation of the IMPACT that these six hundred designers have had on American fashion. Each was asked to submit a statement and images that best document what they believe is their lasting impact on the American fashion industry. These designers are the CFDA, and their participation in this book has been truly invaluable. Together, as you will see throughout these pages, it is an eclectic, artful mix of ingenuity and creativity.

While not our first book, this may be our most important book yet, as it is the ultimate reference on the CFDA. Our past books include *American Fashion*, *American Fashion Accessories*, *American Fashion Menswear*, *Geoffrey Beene: An American Fashion Rebel*, *American Fashion Cookbook*, *American Fashion Home*, and *American Fashion Travel: Designers on the Go*. For the first time, we are working with Abrams, and this partnership has quickly grown into a true friendship and collaboration. The book would not have been possible without the leadership and prowess of senior editor Rebecca Kaplan, with whom we exchanged thousands of emails. Special thanks also to the incredible design team of Sarah Gifford and creative director, Michelle Ishay.

Impact consists of over five hundred photos, and we are very grateful to the photographers, agencies, magazines, models, and everyone who agreed to be part of the book and to celebrate fifty years with the CFDA. We are so fortunate to have such great friends. A huge thank-you also must go to John Tiffany for his enormous help and research, and we are indebted to Monika Tilley, former CFDA board member and one of our most loyal members and supporters, for her historical knowledge and memory.

Thank you to Cathy Horyn, whose illuminating words and anecdotes make up the foreword of this book, and to Patricia Mears, who captured the history of the CFDA so beautifully and accurately. Without Patricia there would be no book. Her research, knowledge, and eloquence are very much appreciated by everyone at the CFDA.

The CFDA books are somewhat of a rite of passage here in the office, and Sophie Marx traveled through the coordination of this book with professionalism and an unerring eye for detail. She deserves much of the credit for getting IMPACT published. And of course, we have the hardest working staff in fashion and they are equally part of this celebration. Along with Sophie, they are: Lisa Smilor, CaSandra Diggs, Catherine Bennett, Karen Peterson, Amy Ondocin, Heather Jacobson, Sara Maniatty, Christine Olsen, Johanna Stout, and Sacha Brown. Thank you also to our extremely organized book interns Lilah Ramzi and Amy Stone, and our other invaluable interns Emilie Fife, Carly Lapidus, Jen Cahn, and Kelsi Rosenberg.

This book is a companion to IMPACT, an exhibit created by the Museum at FIT in collaboration with the CFDA. We are most appreciative of their continued support and guidance as we expand this celebration. Many thanks to Dr. Joyce F. Brown and Dr. Valerie Steele for their belief in CFDA, and to Patricia Mears (mentioned above) and her team, including senior curator Fred Dennis; photographers William Palmer and Eileen Costa; exhibition designer Ken Nintzel; exhibitions manager Michael Goitia; registrars Sonia Dingilian and Jill Hemingway; senior conservator Ann Coppiner; installation stylists Thomas Synammon and Marjorie Jonas; and Karen Cannell and her team in the library at FIT's Special Collections for their immense organization and their appreciation of these American designers.

There is no other organization like the CFDA. Without the insight and perseverance of our founding members, board of directors, and past presidents, we would not exist today. A special thank you to all of them.

And then there is the CFDA's current president, Diane von Furstenberg. Everyone knows Diane for her incredible success as a designer and the IMPACT she has had on empowering women with the way they dress. She has also, without question, greatly impacted the American fashion industry through her dynamic leadership, and we are thankful for the amazing family she has created and for her love for all of us.

Here's to the next fifty.

—Steven Kolb, Chief Executive Officer

EDITOR
Rebecca Kaplan

DESIGNER
Sarah Gifford

PRODUCTION MANAGER
Jules Thomson

Library of Congress Cataloging-in-Publication Data
Mears, Patricia.
Impact : 50 years of the Council of Fashion Designers of America /
by Patricia Mears ; foreword by Diane von Furstenberg ;
introduction by Cathy Horyn.
p. cm.
Includes index.
ISBN: 978-1-4197-0231-0
1. Fashion—United States—History. 2. Council of Fashion
Designers of America. I. Title. II. Title: 50 years of the Council
of Fashion Designers of America. III. Title: Fifty years of the
Council of Fashion Designers of America.
TT504.4.M43 2012
746.9'2—dc23
2011033828

Printed and bound in Hong Kong, China
10 9 8 7 6 5 4 3 2 1

Abrams books are available at special discounts when purchased in quantity
for premiums and promotions as well as fundraising or educational use.
Special editions can also be created to specification. For details, contact
specialsales@abramsbooks.com or the address below.

THE ART OF BOOKS SINCE 1949
115 West 18th Street
New York, NY 10011
www.abramsbooks.com